Blind Oracles

Blind Oracles

Intellectuals and War from Kennan to Kissinger

Bruce Kuklick

PRINCETON UNIVERSITY PRESS

PRINCETON AND OXFORD

Copyright © 2006 by Princeton University Press
Published by Princeton University Press, 41 William Street,
Princeton, New Jersey 08540
In the United Kingdom: Princeton University Press,
3 Market Place, Woodstock, Oxfordshire OX20 1SY

Library of Congress Cataloging-in-Publication Data
Kuklick, Bruce, 1941–
Blind oracles: intellectuals and war from
Kennan to Kissinger / Bruce Kuklick
p.   cm.
Includes bibliographical references and index.
ISBN-10: 0-691-12349-7 (alk. paper)
ISBN-13: 978-0-691-12349-3 (alk. paper)
1. United States—Foreign relations—1945–1989—Decision making.
2. Intellectuals—United States—Political activity—History—
20th century. I. Title

JZ148.K85 2006
327.73—dc22   2005048754

British Library Cataloging-in-Publication Data is available

This book has been composed in Sabon

Printed on acid-free paper. ∞

pup.princeton.edu

Printed in the United States of America

10 9 8 7 6 5 4 3 2 1

For Marc Trachtenberg
and in Memory of Richard Neustadt
Teachers and Friends

So much for a blind obedience to a bludering oracle, throwing the stones over their heads behind them, and not seeing where they fell.

Henry Thoreau, *Walden*

Contents

Illustrations

Note on Citations

I HAVE ABBREVIATED my citations to two important sets of documents. The *Foreign Relations of the United States*, published by the United States Government Printing Office in Washington, D.C., is the standard series of printed official documents (various dates of publication). I have identified the documents I have used, and then abbreviated the title to FRUS and noted the name of the specific volume.

Marc Trachtenberg edited *The Development of American Strategic Thought* (New York: Garland Press, 1988), in four parts: 1. *Basic Documents from the Eisenhower and Kennedy Periods*; 2. *Writings on Strategy, 1945–1951*; 3. *Writings on Strategy, 1952–1960*, in 3 vols.; 4. *Writings on Strategy, 1961–1969 and Retrospectives*. I have cited much material from this collection as Trachtenberg, *Strategic Thought*, followed by the part number, and the volume number if necessary.

The RAND Archives were closed for relocation during the time I was doing this study, but I had access to a multitude of RAND reports from various sources, including RAND websites. I have identified these reports by their RAND numbers when there is no other public collection in which they are available.

I conducted a number of interviews in completing this project, and these are duly noted, but it really got under way in 1978–79 with a series of conversations with Richard Neustadt that initiated my thinking about the topic. In a few instances I have indicated my unorthodox indebtedness by citing my recollections of Neustadt's remarks, never in quotes, as Neustadt conversations, 1978–79.

Blind Oracles

The Social Role of the Man of Knowledge

AT THE END OF 1961 John Kennedy appointed Walt Whitman Rostow head of the Policy Planning Staff in the State Department. Almost fifteen years before, George Kennan had held the same job and provided intellectual leadership for the Truman administration after publishing the famous X-article, "The Sources of Soviet Conduct." From this position Rostow, an MIT economist and the celebrated author of *The Stages of Economic Growth* (1960), wrote a paper, "Basic National Security Policy," that tried simultaneously to elaborate a vision of America's role in the world and to guide decisions. Rostow circulated it among Kennedy's advisors on foreign affairs—preeminently former Harvard dean and then assistant for national security McGeorge Bundy and his staff; Robert McNamara and the "Whiz Kids" in the Department of Defense; and Kennan himself, serving briefly as ambassador to Yugoslavia.

During this period, "the best and the brightest" made learned discussion the common currency of Washington politics, and intellectuals and their ideas stepped from the academy onto a world stage. But the times were rife with ironic tales, one of which was Rostow's. His associates reacted strongly to his essay. Rostow believed that a nuclear war was winnable, but Kennan wrote to him that he would "rather see my children dead" than have them experience such a thing. More important, Kennan told Rostow, the emphasis on economic development was "irresponsible," "reckless[ly] plundering," and "vulgar." McNamara's staff of civilian strategic thinkers did not bother to take issue with the substance but simply said that Rostow's work "should be . . . thrown away." McNamara shared this opinion less openly. The text needed extensive and time-consuming editing, which the secretary of defense did not consider "remunerative." The men around Bundy also doubted that the ideas were "worth the trouble." His deputy, Carl Kaysen, called Rostow's document "bean soup," "blah, blah, blah, blah," "silly," "a lot of nonsense" in which the president "just wasn't interested."[1] In a memo to Rostow, Kaysen mocked the ideas of *The Stages of Economic Growth* that permeated the text of the proposed national security document. Bundy, the most significant critic, persistently objected to the idea that Rostow could write down "doctrine" for the United

---

[1] Kaysen, Oral History (July 1966), pp. 99–102, JFK Library.

States. It was foolish to think a strategy existed distinct from the decisions of the president and the people around him like Bundy.[2]

IDEAS AND POLITICS IN AMERICA

This book examines questions of ideas and foreign affairs on which the Rostow episode touches. What is the role of knowledge in politics? What should learning offer public life? How do political and learned culture contrast? This case study gives limited answers to these questions and others like them by exploring what occurred in the United States from World War II to Vietnam, when men interested in applying scholarly concepts to international policy obtained a distinctive voice in the counsels of state.

Over the course of American history, diplomacy has attracted many thoughtful people. In the nineteenth century we can look to Jefferson, Madison, John Quincy Adams, William Seward, and Richard Olney. In the twentieth century, in addition to the people I will talk about in some detail, there are, for example, Elihu Root, Henry Stimson, Herbert Hoover, James Schlesinger, Zbigniew Brzezinski, Cyrus Vance, Jeanne Kirkpatrick, Richard Perle, and Paul Wolfowitz. International affairs beguile contemplative people concerned with civic life. Diplomacy is often separated from the hurly-burly of domestic politics, and secrecy surrounds it. Questions about the nature of a polity, sovereignty, the role of force in human endeavors, and deep issues of *patria* never need be far from the thoughts of the policymaker. An aura of experience and dignity sets the world of the statesman off from that of the politician.

When we say that a decision was "political," or that something happened "because of politics" or was resolved "on political grounds," we mean to say that even if a good decision was made, it was not made on the basis of the merits. We often assume that there *is* such a basis, though it may be indeterminate. The contesting parties in the disputed election of 2000 sometimes resembled two packs of animals fighting over a piece of meat. Their spokespeople, however, constantly tried to provide legitimacy for the actions of whichever group they represented, despite the fact that they were partisans. Their inability to ratify the behavior of either side was not surprising. Metaphorically, they had a ten-foot ladder with which they were attempting to span a twelve-foot crevasse, and only miraculous or illusory techniques could be successful. There was an unbridgeable gap between the struggle of interests and the laudable. Even when the winner of the election was determined, the victory lacked

[2] The dispute over Rostow makes fascinating reading in FRUS 1961–63, vol. 8, *National Security Policy*. For Bundy and staff, pp. 243, 263, 538; for McNamara and staff, pp. 267n, 268ff., 329, 489. Kennan's criticism is found on pp. 285ff.

authority for many. "Politics" had resolved the conflict—not justice but the structure of power, which might be cultural, military, or intellectual.

THE HISTORICAL SETTING

People who think about civic life worry about this disjuncture between politics and merit. If politics were rational, decisions would be uncontestable, and in the twentieth century American thinkers on war and peace emphasized that knowledge and science might leverage politics into the realm of the right. Within the profession of political science itself an ideal occupation was to sit for a time at the side of leaders, and the prerogatives of thinkers in international affairs were emphasized. But commentators brought both historical and contemporary approaches to bear in the hope of creating a more reasoned foreign policy. From the Greeks to the present, historians of political ideas told college-trained Americans, good leaders had had the assistance of experts.[3]

The Greek Plato headed an institute for statesmen, the Academy. In *The Republic* Plato analogized the harmonious state to the harmonious soul. The just polity and the just individual were for him structurally identical, because reason ruled in each. In the book he outlined the contours of the perfect city led by a class of guardians schooled in Platonic thought. For Plato genuine political understanding was a special sort of knowledge. The guardian-kings would be philosophers, those who studied the nature of life and governance. The guardians would know what was right and good, and would rule their city accordingly. Plato said that the human race would not advance until those who studied philosophy acquired power, or those who had political control became philosophers.

In early-modern and modern Europe, whose traditions were thought to derive from those of the Greeks, political thinkers were also involved in contemporary politics. Niccolò Machiavelli had a minor political career in the small Italian states during the Renaissance. His classic text, *The Prince* (1513), showed how rulers everywhere should use reason and enlightened self-interest

---

[3] In the following account, I have drawn on George H. Sabine's *A History of Political Theory* (New York: Holt, Rinehart, and Winston, 1938), but this text, though the most accomplished work, formulates arguments that can be found in many other texts and contexts; see also Siep Sturman, "The Canon of the History of Political Thought: Its Critique and a Proposed Alternative," *History and Theory* 39 (2000): 147–66; John G. Gunnell, "Philosophy and Political Theory," *Government and Opposition* 14 (1979): 199–203, and Gunnell, *The Descent of Political Theory: The Genealogy of an American Vocation* (Chicago: University of Chicago Press, 1993), pp. 60–145. Herbert Goldhamer's *The Advisor* (New York: Elsevier, 1978) is a descriptive summary of these ideas written by a RAND employee. Another account is in Roman Kolkowicz, "Intellectuals and the Nuclear Deterrence System," in *The Logic of Nuclear Terror*, ed. Kolkowicz (Boston: Allen and Unwin, 1987), pp. 19–29.

to preserve their power. According to the canonical wisdom, *The Prince* began the modern, realistic period of political thought, because Machiavelli was concerned with the statesman's effectiveness. He was ambiguous about whether the model statesman should pursue just policies or should merely be, in the standard phrase, Machiavellian.

One hundred and fifty years after Machiavelli, John Locke and his followers, on the contrary, expounded the essentials of democracy. In addition to drawing up the constitution for the Carolina colony in British North America, Locke wrote his *Second Treatise of Government* (1690). He began a tradition of liberal thought, and his successors spoke for the sane impulses of modernizing Britain, which envisioned that politics would purge itself of the irrational. This became the modest equivalent of Plato's hope that one could square the circle of power and knowledge.

A subsidiary current of the late eighteenth century flowing from Locke— the political development that led to revolution in the British colonies—was particularly interesting in the United States. The American Founding Fathers defended a mixed form of popular government. In the *Federalist Papers* three of these men—Alexander Hamilton, James Madison, and John Jay—pondered the historical experience of the ancient world. They used a rough-and-ready empiricism and common sense of a high order to comment on the Constitution, which had safely navigated the American people thereafter.

By the late nineteenth century, according to accepted views, the social order might pervert the political thinker. Karl Marx indicted Western economic and political life in *Das Kapital* (1867–94). His followers also theorized about society but, by the early twentieth century, showed that the Marxist tradition was equally adept in the world of politics. Lenin, Trotsky, and Stalin brought Communist rule to Russia in the Bolshevik Revolution of 1917 and created the Soviet Union. Although they demonstrated how powerful ideas could be in the real world, as antidemocratic philosophers, these Marxists were, for Americans, crooked instances of Plato's philosopher-kings.

A comparatively mild set of prescriptions about the role of knowledge in politics in the United States paralleled the European developments that gave rise to the Communist state. After the Civil War, a generation of well-to-do citizens advocated the efficient rule of "the best men," devoted to honest government and motivated by the common good.[4] Political machines in American cities, which immigrants and their slightly more Americanized urban leadership dominated, underscored the need for such governance. Its rationale was elaborated by later university-trained generations skilled in new sciences of society. Reformers brought into government individuals who emphasized

[4] See John G. Sproat, *"The Best Men": Liberal Reformers in the Gilded Age* (New York: Oxford University Press, 1968).

scholarship about administration that managers would carry out impartially. The progressive president Woodrow Wilson, himself one of the first generation of American doctorates in the social study of politics, was prepared at the graduate school at Johns Hopkins and called, ultimately, to the presidency of Princeton. Wilson imbibed common ideas of a neutral commitment to advancing public life. In 1912 his future assistant for both domestic and foreign policies, Edward House, wrote a novel, *Philip Dru: Administrator*. In this fantasy set in the 1920s and 1930s, Dru, a former West Pointer who has won a national prize for strategic thinking in war, leads a successful revolution against a corrupted American government. As a dictator, "panoplied in justice and with the light of reason in his eyes," he proclaims himself "Administrator of the Republic," and solves all of the country's domestic problems. Shortly before giving up power and sailing off with his beloved, the Administrator deftly and efficiently establishes a new international order to "bring about the comity of nations."[5]

The closest Wilson himself came to this sort of viewpoint was to create a group of university-based advisors, "The Inquiry," who prepared reports at the Versailles Conference after successful American participation in World War I. This group exemplified the president's idea of the relation between expertise and foreign policy. For the president and these men, the American program formulated at the end of World War I properly fell within the province of scholarship. *Wilsonianism* was "a scientific peace," based on "the disinterested finding of specialists." Wilson famously told a group of these academics: "Tell me what's right and I'll fight for it. Give me a guaranteed position."[6]

The advice of scholars about the virtues of administrative science was vague and talismanic up through World War II. However, after 1945 the discipline changed and so did the goals of the learned involved in politics. Universities emerged from the war with a sense of their scientific character. More hard-headed appraisals for taming the irrationality of politics would replace old nostrums of administrative reorganization. Certainly these ideas antedated World War II, and older students of administration and newer experts on policy shared many beliefs. Nonetheless, a young generation of Ph.D.s argued that real progress warranted innovative claims to authority. Rostow's essay was only one of many such claims, but just as the responses to it suggest the essay's tortured history, so the stories of other brainy attempts to get a purchase on global affairs are similarly convoluted.

[5] Edward M. House, *Philip Dru, Administrator; a Story of Tomorrow, 1920–1935* (New York: B. W. Huebsch, 1912), pp. 46, 95, 148, 153, 181, 297.
[6] I have here relied on Lawrence E. Gelfand's careful work, *The Inquiry: American Preparations for Peace, 1917–1919* (New Haven: Yale University Press, 1963), esp. pp. 16, 33, 328, 330–31.

INTELLECTUALS AND WAR

The "intellectuals" in my title comprise three overlapping circles of scholars and writers thinking about war from 1945 to 1975. The first is a scientifically oriented cadre of experts, usually working in or close to the collegiate world. These men often had a significant association with the RAND Corporation, the think-tank run by the air force. I look at RAND's organizational theory, ideas of scientific management, and forms of economic analysis; and its impact on social science in traditional centers of higher education. I gauge the bearing of RAND's theories on diplomatic practice, and vice versa. Influential economists and political scientists from the university world studied war at RAND, or consulted for it, but of particular importance are the essays of Bernard Brodie in the late 1940s, the reports on strategic "vulnerability" identified with Albert Wohlstetter in the 1950s, and the work of Thomas Schelling on deterrence in early 1960s.

This first circle connected professionally to a second: the foreign-policy academics who were allies of the political scientist Richard Neustadt and the historian Ernest May, particularly in "the May Group" at Harvard and the Kennedy School of Government. My account explores the less formal and more historically grounded social science formulated in Neustadt's *Presidential Power* (1960) and the way the May Group offered advice to those in power. Two events that this circle studied receive detailed attention: the Cuban Missile Crisis of 1962, and the conflict with the British later that same year over the Skybolt missile.

Third, I emphasize as a separate circle those individuals who had bases in the university and who achieved the highest positions of influence from 1947 to 1969. The narrative focuses on George Kennan, Paul Nitze, Dean Rusk, McGeorge Bundy, Rostow, and Henry Kissinger. The discussion converges on events that committed the United States to the fight in Vietnam.

Overall, the men who actually made decisions were least concerned with *scientific* ideas of any sort, and had a multifaceted view of the application of intelligence to society. Kennan and Kissinger, who eschewed much American policy science, were more central than Rostow, who embraced it. Yet all of them interacted with members of the other two circles, and most had close ties to RAND or Harvard. In looking at this third circle, defined by both position and intellect, I scrutinize how the assumptions of the more social scientific strategists affected the truly powerful who had ties to the academy. The question is: how does political practice, for intellectuals, modify theory? I am concerned not so much with the policies that they carried out, as with the fit of these policies to the mind-set of the policymakers.

The book concludes with a twofold analysis. First there is an intellectual history of what came to be known as *The Pentagon Papers*—the huge secret document collection of American involvement in Southeast Asia leaked to journalists in 1971. Rather than focusing on the unauthorized release of *The Pentagon Papers* or on the details of the war that this report revealed, I consider it as a collective enterprise undertaken by men with backgrounds at RAND and the Kennedy School. This multiauthored, forty-seven-volume "book" can be read to uncover the academic presuppositions about war and history governing the thinking of the men whose careers my study traces. Second, and in closing, I examine how policymakers came to perceive their role in the postmortem about Vietnam conducted from the mid-1970s until the end of the century. In writing their memoirs, many policymakers with ties to the intellectuals assisted in the construction of a dominant view of the foreign policy of the United States since World War II. I want to place the historical work of people like former defense secretary Robert McNamara in *In Retrospect* (1995) and *Argument Without End* (1999) in the context of ideas that policy scientists and reflective policymakers created.

The three circles, in my estimation, contain the leading men of intellect who were both interested in war and influential in government from 1945 to 1975. They are the experts or theorists or civilian strategists to whom I refer more generally throughout these pages. My intellectuals were not humanists known for their reading in literature and history, or leaders of popular social science—people more likely to be considered intellectuals in the twenty-first century. Nor were they critics like Linus Pauling or Noam Chomsky, or opinion makers like Reinhold Niebuhr. The aim is only to explicate the views of policy intellectuals in the shadow of the White House. After World War II my students of war brought into existence many organizations for the examination of global politics and fields of inquiry such as international relations and security studies, and carved out new niches in older academic disciplines such as economics and political science. These intellectuals finally transformed some dimensions of institutional life in the most prestigious universities in the United States.

No distinctive style of thought about war was unique to Harvard. Scholars of world conflict at Columbia, Chicago, Hopkins, MIT, Yale, and Princeton often shared the same ideas, which also prevailed at RAND, in the military, and among government-employed doctorates. But while many schools of higher learning contributed to the strategic dialogue, Harvard was still foremost, and its organizational nexus deserves special mention. Its products cast a long shadow over this volume. They were, however, not always the men of the old Harvard that Boston Brahmins dominated, but of the cosmopolitan Harvard that flowered after World War II. Cambridge accepted into its midst Jews, the middle class, the able and meritorious. These intellectuals defined Harvard's commanding position.

Their Intellectual Milieu

Although the three groups of men complexly acted together, and differed among themselves, they were all part of an educated milieu that needs to be made explicit. A patron saint of American thinkers was the philosopher John Dewey, who taught for ten years at the University of Chicago and then from 1904 to 1929 at Columbia University in New York City. His work that bore fruit in the 1920s and 1930s gave a new flavor to the interest in a reasoned politics and, in the eyes of many followers, a revolutionary justification for their ideas.

Knowledge for Dewey was never an inert relation in which a disembodied mind knew the external world. His "instrumental" theory of truth urged that scientific knowledge integrated present experience with guided activity to deliver desired future experiences. Dewey and his successors—loosely known as pragmatists—presumed that the twentieth century should apply to the human world this experimental method that had advanced understanding of the natural.

Dewey made the argument many times but most compellingly in one essay that became required reading for generations of students, "The Construction of Good," chapter 10 of *The Quest for Certainty* (1929). Dewey eloquently called for the "method of intelligence" in human affairs. Earlier philosophy had abdicated responsibility. The intelligentsia articulated the "purely compensatory" to console them "for the actual and social impotency of the calling of thought to which they are devoted." Philosophers had sought "a refuge of complacency in the notion that knowledge is something too sublime to be contaminated by contact with things of change and practice." Philosophy had made knowledge "a morally irresponsible estheticism." Again and again Dewey exclaimed that knowledge must be "active and operative." Only reorganizing the environment, scientifically removing specific troubles and perplexities, would procure human goods. When met with skepticism about the application of "funded experience" and "contriving intelligence" to social life, Dewey contended that if instrumentalism were disallowed in the public arena, the sole options were "routine, the force of some personality, strong leadership or . . . the pressure of momentary circumstances." *The Quest for Certainty* argued against the distinction between (scientific) fact and (social) value, "is" and "ought." Ethical judgments were about the consequences of behavior that people desired. But, for Dewey, people could gauge the outcomes of certain kinds of behavior and attribute causality correctly and, in such rehearsals, would figure out what they wanted. Experience verified the essence of morality. The human sciences could provide us the wherewithal for making more adequate judgments. Dewey assumed that what ought to be desired was no more than what people actually desired when they were clear about what they wanted and how they could get what they wanted.[7]

In a series of short works written in the late 1920s and 1930s Dewey formulated the relevance of instrumentalism to politics in the United States. Of particular importance was *The Public and Its Problems* of 1927. Dewey debated the interest in propaganda among social scientists that World War I had made prominent. The efficacy of democracy depended on a public reared to make decisions about policy. But the Great War had demonstrated to social scientists that deception might sway the people's deliberations from the correct path. Bureaucrats might manipulate information and, as with advertising, appeal to motives that were less than conscious. The political thinker and journalist Walter Lippmann and Harold Lasswell, the political sociologist, captured the contours of these concerns, respectively, in *The Phantom Public* (1925) and *Psychopathology and Politics* (1930). Both men mistrusted the public and, with a bow to the need for the forms of democracy, advocated placing power in the hands of an administrative elite. It would make national policy and, in effect, lead the public for its own good. In addition to Lippmann and Lasswell, a number of thinkers who wrote for journals such as the *New Republic*, the *Nation*, *Common Sense*, and *Plan Age* claimed inspiration from Dewey. They wanted to reconstruct if not abandon democracy in an age of complexity. An educated public, making rational decisions, was a myth. Instead American society must have experts who would act in the name of the public but with access to Dewey's sort of social knowledge.

Dewey did not side with this privileged managerialism even if his ideas were often opaque enough to prop up its prejudices. *The Public and its Problems* argued that America *needed* an articulate public to use pragmatic social knowledge legitimately. Admitting that the United States did not have such a public, Dewey nonetheless insisted that a class of mandarins was not an acceptable substitute. Without an effective democracy to make choices about social issues, experts were "an oligarchy managed in the interests of the few." A public was a precondition to making the scientific method effective in cultural life. Experts gained knowledge, but the public must determine what they investigated and how they employed the results. "The improvement of the methods and conditions of [public] debate, discussion, and persuasion" was mandatory. The technocratic managerial class discovered and made known the facts and experimental knowledge on which policy depended. But democratic debate did the job of the framing and executing courses of action.[8]

---

[7] See Dewey, *The Quest for Certainty* (New York: Minton, Balch, 1929), esp. chap. 10.

[8] Dewey, *The Public and Its Problems* (New York: Henry Holt, 1927), pp. 116–17, 123–25, 196–97, 202–8, quote at p. 209. Robert Westbrook's *John Dewey and American Democracy* (Ithaca: Cornell University Press, 1991) takes up these issues carefully, making the strongest case for the interpretation of Dewey as an antitechnocratic liberal.

Many versions of Dewey's instrumentalism flowered across the United States.[9] As we have seen, some who claimed to follow Dewey believed that scientific administrators ought to direct the culture. Other followers were ardent reformers and placed a compassionate human understanding at the heart of their lives. Still other "scientific naturalists" downplayed reform, stressed the impartial nature of social investigation, and gave priority to the quantifiable aspects of study. A European movement centered in Vienna in the 1920s and 1930s influenced the strictest scientific naturalists. When Hitler came to power in Germany in the 1930s, members of the Wiener Kreis—the Vienna Circle— and their adherents emigrated to the United States and established logical positivism—or just positivism—as an important school of thought. Positivists explored the foundations of the physical sciences and argued that the sort of empirical knowledge that the physical sciences embodied was the only sort. Using the tools of mathematical logic, they set out clear-cut criteria concerning the form of knowledge, and the appropriate techniques for obtaining it.

Dewey and his many adherents ritualistically invoked the scientific method as the means to obtain social knowledge. But whereas they were fuzzy about the precise nature of scientific reasoning, the positivists were not. They looked at the hard sciences and their theoretical underpinnings and urged that a single method dominated all legitimate investigation. Two philosophers, Carl Hempel at Princeton and Ernest Nagel at Columbia, were the leading postwar positivists. Nagel had studied with the naturalist philosopher Morris Cohen of City College and Dewey himself at Columbia. Cohen and Nagel together authored a textbook that showed the spiritual closeness of many pragmatists and positivists, *An Introduction to Logic and Scientific Method* (1934).[10] Nagel's career extended well into the postwar period, however, and reached its height in 1961 with the publication of *The Structure of Science*.[11] Hempel's most significant writings were collected in a work of 1965, *Aspects of Scientific Explanation*.[12]

Dewey and the positivists famously differed about the widely known positivist argument that science was value-free, and that there was a cleavage between facts and values, the world of the scientist and that of the moralist. Positivists then made the denigrating corollary that the empirical meaning of science contrasted to the emotive meaning of nonscientific language, which was strictly meaning*less*. This position conflicted with that of the instrumentalists who refused to distinguish between value and fact and who believed that

---

[9] Varied appraisals of Dewey's influence on political science may be found in the symposium "Dewey's Pragmatism, Social Inquiry, and Democracy," *American Journal of Political Science* 43 (1999): 518–647.

[10] New York: Harcourt, Brace.

[11] *The Structure of Science: Problems in the Logic of Scientific Explanation* (New York: Harcourt, Brace, and World, 1961).

[12] *Aspects of Scientific Explanation, and Other Essays in the Philosophy of Science* (New York: Free Press, 1965).

morality was being made experimental. But the identical emphasis on the one experimental method that promised to give us a purchase over nature minimized these differences, especially among the educated readers of philosophy. Positivists and pragmatists often united in disdain for soft, humanistic inquiry, and in their respect for methodological precision and statistics.

My foreign policy intellectuals were steeped in these writings. Both of my first two groups of intellectuals—the more mathematically oriented RAND theorists of war and the more historically oriented scholars influenced by Neustadt—largely agreed with the dominant credo of their time. Views about the need for advanced training in economics, political science, or sociology and the challenge of using it in a democratic polity were boilerplate in the literature of the postwar period. As one statement of principles put it, Washington officials, "the collective modern prince," "obviously require[d]" social science, which was reason "in its modern dress." Few policy scientists, said a second, "would dispute that decision-makers are in need of assistance from policy science." "No sensible person," wrote the scientific philosopher-strategist Morton Kaplan, "would want . . . a president of the United States unable to understand the restrictions placed upon his possible decisions by correct strategic choice and analysis." But, argued Richard Solomon, a government official and social scientist Ph.D., the decision-making "consumers" often lacked the training necessary to "absorb the insights of the analyst." Max Millikan, who had an illustrious career going back and forth between government and university, nonetheless allowed that if the diplomat had the "intellectual curiosity and persistence" to explore social science tools, he could "substantially improve the wisdom of his own practical judgments." The famous MIT social scientist Daniel Lerner argued that while democratic politics might seem to compromise expertise, social science had to prove "worthy of its mission" by demonstrating the connection between knowledge and democracy. It was, John Steinbruner insisted, a "hard task" to integrate "the abstract paradigms of decision theory into the realities of political life."[13]

---

[13] These rhetorical expressions were conventional and common in the literature and can be found everywhere. In order, Pio D. Uliassi, "Government Sponsored Research on International and Foreign Affairs," in *The Use and Abuse of Social Science: Behavioral Research and Policy Making*, ed. Irving Louis Horowitz (New Brunswick, N.J.: Transaction Books, 1971), p. 287; Richard Smoke and Alexander George, "Theory for Policy in International Affairs," *Policy Sciences* 4 (1973): 410 (the end of the sentence reads, "in coping with the long time horizon"); Kaplan, *On Historical and Political Knowing* (Chicago: University of Chicago Press, 1971), p. 49; Solomon, "Political Culture and Diplomacy in the Twenty-first Century," in *The Political Culture of Foreign Area and International Studies: Essays in Honor of Lucian W. Pye*, ed. Richard J. Samuels and Myron Wiener (Washington, D.C.: Brassey's, 1992), p. 152; Millikan, "Inquiry and Policy: The Relation of Knowledge to Action," in *The Human Meanings of the Social Sciences*, ed. Daniel Lerner (New York: Meridian, 1959), p. 179; Lerner, "Social Science: Whence and Whither?" in Lerner, *Human Meaning*, pp. 29–32; Steinbruner, *The Cybernetic Theory of Decision: New Dimensions of Political Analysis* (Princeton: Princeton University Press, 1974), p. 342.

At the same time, in the thirty years after 1945, and not least in foreign-policy circles, a countertradition hostile to Dewey grew up. It especially disparaged the technocratic aspects of his thought, the "scientism" of university learning, and social-science positivism. But in the American context, this countertradition was a subsidiary current and never fully worked out as a position in the human sciences. It did obtain a hold on some of my intellectuals who achieved positions of power, notably George Kennan and Henry Kissinger, and might serve to focus disagreement. For example, Kennan's outraged response to Rostow's paper "Basic National Security Policy" revealed Kennan's distaste for the social science position Rostow embodied. But it is unclear that this dialogue between supporters and critics of instrumentalist ideas led to consistently different policy prescriptions.

Their Historical Assumptions

In addition to this conversation about the character of social knowledge, my intellectuals all shared important substantive assumptions about the recent past. The first concerned Woodrow Wilson and World War I. The United States joined the Allied Powers to defeat Germany in 1917 and 1918, and then Wilson presided over the Versailles peace conference, on which he imposed his new League of Nations, an organization of states that would band together to prevent war. Despite Wilson's sponsorship, the United States rejected the Treaty of Versailles and did not join the League. Twenty-five years later, commentators believed that the harsh peace imposed on Germany and the American retreat from the world had contributed to the collapse of the state system and had led to World War II. Opinion divided over whether Wilson's political ineptness was responsible for the isolationism in the United States, or whether the domestic opponents who outmaneuvered Wilson must accept the blame. Nonetheless, a consensus existed that the United States was called upon to enter the Great War and that Wilson was central to its outcome. Wilson was a tragic hero for some commentators, while others dismissed his high-flown sensibility as moralistic and naive.

No one gave much thought to the context in which Wilson developed his peace plan—the collapse of Russia, the rise of Bolshevism there, and the public repudiation of European colonialism. Communism and imperialism propelled Wilson's formulations, and appropriate deliberation about them might have made his later critics more sympathetic to his alternative to Leninist revolution and empire. The later critics, too, insufficiently appreciated the impact, on many thoughtful observers, of the trench warfare on the western front. Wilson's concept of world order—even if that of an innocent—can be seen as a reasoned response to the unprecedented failure of traditional diplomacy that World War I represented. Debating the role of Wilson, policy intellectuals assumed by the

1940s that the United States must pursue an internationalist and interventionist role but that the tough-minded must overrule the high-minded.

The second assumption concerned the American entry into World War II. While the rise of an avenging Germany in the late 1930s focused American policy, events in the Far East brought the United States into the conflict. There, most clearly, the Americans resisted the Japanese war against China. From 1937 onwards, and particularly after 1939, the United States opposed Japanese expansionism. Believing for a long time that the Japanese would not go to war against them, the Americans pressured Japan economically. In a strike against American military installations at Pearl Harbor, Hawaii, at the end of 1941, Japan broke out of a system of international politics in Asia that the United States dominated. Following the "sneak attack," the United States was brought into the war against Hitler when, allied to Japan, Germany declared war on the United States.

The specialists of the 1940s, 1950s, and 1960s discounted the context of political strife that formed the background to Pearl Harbor. They paid little attention to the economic competition in the Far East, or the economic diplomacy that the United States used to mold international politics in Asia. With the experts, as for many Americans, the only issue was deceit. Without disputing the American response to the Japanese in World War II—including the use of two atomic bombs at its end—one needs to recognize that students of strategy in the United States had no interest in the role that America played in bringing on the Far Eastern war, or even in the history of the tensions that had led up to the fighting. In the postwar period scholars of strategic studies would assume that war came through malevolent surprise.

The last assumption I call the World War II syndrome. When John Kennedy was inaugurated in 1961, the world learned that the torch had been passed to a new generation of Americans. Those who set the tone of much public life in the 1960s had been, like Kennedy, junior officers in the war. Unlike Kennedy, most had not seen combat, but more articulate than many who had, the new leaders found issues of war and peace unambiguous. They had opposed the Nazis in Germany and the Japanese who had launched the attack at Pearl Harbor. Throughout the "hard and bitter peace" that Kennedy said followed the war a different enemy had emerged in global communism. In a long and furious contest of interest and ideology, the Soviet Union and its allies were assimilated to Nazism under the rubric of totalitarianism. The issues in the struggle against Germany (and Japan) were ethically compelling. The proud sense of being on the side of the righteous in the late 1940s and beyond in the Cold War was continuous with the equivalent sense that had emerged in the late 1930s and early 1940s. My intellectuals *knew* that when the crunch came, America was right and its enemies wrong. They assumed that global politics held little nuance.

As the conflict with the Soviet Union evolved after 1945, the authorities only had to choose between an assertive response to the Russian threat, and an aggressive response. They had few second thoughts, and hardly any agonized about the possibility of American aggrandizement. Defense intellectuals were simplistic in their assessment of Russian strength in Eastern Europe after the war, complementing that of the United States in Western Europe; in their assessment of the extension of Soviet power around the world, again complementing that of the United States; and in their assessment of the emergence of a nuclear arsenal in the USSR, finally complementing that in America. This judgment is not meant to deny the superiority of Western values over those of the communists in the long competition, or to imply that the Russians had a less distorted view of American diplomacy. Rather, it highlights a lasting aspect of the American approach—the lack of complication in the imagination of men who could make complex appraisals in other spheres.[14]

The nature of their reflection about the basic issue of the Cold War had one crucial consequence for most of the period I have considered. The civilian strategists regularly overestimated the power and malignity of their Soviet adversary. After World War II the United States was the most formidable nation in the world. The war had invigorated the American economy, while it had devastated that of other nations. The United States' population was intact, and its technological superiority overwhelming. As the various nations rebuilt after the war, however, American hegemony would undoubtedly lessen. This basic fact underlay America's relations with its European allies in the war, with Germany and Japan, and with the Soviet Union. But however much more powerful the United States was than the USSR, the American policymakers saw the continuing comparative growth of Russian strength as almost fatally compromising their polity. Henry Kissinger's famous book of 1961, *The Necessity for Choice*, began with the flat statement that the United States could "not afford another decline like that which has characterized the past decade and a half," a further "deterioration of our position."[15] The appropriate measure was the supremacy of 1945.

FINDINGS

This book examines the origins and social locus of expert thinking on defense, the trajectory of this thought, its influence on policy, and its grip on political

---

[14] The same kind of balanced point is made by Matthew Evangelista, "Second-Guessing the Experts: Citizens' Group Criticisms of the Central Intelligence Agency's Estimates of Soviet Military Policy," *International History Review* 19 (1997): 593.

[15] Kissinger, *The Necessity for Choice: Prospects of an American Foreign Policy* (New York: Harper and Brothers, 1961), p. 1.

reality. I direct attention to the truth-value of the ideas but also to the culture of the scholars, and the demands that their training, ambition, sense of public service, and the state placed on them. I am interested in foreign policy itself, but more in what my intellectuals made of it. The emphasis is on words more than actions. I am not unconcerned with doing and deserving, but emphasize thinking *about* war. I study the decisions of the powerful, but more closely the ideas of the intellectuals among them and the concepts of scholars close to power. The story begins with the rise of men of knowledge to positions of authority after World War II, and charts the development of more formal concepts during the 1950s when a mentally conservative administration thwarted intellectuals. The history continues with an elaboration of various modes of social science understanding that had become self-congratulatory by the early 1960s, and moves toward the uncomfortable resolution of Vietnam. The book concludes with the perceived discrediting of both scientific and nonscientific visions in the persons of Robert McNamara and Henry Kissinger, but finds that the intellectuals found a new role for themselves conjuring up formulas of expiation.

Nonetheless, the study is more than a history of American knowledge about statecraft, for the text joins narrative with an analysis of the adequacy of our social understanding. My intellectuals include a broad range of thinkers who held a variety of views on an array of topics. Although oversimplification is a danger, some limited generalizations are warranted, and some striking characteristics stand out.

The evidence requires that we be skeptical about the knowledge that all of these men declared to have. While they professed deep understanding, they actually groped in the dark. Much of the time fashion was more important than validity. At the same time, irrespective of the quality of their knowledge, in the usual case the ideas of the cerebral strategists had little causal impact. They served to legitimate but not to energize policies. Intellectuals were most effective when they showed, after the fact, that some endeavors had been desirable. Or they articulated schema that exculpated policymakers—or themselves—from responsibility for action later identified as bad. The basic though not the only function of strategic ideas was to provide politicians with the fictions used to give meaning to policies for the public.[16]

Decision makers often wanted impartial advice from experts, but the notions that had currency frequently only burnished the reputations of statesmen. Scholars wanted to assist leadership in both a realistic and an ethical fashion, but they only credited selected conceptualizations, and government service required constraints on thinking.

---

[16] I use the term *fictions* in the sense of Edmund Morgan, in *Inventing the People: The Rise of Popular Sovereignty in England and America* (New York: Norton, 1988).

A final finding is that many of the strategists I have examined were essentially apolitical, in that they lacked what I must call for want of a better phrase *elemental political sense*. It is almost as if they sought to learn in a seminar room or from cogitation what only instinct, experience, and savvy could teach. They frequently showed themselves blind to the jugular of international affairs. This stance often accompanied a distrust of democratic impulses in foreign affairs and a need to engage in a simplified public information program, or a fear of what a poorly guided polity might do. This collection of traits and beliefs might characterize both social scientists and members of the countertradition.

I have chosen a number of very difficult examples—those concerning destruction and killing—to suggest the irony at the heart of modern political studies. The edifice of social knowledge in the United States presupposes that it can offer something to politics and better lead us to public goods. Statecraft demands knowledge. Yet my philosophers in government knew and understood little, and had little influence qua intellectuals, except to perform feats of ventriloquy. But whatever distortions attached to their commitments and to unyielding attempts to bend the world to their purposes, they seized on a reality that is hard to dislodge. If we give up on knowledge and thus, to some degree, social science as even a partial guide in human affairs, we leave decisions to habit, authority, or chance. What alternatives do we have to the patient and systematic investigation of phenomena and the exploration of causes and consequences? That is, what alternatives do we have to the sort of reasoning in which the theorists of conflict engaged?

Overall, American culture paid a high price for a product of dubious value. But that does not mean that the price was too high. For me the hard lesson is that we do not have any good alternatives to the constricted thinking dominant from the 1940s through the 1970s; and that we cannot do without thinking. The accepted wisdom of the era fell short of what we might want, but I have been hard pressed to offer alternatives. My conclusions are more a meditation than a call for radical change.

CHAPTER 1

Scientific Management and War, 1910–1960

TAYLORISM

One of the most important models in the academic engagement with the Cold War got its start at the beginning of the twentieth century with studies of the competence of business. In that period Philadelphia-born engineer Frederick Winslow Taylor made a reputation as an efficiency expert, assisting organizations in managing their workers. Taylor applied "science" to the shop floor to increase productivity. With a stopwatch and timing methods, associates would examine a workman's jobs to see what he could do more quickly. They also offered incentives, and Taylor looked at an entire manufacturing plant to learn how it could operate more effectively. He explored the distribution of the labor force, the hours of employment and number of hours worked, the job hierarchies, the purchasing, inventory, and routing of materials, and other variables of this sort.

In 1910 labor lawyer Louis Brandeis made Taylor famous in hearings before the Interstate Commerce Commission, called the Eastern Rate Case. Brandeis urged that railroad charges were too high. No revolutionary, however, Brandeis argued that the railroad leaders lacked knowledge of their costs and the basis of their pricing arrangements. Calling on Taylor's notions of a well-run business, Brandeis asserted that the railroads were inefficient and passed their inefficiencies on to the consumer. He gave the name "scientific management" to the "Taylor system."[1]

In the real world of the factory, the analogue of "Taylorism" was Henry Ford's assembly line in the mass production of automobiles, which took the crucial step in creating a consumer culture in the United States. Along a belt that moved from chassis to finished car, Ford placed workers so that each one had a single easily understood function. Managers arranged production so that workmen performed this function as efficiently as possible. As the Germans put it at the time, TAYLORISMUS + FORDISMUS = AMERICANISMUS.[2] Ford's assembly line specially applied Taylor's principles. Taylor had expressed notions that

---

[1] On Taylor there is Robert Kanigel, *The One Best Way: Frederick Winslow Taylor and the Enigma of Efficiency* (New York: Viking Press, 1997).

[2] Thomas Parke Hughes, *American Genesis: A Century of Invention and Technological Enthusiasm, 1870–1970* (New York: Viking, 1989), p. 285.

pertained to a variety of organized activities in which many people acted in concert to achieve a complicated aim.

When Brandeis made Taylorism a household word, the ideas of the man himself were making an impact in two different areas, one in the quasi-scholarly world, the other in the military. Progressives in the first years of the twentieth century believed that knowledge, efficiency, and scientific planning, arrayed against ignorance, error, and economic waste, might achieve social reform. In the academic setting the newly burgeoning social sciences—economics, sociology, and political science—embodied this impulse. The guardians of these emerging disciplines convinced the social elite that they were useful experts who could be entrusted with power, just as they simultaneously distanced themselves from people who did not have their credentials but who could benefit from their wisdom—businessmen, social workers, and the bureaucrats of governmental agencies. These latter groups imbibed the same mentality, and in 1908 the Harvard Business School had consulted with Taylor and added "industrial organization" to its curriculum. For professional schools of business, on the outskirts of academic reformism, Taylorism was translated into procedures that could, at least partially, be conveyed to students before they took up managers' jobs.[3]

Taylor was also making his mark in the War Department. In 1909 General William Crozier, chief of ordnance (munitions), undertook to increase the efficiency of the Watertown Arsenal in Massachusetts. Crozier was interested in military organization and vigorously opposed "soldiering," the malingering and shirking sometimes associated with the armed forces. Although at Watertown he dealt with civilian employees, he intended to make this government-run facility competitive with nonmilitary producers of armaments. Although Secretary of War Henry L. Stimson supported Crozier in bringing in Taylor to revamp the arsenal, the unionized men struck Watertown in 1911 in a dispute over how Taylor's assistants were examining their jobs. A congressional investigation of scientific management in War Department installations followed, and stressed Taylor's promanagement, business paternalism. Among many labor leaders the fame that Brandeis had brought to Taylor in 1910 was, a few years later, turned to infamy. After the congressional hearings in 1915, Taylor's time system was banned in government manufactories.[4] Although the ban was not formally rescinded until much later, changes in the power of the state during World War I supported the importance of Taylorism in the

---

[3] See Edward A. Purcell Jr., *The Crisis of Democratic Theory: Scientific Naturalism and the Problem of Value* (Lexington: University Press of Kentucky, 1973), p. 25; and Michael J. Lacey and Mary O. Furner, "Social Investigation, Social Knowledge, and the State: An Introduction," in *The State and Social Investigation in Britain and the United States*, ed. Lacey and Furner (New York: Cambridge University Press, 1993), pp. 7–8, 42; Kanigel, *The One Best Way*, p. 489.

[4] This story is told in Hugh G. J. Aitken, *Taylorism at Watertown Arsenal: Scientific Management in Action, 1908–1915* (Cambridge: Harvard University Press, 1960).

War Department. Overall, the governmental controls on American industry initiated during the fighting introduced civilian professionals and businessmen to the problems of management on a national scale. War allowed them to test skills and concepts they had developed in the private sphere or learned about in the university, and to experiment with new institutional arrangements and managerial devices.[5]

OPERATIONS RESEARCH

After a fallow era of two decades, World War II invigorated this cooperation between social scientists and the state, and issued in the developments that are the topic of this book. In the special case of economists and generals, the Americans—following the British—constructed a new field of inquiry, which they called operations research. The task was to figure out how the military could use weapons most effectively and integrate them with the men and machines already in the fight. Devotees of OR exploited new applied mathematical techniques and developed other ones to make recommendations based on "optimalization." For example, the operations researcher wanted to know how many tons of explosive force a bomb had to release to do a certain amount of damage to particular sorts of targets. By the time the operations researchers were organized, they had much statistical information and plied their trade by analyzing the quantitative data to increase the destructiveness of the weapons of the Allies and to preserve the lives of their soldiers. Operations research made more systematic the brutal trial-and-error learning that accompanied all wars of any duration. Recognizing that these problems required nonmilitary knowledge, warriors reached out to experts unconnected to the armed forces. Natural scientists interested in the technology that had gone into the development of new weapons first led groups devoted to operations research, but soon nonscientists, led by economists, dominated.[6]

The military was committed to augmenting the effectiveness of GIs and tanks, and of the navy. But it emphasized the most advanced technology in the air. In what formations should bombers fly to minimize risks to pilots and planes? What armor and guns were most effective on bombers? How effective were fighter planes as protection? If bombers were stripped of their armor, would the enlarged range, speed, and bomb-load capacity compensate for their

---

[5] See Robert Cuff, *The War Industries Board: Business-Government Relations during World War I* (Baltimore: Johns Hopkins University Press, 1973); Cuff, "War Mobilization, Institutional Learning, and State Building in the United States, 1917–1941," in Lacey and Furner, *State and Social Investigation*, pp. 400–401, 419; Aitken, *Taylorism at Watertown Arsenal*, p. 240.

[6] An accessible, if sometimes overstated survey, is Stephen P. Waring, "Cold Calculus: The Cold War and Operations Research," *Radical History Review* 63 (1995): 29–51.

lack of armor?[7] Would stripped-down bombers be harder to shoot down?[8] OR looked at the casualty rates of American fliers, the deployment of their equipment (mainly the bombers themselves), and the efficiency of the bombing, measured in straightforward ways such as percentage of targets hit. The new discipline aspired to ascertain how well the bombing went and, if necessary, to alter strategy during the war if some techniques were dubious. Although experts vaguely defined success and restricted the range of variables, they aimed to save American lives and to bring Germany and Japan more quickly to their knees.

OR gave to policymakers an economist's approach to battle. War was "a production process where the outcome is killed and wounded soldiers on the other side. The question was how to kill them more effectively, especially in mechanized combat." Operations research was not interested in "political problems of the goods of war, but how to marry modes of warfare to conflict dominated by new technologies."[9]

In leading operations research, the Army Air Force hoped to become a separate service after the war. In charge of new high-profile equipment, air force chiefs led political leadership to champion a wider vision of their war-making. The way to defeat Germany and Japan was strategic bombing, which did not buttress ground operations directly but destroyed the enemy economies or the enemy's will to fight.[10] The air force promoted not only operations research but also studies of how air power could cripple an adversary. The air force was confident that impartial civilians would appreciate arguments for the independent use of air power, and subsequently for a new service. This meeting of minds between airmen and forward-looking civilians had only one hitch. Early on in the career of operations research, the Army Air Force convened a committee composed of historians to study the efficacy of strategic bombing. The recalcitrant historians urged that the evidence was so complex and the issues so "imponderable" that they could not give the clear-cut answers the air force wanted. They could not, for example, argue that exclusive bombing of key dimensions of the transportation system could rapidly defeat Germany, because they could not know what Germany would do to respond to such bombing, or what the United States would give up in focusing its energies on transport; nor could they judge that other strategies—bombing essential industries

---

[7] This discussion derives from Fred Kaplan, *The Wizards of Armageddon* (Stanford: Stanford University Press, 1983), pp. 52, 57.

[8] Edward S. Quade, ed., *Analysis for Military Decisions: The Rand Lectures on Systems Analysis* (New York: Rand McNally, 1967), introduction, p. 7.

[9] Interview with Carl Kaysen, March 27, 2004.

[10] On strategic bombing there is Conrad Crane, *Bombs, Cities, and Civilians: American Airpower Strategy in World War II* (Lawrence: University Press of Kansas, 1993), and Tami Davis Biddle, *Rhetoric and Reality in Air Warfare: The Evolution of British and American Ideas about Strategic Bombing, 1914–1945* (Princeton: Princeton University Press, 2002).

or concentrated tactical support of ground action—would be a worse use of resources.[11] Air force leadership then jettisoned historians for more decisive men. Lawyers and economists were soon prominent in operations research, and next statisticians and scholars in the harder social sciences. They were more willing to draw conclusions on the basis of imperfect evidence, a necessary ability when working in the real world under stressful circumstances. During the fight against Germany and then Japan, the airmen did not have the time to mull over the difficulties posed by historians and believed that the more practically minded experts would see the future in strategic bombing.[12]

By 1945, a new entity, the United States Strategic Bombing Survey, was engaged in the broader strategic calculations as the Americans looked at the whole German economy and how air warfare had affected it. In the immediate postwar period the USSBS climaxed its activities with volumes exploring how and at what cost the American effort had changed the structures of economies around the world.

Central to the study of Germany was the expertise of Albert Speer. Successful as the architect for the Reich, Speer was the czar of the German economy by 1942, organizing defense production, settling disputes among the armed forces, and maximizing the effectiveness of the military effort. Through 1944 he was deemed to have worked miracles to have kept Germany in the war.

The Americans who debriefed him, including George Ball and Paul Nitze, highly placed in the USSBS, and John Kenneth Galbraith, another student of the German economy, all went on to positions of authority in the United States. Nitze in particular promoted federal support for military use of operations research and, in the 1950s and 1960s, its more elaborate descendent, systems analysis. In April and May 1945 Nitze and his colleagues listened to Speer's recitation of facts and figures pertinent to the German endeavor.[13] His information proved critical in the examination of the German economy and in the re-creation of operations research as an approach to more intelligent management of large-scale economic and strategic enterprises. George Ball recalled that Speer "evoked in us a sympathy of which we were secretly ashamed."[14]

---

[11] Richard Overy makes this point in his analysis of the views of Albert Speer and Hermann Goring in *Interrogations: The Nazi Elite in Allied Hands, 1945* (New York: Viking, 2001), pp. 134–40, 148, 448, 470.

[12] Gian P. Gentile, *How Effective Is Strategic Bombing? Lessons Learned from World War II to Kosovo* (New York: New York University Press, 2001), pp. 12–13, 18, 32, 41–42.

[13] Gitta Sereny, *Albert Speer: His Battle with Truth* (New York: Knopf, 1995), pp. 548–54; Michael S. Sherry, *The Rise of American Air Power: The Creation of Armageddon* (New Haven: Yale University Press, 1987), pp. 162–66.

[14] George Ball, *The Past Has Another Pattern: Memoirs* (New York: Norton, 1982), pp. 63, 66. Galbraith has a withering account of both Speer and the allied bombing in "A Retrospect on Albert Speer," in *Economics, Peace, and Laughter* (Boston: Houghton Mifflin, 1971), pp. 220–30. Nitze, on the other hand, admired Speer: see Speer, *Spandau: The Secret Diaries* (New York: Macmillan, 1976), pp. 176, 359.

The complex task that engaged military planners went beyond what fact or oral history could establish and required interpretative commitment, as the rejected historians knew. The Bombing Survey postulated what would have happened in the absence of certain kinds of bombing, and decided if certain occurrences were the effects of bombing and not consequences of other events. To evaluate the role of strategic bombing, said Nitze, was to place "calipers" on the destruction of a social order, quantifying "something that was considered immeasurable."[15] A positive evaluation of the bombing also made a case for the endeavor and so for an independent air force.

RAND

After the war, under the leadership of the air force, the Douglas Aircraft Company organized civilian scientists who would carry on this sort of research, think about scientific discoveries in relation to new weapons, reflect on the possible effectiveness of the weapons, and measure this effectiveness. This outfit was called the *RAND* Corporation, after *r*esearch *an*d *d*evelopment. Although its employer was the air force, it would hire civilian scientists and, through Douglas, function as an independent center for investigation. Soon Douglas dropped put of the picture, but after initial funding from the Ford Foundation and the largesse of backers interested in air defense, RAND flourished as a scholarly center funded by the air force. Located in Santa Monica, California, this early "think tank" was the most prominent of many quasi-governmental institutions—for example the Weapons Systems Evaluation Group of the new Department of Defense and the Office of Naval Research—to study the use of weapons systematically. Although also most well known, RAND was also conventional in developing the techniques of mathematical economics that World War II had initiated.[16]

Relishing RAND's special connection to the worlds of politics and of the academy, its director in the early years described RAND as "a secret air force scientific organization."[17] It initially employed natural scientists and engineers but gradually hired economists and finally sociologists and political scientists with methodological leanings who might migrate back and forth between vari-

---

[15] Gentile, *Strategic Bombing*, quoting Nitze, p. 45.

[16] For a sense of these developments see, for example, Norman Schofield, "Chaos or Equilibrium in Preference and Belief Aggregation," in *Competition and Cooperation: Conversations with Nobelists about Economics and Political Science*, ed. James E. Alt et al. (New York: Russell Sage Foundation, 1999), pp. 33–50; and Paul N. Edwards, *The Closed World: Computers and the Politics of Discourse in Cold War America* (Cambridge: MIT Press, 1996).

[17] Collbohn to Seymour, Telegram, April 26, 1948, Box 87, Folder 757, Seymour Papers, Yale University.

ous university positions and RAND. In June 1949 RAND helped to sponsor a strikingly successful conference in Chicago at the Cowles Commission that alerted many thinkers to the challenge of RAND's approach.[18] Although the bulk of its research was always focused on problems of military hardware, by the 1950s RAND had a notable group of social scientists more interested in strategic questions of national security.

The flourishing of RAND rewarded farseeing air force leadership, including Generals Henry "Hap" Arnold and Curtis LeMay, who were notably not intellectuals but who recognized over the long run how useful the expertise, weight, and prestige of such an organization could be. But the connection to RAND was never easy for the air force. For years it endured the almost reflexive distaste and patronizing arrogance of the civilians. From the start RAND denigrated the intellect of the military and eagerly took the opportunity to argue that, without RAND advising, the air force was capable of only the most primitive thought.

On their side the civilians benefited greatly from the alliance. They enjoyed salaries at least equal to their peers in universities, and freedom from teaching and administration. There is only indirect evidence that they chafed at their link to the military or to the national government. Certainly they did not object to the Cold War verities that justified the air force funding, although they might have winced at the air force's platitudinous publication of these verities. It can be speculated, however, that the warriors' financing of the RAND professoriate made it psychologically uncomfortable. At least RAND's persistent celebration of its own mental prowess, in contrast to that of its employers, suggested a problematic marriage. In the second half of the twentieth century, in addition, the civilians were explicit about another problem. They thought that their association with the air force would taint their scholarly reputations for impartiality, and worried that they would be identified as academics who provided intellectual respectability for a government position.

Three connected strands contributed early on to the mind-set of the self-described RAND "philosophers":[19] a reliance on a certain style of mathematical-economic reasoning, an interest in organizational theory, and a commitment to what came to be known in political science as rational choice. Together these impulses and the men who championed them developed a perspective on world politics that in the 1950s made RAND the chief institution analyzing military strategy.

---

[18] For an overview of these developments see Michael A. Bernstein, *A Perilous Progress: Economists and Public Purpose in Twentieth-Century America* (Princeton: Princeton University Press, 2001), pp. 46–47, 80–82, 95–99; and the rich set of notes to these pages.

[19] See R. D. Specht, "RAND: A Personal View of its History," P-1601, October 23, 1958, Rand Corporation.

JOHN VON NEUMANN AND GAME THEORY

RAND initially convened mathematicians and physical scientists of the sort who had built the atomic bomb to have them think about newer weapons. An early RAND consultant, who had worked on the atomic bomb, was mathematician John von Neumann, a central European who fled the Nazis for the United States and who thought about politics in terms of apocalyptic extremes. In 1928 von Neumann had published an essay, "On the Theory of Economic Games," that was relevant to the work operations researchers undertook during the war. In 1944, at Princeton, he coauthored, with economist Oskar Morgenstern, an expanded version of his ideas in *The Theory of Games and Economic Behavior*. At RAND, *The Theory of Games* focused the energies of its employees.

For von Neumann classical economics fallaciously assumed buyers and sellers to be independent entities, whereas they formed an interacting unit, in which what one did depended not only on what the other did, but also on the one's expectations of what the other would do. Von Neumann proposed to model the activities that a buyer and seller might undertake, making their decision on the basis of the anticipated decision of the other. The model could be generalized to explain the decisions of any two "players" in a situation where the conflict of interest made the outcome uncertain.

This systematic thought was designated "game theory," and its paradigm example became a game of 1950s vintage, Prisoner's Dilemma. Suspected of participating in the same crime, two prisoners are kept in separate cells, unable to communicate. Each is told independently that if both confess, they will serve half sentences. If neither confesses, they will serve minimal sentences, but if one blames the other who remains silent, the silent one will receive a maximum sentence and the accuser go free. The prisoners are best served if each remains silent (and thus serves minimal sentences), yet fear that the other will talk and try to get off completely makes it likely that each will talk (and serve a half sentence).

If we let 10 be the value to each of going free and −10 the value of the maximum sentence, 0 the value of the minimal sentences, and −5 the value of half sentences, then we can construct a two-by-two diagram of alternatives (Table 1).

TABLE 1
The Prisoner's Dilemma

		Prisoner 1	
		Talk	Don't Talk
Prisoner 2	Talk	−5, −5	10, −10
	Don't Talk	−10, 10	0, 0

There are four possible outcomes: each talks, neither talks, prisoner 1 does and prisoner 2 does not, or prisoner 2 does and prisoner 1 does not. The results to each player are exhibited in the table. For the game theorists if each prisoner devised a "rational" policy, each would talk, for either one would say: if I talk, then no matter what the other guy does, I come out better than I would were I to keep quiet. The table shows that each would get a half sentence. Nonetheless, the table also shows that had neither talked, each would have served the minimal sentence. Thus, maximizing value is not a transparent definition of rationality. Such an outcome depended on each prisoner's trusting the other not to confess, and Prisoner's Dilemma elevated self-interest above trust.

For game theorists, talking was rational for each prisoner. Each had to assume that the other would do what was best for himself. The best move for each was to do what was best for himself, given the best move of the other. Game theory postulated that people acted rationally when they acted with some sense of what opponents might do and then tried to achieve the best for themselves. The rational actor did not necessarily achieve the maximum gain, nor even avoid serious loss, but did arrive at the "minimax" solution, the outcome that minimized losses and maximized gains.[20]

In this example, scholars used game theory to examine loyalty between thieves, but von Neumann's way of thinking also applied to poker, business transactions, and a range of social activities—for example, in another favored instance, international conflict between two rivals. But while Prisoner's Dilemma represented a simple "game theoretic" situation, von Neumann was more interested in multiperson games *and* circumstances in which the options were more numerous than talking or keeping silent—more than two variables. Furthermore, the simple game assumed that each criminal put the same value as the other on spending time in jail. The first could assume that the second felt about incarceration the way the second did, and decide accordingly. In real life, different people had different values. A rational approach did not mean making decisions based on what one would do oneself in the position of the opponent, but of adjusting them to what one thought a differently minded opponent would do. Rational behavior hinged on "the utility functions" of the other actors.

Von Neumann's genius at RAND was applying the mathematics formerly limited to economics to social activities. Economists and mathematicians gave his ideas greater complexity, and contributed to the work in the institution that was not oriented to weapons. The organization could also employ other social scientists who could examine the preferences and values of consumers, crimi-

---

[20] The article appeared as "Zur Theorie der Gesellschaftsspiele," *Math Annalen* 100 (1928): 295–370. My discussion in part follows Kaplan, *The Wizards of Armageddon*, pp. 65–67, but compare von Neumann and Morgenstern, *Theory of Games and Economic Behavior* (Princeton: Princeton University Press, 1944), pp. 175–78.

nals, poker players, businesspeople, or international rivals. So RAND widened its scope from considerations of the use and effects of weapons to broader social scientific consideration of strategy.

HERBERT SIMON AND ORGANIZATIONAL BEHAVIOR

The second intellectual stream that influenced RAND emerged in organizational behavior, a subdiscipline in political science, psychology, and graduate schools of business. Herbert A. Simon's *Administrative Behavior*, a book published in 1945, typified the endeavor and enjoyed a long-lasting reputation.[21] Literate and philosophically sophisticated, Simon later received the Nobel Prize in economics. In addition to citing his debt to Frederick Taylor, Simon claimed von Neumann as an intellectual collaborator. While describing his views as those of a "stubborn positivism," Simon also grounded his work in American instrumentalism, and consciously showed how the social scientist could apply the schema of John Dewey's *The Public and its Problems*.[22]

Administrative Behavior was a study of "the logical foundations of administrative science."[23] Human activity in any organization, said Simon, positioned individuals to reach goals through intelligent action. Rational behavior most effectively brought into existence the postulated ends. Rationality was relative— the use of "appropriate means to reach designated goals."[24] Organizations should aim at efficiency. They must ascertain the most economical ways to maximize the institution's various subgoals; they should strive to find quantitative measures of what they were about and define nonconflicting routes to their ends. Quantification might not be possible in all circumstances, but experienced managers articulated such reckoning even when relying on intuition.

Simon argued that the ultimate goals of an organization, its highest values, existed only by "human fiat." But once they were accepted, the functional rationality of the organization consisted in employing verified generalizations that allowed the organization to meet the goals. A continuum of means and ends existed, the processes of an organization and its purpose. The low-level processes were stipulated once the purpose had been designated. The purpose was high-level, an undisputed preference for some end.[25]

---

[21] For Simon see Stephen P. Waring, *Taylorism Transformed: Scientific Management Theory since 1945* (Chapel Hill: University of North Carolina Press, 1991), pp. 49–77.

[22] Herbert A. Simon, *Administrative Behavior: A Study of Decision-Making Processes in Administrative Organization*, 4th printing (New York: Macmillan, 1945, 1947, 1949), pp. 23, 43, 67, 80n, 88–93, 181, 195n, 208. Simon gives a more subtle account in "A Behavioral Model of Rational Choice," *Quarterly Journal of Economics* 69 (1955): 99–118. The self-description is from Simon, *Models of My Life* (New York: Basic Books, 1991), pp. 53, 86.

[23] Simon, *Models of My Life*, p. 53.

[24] Simon, *Administrative Behavior*, pp. 61, 69, 75.

[25] Simon, *Administrative Behavior*, pp. 32, 56, 65, 74–75.

This end (a value) was absolutely distinguished from the process (in the factual environment) that the analyst explored. In defense of his position Simon cited the latest philosophical scholarship on logical positivism: the final goals or values had no further justification and were emotional in character. In contrast to them, the factual environment was an objective, scientific realm whose relevant aspects came into focus once goals were set.[26]

Simon paradigmatically blended pragmatism and positivism. Like other organizational theorists, he was unconcerned about ends, basically accepting what American society had on offer. Both Dewey's pragmatism, which argued that social ends were empirical, and American positivism, which found such ends to be nonempirical, did little to look into the premises of their culture. Both pragmatists and positivists were committed to American life. The pragmatists believed they could show democratic culture to be empirically desirable. The positivists thought such a demonstration impossible but nonetheless accepted the preference for such a society. Another theorist, Albert Wohlstetter, explicitly wrote about how organizational theory might amalgamate the two moral positions. Wohlstetter had worked in the philosophy of science under Ernest Nagel at Columbia and was as astute a philosopher as Simon. Wohlstetter, however, took issue with the positivist disjunction between fact and value. Instead, citing John Dewey in the famous chapter 10 of *The Quest for Certainty*, he argued that individuals should not confuse ultimate goals with simple preferences and that we should argue about such goals. Nonetheless, Wohlstetter did not find that this conclusion conflicted with Simon's analysis. Rather, Wohlstetter thought his position reinforced it. Accepting the continuity between means and ends that Simon had defined, Wohlstetter said that the organizational researcher began by inspecting the means necessary to achieve a given subgoal and its compatibility with other subgoals. In this way, the researcher could expand agreement, point out the information needed to reach certain subgoals or appraise their costs, or prove that some could not be made compatible with others. Working outward to the ultimate ends of the organization, the researcher not only examined the way these ends might be most resourcefully met but, by looking at the process, demonstrated that they were worth meeting.[27]

Neither Wohlstetter nor Simon spent much time worrying about the ultimate ends. For Simon they were not an object of reasonable concern. For Wohlstetter the process validated the ends. Both men were enamored of the process, and to the extent the goal was definable, it was in terms of the process.

---

[26] Simon, *Administrative Behavior*, pp. 45–46, 184.

[27] Albert Wohlstetter, "Analysis and Design of Conflict Systems," in Quade, *Analysis for Military Decisions,* p. 122. Wohlstetter's essay dates from 1955. To see how closely he follows Dewey's argument compare his essay to Dewey, *The Quest for Certainty*, chap. 10. In 1968, responding to criticism of RAND's role in Vietnam, Wohlstetter recalled that he had always thought reflec-

KENNETH ARROW'S IDEAL STATE

The final stream that carried RAND through the 1950s and 1960s was what came to be called rational choice theory, and in the late 1940s had an outstanding exemplar, on a par with von Neumann's *Theory of Games*. Kenneth Arrow's Columbia doctoral dissertation of 1949 was published in 1951 as *Social Choice and Individual Values*.

Arrow was a theoretical economist and RAND consultant, whose book also later won him a Nobel Prize. He was indebted, however, not just to von Neumann but also to Ernest Nagel and the mathematical logic associated with logical positivism. Many considered Arrow otherworldly, and his own career turned away from practical problems.[28] But *Social Choice and Individual Values*, a twentieth-century version of Plato's *Republic*, argued that rational decisions occurred in a dictatorship. The dictator could choose the society's ultimate ends, which had no further justification than the choosing of them anyway, and knowledge might provide him with the best means to achieve them. The ability to make such consistent decisions marked "an integrated personality," and Arrow set as his task a search for rational decision-making if multiple wills were involved. In a democratic social order where varied individual tastes were at issue, how could we achieve "an integrated society"?[29]

Arrow investigated the "formal aspects" of this question because of the "great advantages of abstract postulational methods." He hoped to construct a procedure for passing from a set of known individual preferences to a pattern of decision making that would maximize the preferences of many individuals in an equitable manner.[30] Thus, Arrow assumed that every individual had "a definite ordering of all conceivable social states, in terms of their desirability to him," and the social scientist assigned "a numerical social utility" to each social state based on the preferences of all of society's members. "The aim of [a just?] society" was "to maximize the social utility or social welfare" subject to relevant technological or resource constraints. The politician acted to bring this state into existence.[31]

After imposing some reasonable conditions on his theorizing, Arrow proved mathematically that no such "social welfare function" could be constructed. "Collective rationality" was incompatible with a full range of con-

---

tions on ends to be important. See "On Vietnam and Bureaucracy," RAND Corporation, D-17276–1-ISA/ARPA, July 17, 1968, pp. 4, 8.

[28] See the remarks on Arrow in George R. Feiwel, ed., *Arrow and the Foundations of the Theory of Economic Policy* (New York: New York University Press, 1987), pp. 36–37, 652, 681, 696.

[29] Kenneth J. Arrow, *Social Choice and Individual Values* (New York: John Wiley and Sons, 1951), pp. 2–3.

[30] Arrow, *Social Choice*, pp. 6, 87.

[31] Arrow, *Social Choice*, pp. 17, 22.

sumers' and workers' choices. To attain such rationality, there must be a far greater similarity of attitudes toward social alternatives than the social scientist could bring into being with the multitude of preferences of varied individuals. The possibility of such a "function" depended on muting the divergence of preferences. Under the doctrine of "voters' sovereignty," free discussion and the expression of opinion were the best techniques for arriving at "the moral imperative" that might make this function possible.[32] Arrow did not applaud democratic deliberation in order to let a thousand flowers bloom. Democracy could only produce a good society if it inculcated similar attitudes toward alternatives—a certain cultural homogeneity—that mimicked the unified will of a dictatorial society.[33]

CRITIQUES

RAND posited a world defined by autonomous, self-sufficient individuals each of whom acted out of self-interest. The belief that social policies were acts of some supreme or collective will did capture the notion of the sovereignty of state power in the international system of the nineteenth and twentieth centuries, but an array of criticisms became conventional. One commentator wrote that RAND's language and standard of measurements were not those of science, but of "the balance sheet mentality of capitalism."[34] Another critic called the approach "the image of the game-theoretic man" who made a "sharp distinction between inter-subjective means and private ends—between social instrumentalities and the personal satisfactions that they serve."[35] Even when, in a variant of Prisoner's Dilemma, scholars might designate the two participants as the United States and the Soviet Union, each behaved as an individual and had a psychology usually thought to be attached to a single person. Self-interest was analyzed in terms of functional rationality: the individual's behavior was rational if it used appropriate means to reach stipulated ends. Although one could not "rationalize" the ends and had to accept them by fiat, RAND investigators rarely postulated anything more than an impoverished, predictable, and cramped psyche in inventing the goals that generated rational self-interest. People wanted money; they would squeal to stay out of jail. They didn't often have, say, moral scruples in favor of truth-telling no matter what the costs, or feelings of guilt or honor that might motivate them. Nor did a network of social obligations and cultural norms complicate what they wanted or encumber

[32] Arrow, *Social Choice*, pp. 31, 33, 37, 60, 85.
[33] Arrow, *Social Choice*, pp. 63, 69, 81.
[34] Sherry, *American Air Power*, pp. 234–35.
[35] Robert Paul Wolff, "Reflections on Game Theory and the Nature of Value," *Ethics* 72 (1962): 174.

them.[36] Even a committed game theorist urged that the RAND sensibility was pinched. Prisoner's Dilemma represented "the psychology of a timid man pressed into a duel," and there were many ways to be rational.[37]

RAND's outlook had diverged from the "institutionalist" economics that had been an aspect of Taylor's scientific management. The institutionalists suspected classical economic reasoning and explored instead how organizations functioned, drawing generalizations about behavior from their observations. But the desire to reform the institutions led economists to theorize about how they could be made better, to reproduce the better institutions that existed in the minds of the scholars. The mathematics available thirty to fifty years after the heyday of Taylor's scientific management made such formalism possible. RAND in many ways had priorities that were just the reverse of the institutionalists; it prized theorizing. Belief in the one best scientific way drove Taylor too, but the shop floor grudgingly called him back. At RAND there was less of a shop floor.

To little effect commentators pointed out the abstractness of the approach. More significantly, while the civilian social scientists fretted that their attachment to the air force might be suspect, they did not grasp that their commitment to the United States might also compromise their science. RAND held standard and unnuanced beliefs about how human beings, conceived as American customers, behaved. Monochromatic individuals with nonidiosyncratic goals were also consistent with Arrow's desideratum of people who could make for a successful democratic society.[38] As one minor RAND-influenced theorist said, only "ideological viewpoints distinctly outside the range of the basic American consensus on political values" might lead to criticism of RAND's ideas.[39]

In any event, RAND hoped to "model" how individuals would behave in a variety of situations requiring decision. On the one hand, criticism might not matter if the model could account for the behavior under scrutiny. On the other hand, a more serious conceptual problem might have existed. Game theory might not involve science at all, but merely a generalized depiction of behavior that put a peculiar ethical cast on it as rational, or not. To qualify as a genuine theory in terms of the (positivist) canons of the philosophy of science that the civilian strategists accepted, game theory had to generate predictions whose

[36] For a more extended critique see Elizabeth Anderson, *Value in Ethics and Economics* (Cambridge: Harvard University Press, 1993).

[37] Daniel Ellsberg, "Theory of the Reluctant Duelist," *American Economic Review* 46 (1956): 923.

[38] RAND-bashing is a common academic sport, but does not seem to have had much of an effect. A measured early study is Hedley Bull, "Strategy Studies and Its Critics," *World Politics* 20 (1968): 593–605.

[39] Richard Smoke, "National Security Affairs," *Handbook of Political Science*, vol. 8 (Reading, Mass.: Addison-Wesley, 1975), p. 327.

truth (or falsity) would tend to confirm (or disconfirm) its accuracy. Indeed, von Neumann and those around him might be able to do this when asking subjects to play Prisoner's Dilemma, and might accurately construe how people played some *games* or responded in experiments under controlled conditions. But RAND needed to know, for example, what two people implicated in a real robbery might do under questioning. Game theorists did not test theory in this matter. They might justify their theory as an explanation of reasoning in games, but it might not have relevance outside this setting.

Finally, game theory might not qualify as an explanation of behavior as positivism defined explanation, but conceivably be useful for understanding human activities under some looser criteria that, for example, some thinkers claimed operated in history. But such a relaxed position did not comport with RAND's hard-science attitude. Nor did the game-theoretic sensibility connect with that of a humanist understanding.

The limitation appeared in the political gaming that RAND took up to illustrate its theories. In various political and war "simulations," groups of knowledgeable specialists acted as countries, and countries made moves against each other.[40] Another group represented nature—to provide for events that happened in the real world but were not under the control of any government; and another group were referees—to rule on the feasibility of any move that might not be within the constitutional or physical power of a country. These games were a mesmerizing intellectual exercise, but the assumption that judges might decide what could happen in war ignored the crucial unpredictability of political life, as did the view that some people might control nature. In a connected constraint, RAND justified the study of history because it provided a reservoir of information for various groups to use. History could assist in the way one structured the conclusions drawn from simulation, for the discipline was a collection of facts that might assist the gamer. More important, history might then be superseded, for the results of gaming themselves became "synthetic history" or "hypothetical history."[41]

Much of this criticism was beside the point from the point of view of the strategists. Carl Kaysen, a longtime RAND consultant, recalled that they recognized the difference between the world of the classroom and that of real politics. They knew their theories could not act as predictors and were often simplified prescriptions. The civilians' brand of theorizing, rather, gave them a systematic way of talking about problems: is this like a game of chicken, or

[40] Smoke and George, "Theory for Policy," p. 388.

[41] See Herbert Goldhamer and Hans Speier, "Some Observations on Political Gaming," *World Politics* 12 (1959–60): 71–83; and William T. R. Fox's comment in "Frederick Sherwood Dunn and the American Study of International Relations," reprinted in *The American Study of International Relations: Essays by William T. R. Fox* (Columbia: University of South Carolina Press, 1968), p. 54.

is it like haggling over a price? The theorists may not have been very good, said Kaysen, but they were certainly no worse than anyone else.[42]

To lend the greatest reality to game theory RAND had created a social science division that appointed noneconomists. In the early years of the Cold War conflict between the United States and the Soviet Union, "Kremlinologists" worked on the social psychology of Russia. But these less quantitatively oriented men confirmed the view of economists and mathematicians that a priori models were rich enough to account for human activity. They bolstered the popular view of the late 1940s and early 1950s that evil geniuses intent on the destruction of the West led the USSR.

NATHAN LEITES AND POLITICAL PATHOLOGY

The early book of Émigré thinker Nathan Leites, *The Operational Code of the Politburo*, exemplified this impact. Leites' father had been a revolutionary purged by the Bolsheviks, and the son had been educated all over Europe, ending up with a degree in economics from Freibourg in Switzerland. Leites had then taught at Chicago, where he blended the logical positivism he had picked up in Europe with political analysis. He collaborated with Harold Lasswell, whose multifaceted efforts in the social sciences assumed that the displacement of private motives explained (most) politics and that public affairs needed an elite administrative cadre. During the war Lasswell's Division for the Study of Wartime Communications employed Leites. He partly aimed to uncover the psychopathological roots of political belief. He also analyzed the worldviews of the leadership groups in various nation-states, desiring to predict behavior by understanding how a national mind worked. His "operational code" later became a leading idea among political scientists, and his RAND study assembled numerous facts about the Soviet mentality, drew from them generalizations about that mentality, and forecasted how the Russians might negotiate. The publishers claimed that "few books since Machiavelli's *The Prince* . . . [had] set forth rules of political conduct which so completely dictate a strategy of power." Like von Neumann and many intellectuals who had left Europe for America both before and after the war, Leites' experience was of totalitarian political systems. He had a heightened sense of political fanaticism, and *The Operational Code* painted the Soviet Union black, validating the doggedly uncomplex RAND view of the Russian psyche. A machinating USSR was out to do in the globe.[43] With this sort of social-science

---

[42] Interview with Kaysen, March 27, 2004.

[43] Nathan Leites, *The Operational Code of the Politburo* (New York: McGraw-Hill, 1951). The quote about Machiavelli is taken from the book jacket. For Leites' life and career see Charles Wolf Jr., *Remembering Nathan Leites: An Appreciation, Recollections of Some Friends, Colleagues, and Students* (Santa Monica: RAND Corporation, 1988).

assistance in discovering the values of other nations, the RAND economists and mathematicians believed they could construct frameworks to guide them in international politics.

RAND AND THE MANAGEMENT OF DEFENSE

Equipped with this perspective, the RAND social scientists first set forth ideas about how the United States could mount a more scientific defense, and also devised strategies for the military that would enhance the prestige and budget share of its employer. This was not an impossible or implausible task, because after the war the air force anchored American security. By the late 1940s the number of Americans under arms had shrunk. The administration of Harry Truman (1945–53) and later that of Dwight Eisenhower (1953–61) emphasized nuclear weapons and air power as a way of containing defense costs and of negating the advantage of Russian land forces. RAND easily made the case that rational defense management entailed giving more to the air force. At the most general level RAND reinforced accepted ideas of defense. Its service mission was compatible with its scientifically objective appraisal of what strategy the United States ought to pursue.

On the other side, RAND eventually offered people outside the military a way to judge service requests for weapons and to evaluate how well soldiers were doing their job. The RAND Social Science Division also matured when the foreign-policy public debated the defense budget and the parochialism of the armed forces. The Truman and Eisenhower administrations struggled to maintain an adequate defense without, as they saw it, bankrupting the nation. They suspected service leaders of inflating their needs and contributing, wittingly or not, to a militarized society. Finally, the politicians worried that interservice rivalries prevented the generals and admirals from presenting a coherent, overall strategy for the United States. In the middle and late 1940s ongoing battles between the War and Navy Departments often led Truman and his associates to believe that the brass cared little for what a *national* defense might require.

Under these circumstances, in 1947, Congress had passed a National Security Act that was to put the military on a new footing. Previously defense had been in the separate hands of the army and air force (in the War Department) and the navy and marines (in the Navy). In the postwar period the navy felt beleaguered over its diminished role, while the army and the air force only stopped bickering to assert their supremacy against the navy. Civilian authority believed these conflicts wasteful; they made an overall defense posture difficult. Civilians also believed the structure gave too much power to the military. Under the terms of the National Security Act the State Department remained in existence, but there was to be a National Security Council, a new executive department (the National Military Establishment, soon renamed the Department of Defense), and a secretary of defense, who was to represent the values of civilian life. The politicians disbanded the old departments of War and Navy; but despite the fact that independent services remained—an army, navy, and a new air force—elected officials hoped that the military would speak with a single voice under civilian control. Historians have studied the governmental infighting of the era and pointed to the ambiguity of the outcome in the National Security Act and its amendments. There is, in addition, a certain nonrational aspect to the worldview out of which all the participants acted. The "security of the United States" was an unlikely scientific idea. Was there a national interest that a secretary of defense and an NSC could articulate more adequately than the secretaries of state, war, and navy had previously done in the State, War, and Navy Coordinating Committee? How could threats to national security best be met? Could security be absolute? How much would that cost? Would a higher level of taxation undermine the economic strength that made it possible to consider increasing security in the first place? What consequences would more spending on guns have for life inside the United States, for American businessmen, for citizens who might be called on to serve in the armed forces, for the size and power of the federal government, for political expression?

RAND's thought about defense developed during this national conversation of the late 1940s, but the construction of security was less like what RAND presupposed it was, say, building a four-lane bridge for automobile traffic, than it was like creating a flower garden on inhospitable ground. Moreover, even if the connection to the air force imperiled the RAND ideal of rational civilian control of defense, the ideal was not undesirable in an era when military expertise allowed soldiers to make gigantic claims on American society.

SYSTEMS ANALYSIS

Out of this mix of intellectual and cultural elements arose RAND's "system analysis," which defined the organization's interest in defense management and war strategy. Systems analysis was a kin of operations research, but a more grown-up relative. It answered complex questions of choice that arose in all areas of life, but especially in industrial and managerial enterprises, which at RAND concentrated on defense. Unlike operations research, which dealt only with tactical problems involving the immediate future use of equipment, the systems analyst examined holistically the development of weapons, disarmament, and deterrence, and sought intelligence about American allies and adversaries—mainly the Soviet Union.

The systems analysts looked at the actual and possible armaments available to the United States and it allies, and to its chief opponent. Then analysts figured out the best strategy that the opponent might come up with. This projection might include estimates of how much money the opponents had to spend, and how they would use it. The investigators would look at manpower and equipment use, the industrial system, and geography. They would calculate the sort of defense it would take in the United States to meet this theoretical enemy strategy, and would make the same sorts of evaluations for both the United States and other countries. But since costs were never indefinitely elastic, the RAND professionals would also reckon the best defense available for given expenditures. The results might be compared to the actual defense in place. Here, RAND's formalism made common cause with reformist ardor. The organization might criticize existing defense postures and argue for improvements, through either efficiency or greater spending.[44]

An interdisciplinary team—economists, engineers, and sociologists—best undertook this job. Using the methods of science, they would be "objective and quantitative." The military, which relied on experience of the last war, was unequipped to think about conflict in the new age. Soldiers would be strategically outmoded if they did not heed the scientific method. The services must learn "to 'do' this sort of philosophy."[45] In later years, with the assistance of computer technology, the reasoning became common in a range of activities from the scheduling of professional sports teams to the invention of adolescents' computer games.

RAND could quantify much of the material it examined—the number of bombers and the destructive power of weapons. Some of it could be statistically determined—the percentage of bombs reaching targets, the number of planes with mechanical failures. Some had to be guessed at—the expertise of the enemy soldiers, or the morale of the American people in the face of an attack. Nonetheless, RAND stressed, and prided itself on, its mathematical results, especially by the late 1950s when machines did the complex arithmetic necessary to solve the multivariable equations that were part of the analysis.

Civilian social scientists almost ritualistically acknowledged that many questions resisted quantification. But they also adamantly supported quantifying what was possible. As C. J. Hitch, a leading RAND economist and president of the American Society for Operations Research, said in 1960, the economist's way of looking at problems raised "the thrilling hope that [economics] could point the way toward solutions of some of the great public policy problems of our age."[46] "Every bit of the total problem that can be confidently analyzed," said Hitch, "removes one more bit of uncertainty from our process

---

[44] My summary is taken from Quade's preface and introduction to *Analysis for Military Decisions*, pp. v, 4–7.

[45] Quade, introduction, p. 10; and "Recapitulation," p. 321, in *Analysis for Military Decisions*.

[46] Hitch, "The Uses of Economics" (RAND paper, November 17, 1960) in Trachtenberg, *Strategic Thought*, pt. 3, vol. 3, p. 215.

of making a choice. . . . [A]nalytical techniques can allow us to make significant choices with a very real increase in confidence." Another social scientist argued that national policymakers who must "integrate" all factors in making political decisions for the state were "really doing systems analysis, but are at a level so high it is hard to consider it as such."[47]

RAND's formal conceptions of defense would gain a critical hearing in Washington. But the national debate about the Cold War, which was occurring as RAND established itself, initially required intellectual understanding of a kind different from that which the institution could provide. It waited in the wings until intellectuals better able to command the attention of the public and of politicians outlined the new American role in the world.

---

[47] Hitch quoted in Quade, "Recapitulation," p. 326; and Quade, "Methods and Procedures," p. 175, in *Analysis for Military Decisions*.

CHAPTER 2

Theorists of War, 1945–1953

WORLD WAR II had ended with the armies of the Soviet Union spread across Eastern Europe and the eastern part of Germany, while the United States had before long brought many of its troops home. Soon the two nations were at odds, as the Americans accused the Russians of snuffing out the freedom of the eastern Europeans, and the Soviets accused the United States of capitalist imperialism in reconstructing the global economy in its own favor. Americans also struggled to understand why the successful detonation of atomic bombs over Japan, which had concluded the war in the Pacific, had not put a stop to foreign problems. Finally, by the late 1940s a fearsome debate about the Soviet ideology of Communism even gripped many Americans who had no pretensions to higher education or book learning.

THE SHAPE OF POSTWAR POLICY

In the State and War Departments of the United States the strategy of the postwar period was simple. American diplomats did not worry that conflict was imminent, and assumed that it would not come in the foreseeable future—the Russians were too weak, their energies occupied in areas already conceded to them, and signs of extreme tension nonexistent. Yet if there were to be war, the new atomic weapons, which the Americans alone possessed, would match the Soviet advantage in conventional troops. In case the Russians tried to overrun Western Europe, the United States would counter with nuclear bombs and destroy the Soviet's military forces or its society, or both. The planes of the air force would drop the weapons. To achieve this goal, the United States built and stockpiled atomic bombs, and the air force planned for strikes against the Russians. Until the Soviets broke the American monopoly when they tested their own atomic device in 1949, thinking in the United States did not rise much above this policy.[1]

Indeed, the Americans emphasized political-economic programs for the reconstruction of Western Europe such as the Marshall Plan of 1947, named after Secretary of State George Marshall. The United States gave West Europeans

---

[1] See, for example, Walter J. Boyne, *Beyond the Wild Blue: A History of the U.S. Air Force, 1947–1997* (New York: St. Martin's, 1997), p. 28.

aid to rebuild their war-devastated economies. A prosperous Europe, oriented to the folkways of American capitalism, would limit Soviet expansion. Washington saw the danger of Russian Communism as political and ideological, and the export of American-style political economy would blunt it. War by the Russians was unlikely, and the American military was relegated to a secondary role. Although as custodian of the "air-atomic" power of the United States, the air force became the all-important service, President Truman restricted the defense budget in the middle and late 1940s.

To gain public support for its expensive and unglamorous courses of action such as the Marshall Plan, the Truman administration exaggerated the propensity of the Soviet Union, and Communist ideology in general, for military adventure. Such an information policy may have been disingenuous, but in 1946–48 the Truman administration found it necessary, facing a public with little stomach for more international engagements and a hostile, almost isolationist Congress. The centerpiece of this information policy, the president's address in March 1947, announced "the Truman Doctrine" and told of a global contest between democracy and totalitarianism, but left ambiguous the nature of the contest and the need for military action.

In this context various intellectuals described for the foreign-policy public the altered international environment in which the United States operated. RAND social scientists made their voices heard, but at first educated Americans listened to other strategic thinkers, less moved by quantitative measures of security and the problem of atomic weapons.

George Kennan

The most famous essay published in America on issues of war and peace was George Kennan's "The Sources of Soviet Conduct," in *Foreign Affairs* in June 1947. From a well-to-do midwestern family, Kennan had gone to Princeton in the early 1920s and then joined the State Department. Among the first of the first generation of foreign-service professionals, he received what amounted to graduate training in Europe in Russian studies, and early on had a propensity to meditate on the history of political systems. He read Oswald Spengler's *Decline of the West* (1918), the treatise on the cyclical rise and inevitable fall of civilizations, in its original German, and imagined himself in the nineteenth-century mold of an aristocratic diplomatic author of belle lettres. In the late 1920s, 1930s, and early 1940s, as a midlevel career diplomat, Kennan fastidiously analyzed the limitations of American diplomacy and its foreign policy. He lived in Europe most of the time, although—if his writings were evidence— he was mostly concerned with his inner life and his reactions to the collapse of a peaceful order. Sensitive, intelligent, and learned, he was culturally conservative if not reactionary. Ten years before his ideas became widely known, he had ruminated on how the disenfranchisement of women, blacks, and immigrants, and the limitation of white male suffrage would solve American problems; and in the 1970s he advocated abolishing the direct election of the Senate in favor of a less democratic procedure.[2] Yet Kennan also yearned for a position in which grateful statesmen would implement his concepts and the public would accept his acumen.

Although he looked on his work in the State Department as creating "a logical program," no technician would construct it. Global politics was "not a science," Kennan said. Nor did political judgment depend only on rational deduction but required an affective and aesthetic element. When "international relations" imbibed social scientific constructs and became an academic enterprise, Kennan disdained its intricacies and dissociated himself from its conundrums. In diplomacy he promoted decision making by a select priesthood, educated at prestigious universities, schooled in languages and the humanities, and at ease in the high cultures of Europe. He sought the perspective of these few people of wisdom. They were more valuable than the most elaborate synthesis of demonstrable fact and syllogistic deduction.[3] Kennan's ideas were eventually to anchor a constellation of views about the conduct of foreign affairs distanced from RAND's emphases and a tradition counter to that of the followers of social science. But both he and RAND held their noses at democratic dialogue and were certain they knew how to improve American foreign policy—if only those in power had the wit to listen.

Reporting to Ambassador Averell Harriman during World War II in Russia, Kennan noted that Harriman must have found him a trial, "running around with my head in the usual clouds of philosophic speculation."[4] In 1946 and 1947 he worried that the United States was not up to the challenge posed by its totalitarian enemy and gloomily argued with himself about the future of the West.

Naval Secretary, later defense secretary, James Forrestal was a brooding and self-conscious explorer of the ideological foundations of the East-West struggle. Determined to understand the Marxist polity the United States confronted and how its evil place in history might be challenged, Forrestal knew he could not intelligibly formulate the issues himself. He favored Kennan's writing on the USSR, which he found in a report by Kennan on the Soviet Union. Playing into Forrestal's needs, Kennan ingratiatingly shaped a more finished work,[5] "The Sources of Soviet Conduct." It told politicians how the United States must

[2] David Mayers, *George Kennan and the Dilemma of US Foreign Policy* (New York: Oxford University Press, 1988), pp. 51–53, 290–91.

[3] Anders Stephanson, *Kennan and the Art of Foreign Policy* (Cambridge: Harvard University Press, 1989), pp. 150, 181; Mayers, *Kennan,* p. 316.

[4] Kennan, *Memoirs, 1925–1950* (Boston: Little, Brown, 1967), pp. 109–12, 232.

[5] See the exchange of letters in the Forrestal Papers, 1946, Box 70, Kennan, Mudd Library, Princeton University.

comprehend its chief enemy. In part, the article was a social-psychological portrait of the Soviet leadership, pathologically absorbed in its rigid Communist belief system. Kennan painted a picture of the Soviet political elite as neurotic, even paranoid in its suspicion and hatred of the West. A zealot's worldview had become institutionalized in the USSR, and meant that the United States could not look to any normal accommodation with Russia.

At the same time, Kennan's reliance on an evil ideology and mental pathology to explain Russian wrongdoing, an approach prompted by his desire to come up with a line that Forrestal would find acceptable, inverted his long-term beliefs. Kennan usually emphasized the secondary role of Marxist-Leninism for the Soviet leadership. Instead, he thought, balance-of-power principles that had defined Russian foreign policy for generations guided the USSR. This realpolitik, more central to Kennan's views, even had a place in "The Sources of Soviet Conduct."[6]

Positively, the essay argued that the United States could "contain" the Soviets, who would eventually self-destruct if opposed with "unalterable counter force" wherever they intruded on the interests of the free world. But Kennan also assessed whether the American people could muster the courage and moral excellence needed to defeat such a malign rival. He initiated a tradition of ominous reflections by American foreign policy savants about the staying power of the American people. This analysis became conventional in American studies of the Soviet Union, and indeed was a cerebral version of the views found in the Truman Doctrine speech of the president. The essay contributed to the impulse to overstate the hostility of the Soviets to the United States, their military capability in respect to America, and their interest in an armed contest. The outlook also intellectually legitimated and energized the worldwide series of challenges and responses that became the Cold War.

Scrupulous at the time in his estimate of the forces at work against the United States, if also aware that high officials wanted a lurid characterization of the Soviet Union, Kennan soon lamented what he saw as the exaggeration of this work for hire. Reflecting his ultimately more passive commitments in respect to international politics, his later *Memoirs* also acknowledged that his writings of the middle and late 1940s sounded like those of the strident right-wing anti-Communists of that era.[7]

Kennan became the first intellectual middleman of postwar national security studies, someone with an interest in ideas and with a knack for conveying them to a less scholarly audience in Washington and elsewhere. "The Sources of

---

[6] This analysis of Kennan is indebted to David C. Engerman, *Modernization from the Other Shore: American Intellectuals and the Romance of Russian Development* (Cambridge: Harvard University Press, 2003), pp. 253–71.

[7] "The Sources of Soviet Conduct," in *Foreign Affairs* (July 1947) was originally published under the pseudonym "X," and has been reprinted in Kennan, *American Diplomacy, 1900–1950* (Chicago: University of Chicago Press, 1951); see also Kennan, *Memoirs,* pp. 294, 354–60.

Soviet Conduct" was a remarkable achievement. It brought together strands of thought floating around Washington, blending a no-nonsense program for political action with moralistic denunciation of a dangerous but beatable enemy. Kennan took his place in a long tradition of American calls to arms, from John Winthrop to Manifest Destiny. More important, while his essay assisted the administration's public information program, he also contributed to a strategic concept: a formula for action applicable to a range of cases in pursuit of a long-term goal that recognizes the contingency in the experience to which the concept is meant to apply. Diplomats and the intellectuals who served them can often be seen as expounding or typifying such concepts.

Kennan came back from Moscow, soon to head Secretary Marshall's planning staff, a new position that he made famous as the job in the State Department going to a thinker on foreign policy. Kennan gave modern meaning to a role for intellectuals in high politics. But this job did not require him to worry about obligations to ends that were politically achievable, and almost immediately the otherworldly aspects of his personality were displayed. One biographer saw Kennan as an organicist conservative who took legal or universal solutions to the clash of nations as artificially tampering with the world. For Kennan such activities were odious, almost perverse. His "realism" lay in understanding the inherent limits of things, the futility, indeed blasphemy, of extending beyond the existing, the real.[8] There was, in Kennan, a quietist if not pacifist dimension. Most of his advice in crises was about how Americans should look inward, resolve to rebuild their own character and to pull up their own socks, positions consonant with his repudiation of the article, the one piece of writing that promoted conflict and action. His reputation was ironically built on ideas that he could barely stomach. Although the paper was idiosyncratic for Kennan, it does typify the indirect connection the ideas of experts had to the policy they pursued in power.

Truman had assumed office on the death of Roosevelt, and after he was elected in his own right in 1948, Dean Acheson, the most influential diplomat of the era, became secretary of state. Kennan immediately ran afoul of the new secretary's assertive style in foreign affairs. Acheson was less tormented than Kennan in admitting the perceived need to simplify in order to educate the American public. From Acheson's perspective, his theoretician-assistant took an overly highbrow view of the quarrel with the Soviet Union, and was not up to dramatizing a hard line. Indeed, the secretary believed Kennan was unfit to have any role in the making of policy.

For Acheson, Kennan's chief problem was that even in the late forties the military horrified him. During that period, nonetheless, Kennan outlined circumstances in which violence was legitimate, although even then his hatred of atomic weaponry was noticeable. He thought that the problem of nuclear

[8] Stephanson, *Art*, p. 176.

bombs was "metaphysical," their development "a philosophical mistake." Trying to find a "logical" place for them would lead the United States to "a realm of total confusion."[9] As Acheson put it, Kennan had an "abstract" sense of the national interest and a "Quaker gospel." Acheson told him that one must face issues "to be decided . . . under a sense of responsibility." Diplomats had to deal with concrete security problems and the immediate choices to be made about such problems. Acheson meant that, from his perspective, Kennan put forward impractical total solutions that did not speak to the mix of interests demanding attention. If Kennan wanted to concoct utopian schemes, Acheson believed, he should resign.[10]

Acheson, perhaps even consciously, distinguished between an ethic of responsibility and an ethic of ultimate ends, as the German sociologist Max Weber had done in his famous essay "Politics as a Vocation." In this framework, politics was process, and when called on to serve, the politician was always *in medias res*. He made an indefinite series of decisions designed to extend the life of the system into which he had entered. This was, for Weber, the ethic of responsibility.[11] The ethic of ultimate ends was reserved for personal moral decisions, and was not a framework usually pertinent to political decisions. On the contrary, Kennan urged that only the acceptance of his "theoretical groundwork" and "philosophy of foreign affairs" could salvage American diplomacy.[12] As one of his staff members put it, he "had a sense of being the philosopher king."[13]

After crises in Berlin and Czechoslovakia, the Soviets exploded a nuclear device in 1949, and commentators more easily deplored the centrality of foreign economic policy in the Truman administration and the peripheral role of its atomic strategy. A public relations program grounded in hyperbole now supported more rational suspicions that the Soviet Union, with nuclear weapons, would expand its domain through force of arms. A worldwide threat from Communism now was taken seriously, and questions arose concerning the adequacy of the American defense, if the Russians had bombs also. Even if the United States built more weapons, what would happen if the Russians attacked first and destroyed what the Americans had? By the end of 1949 a vision of a

[9] See the discussions in Mayers, *Kennan*, pp. 11, 122, 233–35, 307–16; Wilson D. Miscamble, *George F. Kennan and the Making of American Foreign Policy, 1947–1950* (Princeton: Princeton University Press, 1992), pp. 299–304.

[10] For discussion of this altercation see Miscamble, *Kennan,* pp. 175, 341–42; Mayers, *Kennan,* pp. 233–35, 307–9; and David S. McClellan, *Dean Acheson: The State Department Years* (New York: Dodd, Mead, 1976), pp. 157–59, 415–16.

[11] "Politics as a Vocation," in *From Max Weber*, ed. and trans. Hans Gerth and C. Wright Mills (New York: Oxford University Press, 1958), esp. pp. 120–28.

[12] Kennan, *Memoirs,* p. 468.

[13] As quoted in David Callahan, *Dangerous Capabilities: Paul Nitze and the Cold War* (New York: HarperCollins, 1990), p. 70.

new militarily potent totalitarianism had shifted the premises of foreign policy. Many people—though not either Kennan or Acheson—came to believe what might be best described as the oratory of foreign policy. But Acheson did see the need for a more forward stance by the United States. The explosion of the Russian bomb confirmed such a need. At the same time, the ascension to power of Communists in China after a long civil war in which the United States had supported their opponents, the Chinese Nationalists, added to the credibility of a universal threat.

Eased out of his job, Kennan went on to a quasi-academic career at Princeton's Institute for advanced study, respected as a Guru of foreign affairs but with no practical influence. His brief stints as a diplomat—in Russia in the 1950s and in Yugoslavia in the 1960s—were pedestrian. When in office he yearned for a different, more scholarly, environment, and when out of office, at Princeton, he was discouraged that the State Department got along without him.[14]

PAUL NITZE AND THE HARD LINE

Acheson replaced Kennan with Paul Nitze. With many connections at RAND, Nitze had a great respect for quantification and had reflected on the new bombs. He emerged as perhaps the most important intellectual middleman of the Cold War period. Not as original or as intelligent as Kennan, Nitze did have an excellent sense in trumpeting his greatest fear, the unpreparedness of the United States in facing a ruthless Soviet adversary.

Nitze was raised in Chicago, the son of a successful and prosperous professor at the University of Chicago. Nitze was himself interested in the professoriate, but on one account an illness that occurred after his graduation from Harvard in 1928 delayed his entrance into a doctoral program and altered his career plans. But Nitze also recalled that he desired to make an impact on affairs and believed the scholarly realm restricted the leverage that even action-oriented academics could have on public policy. In any event, though the world of learning and of international relations still attracted him, he became an investment banker in New York through his family connections. In the 1930s he traveled on the continent, a witness to the collapse of the European democracies. His fearful yet respectful evaluation of Hitler's Germany, which some attributed to his family's German heritage but which really displayed the value he placed on authority and discipline, earned him the reputation of being pro-Nazi.[15] In 1937 he took a year off from the firm of Dillon, Read to do graduate work at Harvard. There he pondered Spengler's *Decline of the West*, like Ken-

[14] Miscamble, *Kennan*, pp. 36, 343; Mayers, *Kennan*, p. 294.
[15] Nitze, "My School Days in Hyde Park," *Hyde Park History* 3 (Winter 2001–2): 3.

nan before him, and took a constellation of courses that asked large questions about the nature and growth of world cultures.

In 1940 James Forrestal, with whom Nitze had worked in New York, joined the Roosevelt administration as an assistant to the president. Forrestal became Nitze's political mentor (as he was later to become Kennan's) when he asked Nitze to move to Washington as his aide. Nitze was one of many international businessmen to become part of the foreign policy establishment in the capital at the start of World War II. He later worked with economists on making the American bombing campaigns more effective. Then as a member of the Strategic Bombing Survey, he analyzed the performance of the German war economy immediately after the war, where we have already met him. Nitze believed in air warfare and chaired the groups that later wrote the Survey's reports on the bombing of Japan after the surrender in the Pacific. He authored the view that neither an invasion of Japan nor the atomic bomb would have been necessary to conclude the war in the Far East before the end of 1945. Although the most authoritative scholarship about the bombing surveys has argued that previously held prejudices shaped Nitze's conclusions, he thought that a policy of heavy bombing alone would have secured Japan's defeat.[16] This estimate later gained Nitze the appreciation of many commentators who denounced the American use of the bombs to end the war but, more important, his style of reasoning made him one of the chief policymakers to press RAND numbers and conclusions on politicians.

Nitze was in and out of government service for the next fifty years, never reaching the highest appointed positions, but always recognized as a critical member of the decision-making class.

In 1943 Nitze and his friend, Congressman Christian Herter, established a Foreign Policy Center in Washington that offered practical training to men in careers in international commerce or diplomacy. This "School of Advanced International Studies" promoted "mutual understanding between corporation executives and government officials in the foreign field." It borrowed its tiny faculty from other Washington institutions or from government agencies. The organization relied on donations from large businesses, and in the 1940s fulfilled Nitze's desire to provide those interested in foreign affairs with some intellectual guidance.[17] It also displayed Nitze's concept of higher education in this field—a mix of historical precepts and a working sense of the needs of American business. Although Nitze was a more centered and healthy individual than his patron Forrestal, their liaison was not accidental, and the younger

[16] Robert P. Newman, "Ending the War with Japan: Paul Nitze's Early Surrender' Counterfactual," *Pacific Historical Review* 64 (1995): 167–94.

[17] 1952 Support Program, Minutes May 10, 1950–June 28, 1955, Foreign Service Educational Foundation Records, Johns Hopkins University.

Figure 1. *Left to right,* President Lyndon B. Johnson, Secretary of Defense Robert McNamara, Secretary of the Navy Paul Nitze, General Earl Wheeler at a National Security Council meeting (LBJ Library photo by Yoichi R. Okamoto)

man adopted rhetoric that Forrestal reinforced. Nitze recalled that they had many "philosophical" discussions about international conflict. He had the same sort of vision as Forrestal about the evil of the Soviet Union, and of the world-historical contest that engaged the United States. Following Forrestal, Nitze believed in a Manichaean Universe and in an American exceptionalism and destiny, notable even in a culture whose roots lay in the Puritans. The outlook served Nitze well as policymaker, but critics also said that he overstated his guiding maxims: the softness of democracy, the strength of its adversaries, and the sinister quality of the other side. Early on, of course, Kennan had given Forrestal the ammunition for this point of view. But Kennan was more opportunistic in joining ideology to foreign policy and barely found acceptable what he wrote for Forrestal; Nitze was a true believer.

Yet this judgment is oversimplified. Throughout his career Nitze may have overestimated Soviet power, and—coincidentally—accused his opponents of almost traitorous motives. He pointed out the weakness and flaccidity of other policymakers who did not have his fortitude and will. Nonetheless, he also found the Soviet threat more bounded when he was in power than when he was out. Some thus disliked Nitze as a dealmaker and fixer. When he had a government position, Russian iniquity diminished and became manageable.

Nitze talked about negotiation, not apocalypse. He may have justified the need for strength, but far more so when he did not have authority.[18]

Assisting Kennan in the late 1940s, Nitze had advanced himself in Acheson's eyes by being more aggressive than his immediate boss. Moreover, although in the State Department, Nitze befriended the social scientists at RAND and their air force supporters. He encouraged their study of defense management and the expansion of techniques to the study of actual war-making. Moreover, he was not afraid of atomic weapons. His work on the USSBS convinced him that the conventional bombing of World War II was just as dreadful as that which atomic armaments could produce. For him they were just new bombs, and he dismissed the cares that, he believed, regulated the thought of many overwhelmed by the prospect of an Armageddon.

Although Nitze was less cynical, he shared Acheson's change of mood in 1949–50. Nitze took to heart the secretary's view that the administration would have to bludgeon the mass bureaucratic-legislative mind to move policy from its political and economic orientation to a military one. In early 1950 Nitze responded to the novel problems of weaponry and perceived Soviet aggressiveness by drafting a new statement of policy prepared by Truman's National Security Council, NSC-68. The document made an ideological call to protect freedom in the United States and to secure Europe from a military threat. The defense budget was to be tripled. Although NSC-68 was a secret study, Nitze heated up the anti-Communist climate.[19]

Nitze had read and relied on the publication of the RAND social scientist Nathan Leites. From Leites' study for RAND, *The Operational Code of the Politburo*, Nitze adopted the ideas about the implacable and global nature of the Communism that permeated NSC-68.[20] A chief interest of Leites was in applying psychoanalytic ideas to politics, and *The Operational Code* was in many ways a more academic restatement of Kennan's earlier speculations about the underside of the mental world of Soviet officialdom—Leites' first footnote cited Kennan. But whereas in 1947 Kennan had lamented the confrontation with the enemy and worried about how America should respond, in 1950 Nitze was more optimistic about how the United States could strike back at the enemies Leites had explained to him. Nitze was fairly certain that a mailed

---

[18] For Nitze's career I have relied on Callahan, *Dangerous Capabilities*; Strobe Talbot, *Master of the Game: Paul Nitze and the Nuclear Peace* (New York: Knopf, 1988), pp. 8–12, 23–31, 62; Paul H. Nitze, *From Hiroshima to Glasnost: At the Center of Decision: A Memoir* (New York: Grove Weidenfeld, 1989), pp. ix–xxii, 3–7, 153–59; and *Tension Between Opposites: Reflections on the Theory and Practice of Politics* (New York: Charles Scribner's Sons, 1993).

[19] In "NSC (National Insecurity) 68," in *Critical Reflections on the Cold War*, ed. Martin Medhurst and H. W. Brands (College Station: Texas A&M University Press, 2000), pp. 55–94, Robert P. Newman is hyperbolic and moralizing but does capture accurately Nitze's style of operating.

[20] For Leites see the citations in chapter 2; and Gregg Herken, *Counsels of War* (New York: Knopf, 1985), p. 75.

American fist would do the job and confidently called for more weapons and the will to use them.[21]

Nitze wanted to etch into the policymaking psyche an enlarged sense of the villainy of the Russians, their ability and intent to harm the United States, and the faintheartedness of the American people, whose inclination to pacifism had to be restrained. Although extreme, Nitze typified an approach that came of age in 1950 and was a core element in foreign policy for four decades. Acheson, at least, thought that NSC-68 exaggerated, but he and others did believe that there was an added threat, and the Soviet atomic bomb did portend major changes in the strategic balance. NSC-68 used hyperbole in order to raise the consciousness of decision makers about a fresh level of Russian aggression.[22]

Nitze and like-minded individuals were far from fools, and their experience in foreign policy—although more ambiguous than they credited it—did lend support to their views. The major event was the attack of the North Koreans on the South in June 1950, a crisis in which the North, with the sanction of both Russia and China, hoped to take control over an area that the United States had signaled as secondary to its concerns. When confronted with the attack, however, the Americans quickly saw their interest in maintaining a foothold on the Korean peninsula, and recognized the issues of prestige at work. In the elevated mood of the era, they embraced what was known as the Munich Analogy. In his 1938 conference with Hitler, British prime minister Neville Chamberlain had given in to the dictator's demands over Czechoslovakia, thus insuring, so the narrative went, that Germany would ask for more. Had Chamberlain confronted Germany, Americans believed, Hitler would have backed down. This incident taught that diplomats should not reward aggression, that standing up to bullies was easier in the long run than capitulating. And so the United States in 1950 should not repeat Chamberlain's performance. America must resist at once the North Korean takeover of the South.

The United States hoped for an easy victory. Instead, the North Koreans and their Chinese Communist friends fought a war of attrition against the South Koreans and their American allies that established real boundaries for the North and South at just about where there had previously been an administrative divide. In falsely assuming that the Chinese would stay out of the conflict and that the North Koreans would turn tail, the Americans found that assertiveness had its complications. The United States had involved itself in a costly and ambiguous conflict and became committed to a weak ally in Asia on the borders of the great Communist states. Finally, the Americans continued to

[21] For NSC-68 the best source is Ernest R. May, ed., *American Cold War Strategy: Interpreting NSC-68* (Boston: Bedford–St. Martin's, 1993).

[22] On the complexities of this debate see Jerald A. Combs, "The Compromise That Never Was: George Kennan, Paul Nitze, and the Issue of Conventional Deterrence in Europe, 1949–1952," *Diplomatic History* 15 (1991): 361–71.

believe in a policy that put Europe first. They did not want to make land war in Asia a military priority, and judged that a Korean probe might portend real trouble in Western Europe.

NSC-68 was a tightly held study when the Korean War gave it political life. Before that time the administration doubted that even a trumped-up danger of the Russian military could persuade the Congress to enlarge United States military spending and, thus, taxes. In the context of the Korean War, however, the concerns of NSC-68 appeared vivid to opinion makers in foreign affairs, and the administration greatly increased the military budget, although much money went to fortify defenses in Western Europe. Diplomats transformed into an armed alliance the North Atlantic Treaty Organization, which had been created the previous year but which had had a partially economic function. By 1951 the United States had set up NATO as the first line of defense in the primary arena of conflict, Western Europe.

Although the Truman administration shifted from economic to military priorities, the Soviet A-bomb perhaps made the nuclear strategy based on sole possession of atomic weapons obsolete. The Korean War additionally demonstrated that the United States might need to think not only about launching such weapons against the Russians, but also about waging little wars against Communist satellites such as North Korea, which were not worth major conflicts. The Korean War itself was not fought with atomic bombs. It was known in the 1950s as a "limited" or "conventional" war. Some strategists easily took from Korea the lesson that the United States should not focus on fighting with atomic bombs, but evolve responses to lesser threats, which might not demand "going nuclear." The stage was set for a new role for RAND.

CHAPTER 3

RAND in Opposition, 1946–1961

The Korean War dragged on from June 1950 through the congressional elections of November and then through the presidential campaign of 1952. The inconclusive nature of the contest helped to discredit the Truman administration and Democrats in general. The war and a heightened sense of ideological threat contributed to the election of Dwight Eisenhower and the Republicans in November 1952.

The change in political climate was coterminous with a change in the intellectual climate. In the immediate postwar period, reflective writers had made Americans understand what the world outside their borders was like. But the men who successfully purveyed ideas about war and diplomacy were gentlemen scholars like Kennan and Nitze. Moreover, their paradigmatic statements of principle did not make policies but rather justified policies that circumstances later propelled into being. The use of force intimated by "The Sources of Soviet Conduct" was metaphorical until the Soviet A-bomb and the fall of China made military options real. Although NSC-68 was top secret, its reasoning did not get a purchase on decisions until the Korean War broke out.

In the 1950s, a more professionalized group of expert-academics hoped for greater real command of the levers of power. Chief among them were the RAND civilians and the university-based social scientists who consulted for the organization. By the 1950s RAND's scope had grown beyond providing advice to the air force about new weapons. Additionally, the framing of the stakes in the Cold War had given RAND and its acolytes ideological space in which to operate. Because the air force had become the keeper of American nuclear weapons, RAND moved directly into calculations about the war strategy of the United States.

The road to Washington was nonetheless circuitous. The Republican administration, the first in twenty years, was committed to shrinking the federal government, swollen, the GOP believed, through two decades of taxation and expenditures by the free-spending Democrats of Franklin Roosevelt's New Deal. Not only did the GOP wish to contain federal agencies; it also had a mandate to cut taxes and spending. The focus, for Republicans, was the domestic welfare state, but Eisenhower worried that defense too manifested rapacious government. With the prestige that he had acquired leading the western forces in Europe in World War II, Eisenhower determined to trim both welfare and the military.

RAND social scientists had two overlapping but not necessarily consistent goals. One was a rational defense, in which RAND could quantify threat, calculate the most effective strategy to combat the threat, and realize the strategy through the allocation of funds and the reconfiguration of the armed services. In the 1950s the policy intellectuals agreed that the United States must plan for limited wars such as had occurred in Korea and that such planning must look carefully at the nuclear options. The other goal was to enlarge the air force budget. Thus RAND was at odds with the overall design of the Eisenhower administration and with Ike's well-known distaste for ideas of limited war. Part of RAND's complaint about the cost-cutting Republicans reflected the prejudices of its employer. The RAND civilians worked for the air force and satisfied its need for a rationale that would obtain the service more money. Nonetheless, the leadership of a mentally inferior general confirmed the belief of the strategists that their arguments were correct.

Thus, just when RAND felt it might be most useful to the nation, the civilian theorists faced not just the sort of military figure whose sort of ability they deprecated. They also had a president interested in slashing costs. Moreover, while in power, the Democrats had a use for men like Kennan and Nitze. Eisenhower Republicans were more suspicious of such intellectuals.

EISENHOWER'S STRATEGY

Eisenhower gave much thought to American security and wanted it overhauled. Despite what educated Democrats said, the president was not a foolish or obtuse man. Although burdened by the fear of Communism and often unwilling to surrender even minor tactical advantages, he was sensitive to the appalling dilemmas that nuclear arms had created, and from the mid-1950s on struggled to find a way to disarm.[1] The president had met von Neumann and was familiar with RAND. He had some understanding of game theory, which he saw as the formalization of basic strategic reasoning—planning on the basis of what one thought the other side was likely to do.[2] But Eisenhower's style differed. He did not think, on the one hand, that risks and benefits could be arithmetically calculated and, on the other, he was not interested that RAND or the university community should validate his ideas. Eisenhower said he

---

[1] This is the clear message of Charles A. Appleby, "Eisenhower and Arms Control, 1953–1961," Ph.D. diss., School of Advanced International Studies, Johns Hopkins University, 1987.

[2] Kaplan, *The Wizards of Armageddon*, p. 178; Robert R. Bowie and Richard H. Immerman, *Waging Peace: How Eisenhower Shaped an Enduring Cold War Strategy* (New York: Oxford University Press, 1998), pp. 48, 268n.

tired of "abstractions" and disliked the "idea of . . . generalized definitions" of which intellectuals were so fond. His brief tenure as president of Columbia University had crystallized his lack of ease with, and his mistrust of, the scholarly world. He did not want "a lot of long-haired professors" to examine nuclear policy. "What the hell do they know about it?" he is reported to have said. His secretary of state, John Foster Dulles, found theoretical issues "utterly academic," while Eisenhower's confidant C. D. Jackson said they were "dream stuff."[3] The administration particularly disliked Nitze, who as a conduit for RAND ideas had looked forward to a larger role in post-Korea Washington. Over his years in office Eisenhower made policy in a remarkably open series of national security meetings, where scholars and university concepts were conspicuous by their absence. Ike's planning was a standard against which the defense strategists reacted.

An important part of Eisenhower's perspective was the money allocated to the military. Central to national security, Eisenhower reasoned, was a sound economy, and although he curbed domestic (welfare) spending, he also was afraid that the higher taxes associated with NSC-68, which Truman partially implemented, threatened to bankrupt the nation they were supposed to shield. Finally, Eisenhower skeptically viewed doctrines that had emerged from Korea. Although the contest may have been necessary, Eisenhower had no stake in believing that American policy in Asia was shrewd and efficacious. Not a party to the strategy in the Far East in the late 1940s and early 1950s, the new president was not invested in justifying conventional ground warfare in north Asia, still tangential to American concern. Truman and Acheson could have circumvented such a costly policy had they been more competent. Eisenhower also suspected the gradual application of force. Military doctrine demanded clarity in the definition of a mission and the resources to prevail. The president believed that, as a great power dedicated to peacekeeping in the 1950s, the United States must not involve itself in costly, ambiguous conflicts. America should not intervene unless it was certain that the United States would overcome the enemy, and irresistible power should be designed to bring about quick victory. Korea taught Ike not that the United States had to plan for limited war but that his predecessors had made a mistake, which he could avoid with the appropriate consideration of nuclear weapons.

---

[3] NSC Meetings, March 4, November 24, 1954, FRUS, 1952–54, vol. 2, *National Security Affairs* (in two parts), part 1, pp. 642–43, and 799 respectively. Memo of Conversation with President, July 2, 1959, FRUS 1958–60, vol. 3, *National Security Policy, Arms Control and Disarmament*, pp. 228, 235. On Columbia see Travis Beal Jacobs, *Eisenhower at Columbia* (New Brunswick, N.J.: Transaction, 2002), and especially the summary judgment at p. 205. "Long-haired professors" is quoted from Campbell Craig, *Destroying the Village: Eisenhower and Thermonuclear War* (New York: Columbia University Press, 1998), an outstanding treatment, p. 56. Reported comment from David L. Snead, *The Gaither Committee, Eisenhower, and the Cold War* (Columbus: Ohio State University Press, 1999), p. 80.

The president also vetoed limited war because of its cost. Weighing alternative strategies to obtain a better defense for the least outlay, Eisenhower turned to "the New Look," or what Secretary of State Dulles spoke of as massive retaliation. The Republicans would eschew the expense of conventional conflict and save on defense by underwriting atomic war. To prevent the nibbling away at the edges that Korea represented, the United States would concentrate on instruments of terror such as the new H-bomb. The threat of such weapons could prevent war, when no other nation had much of a nuclear arsenal. Attention to the relatively inexpensive strategy of building up the air force and nonconventional arms (and of economizing on costly ground troops) would solve Eisenhower's "great equation" that connected defense expenditure to a sound economy and a balanced budget.

Much of this was old hat. On the one hand, Truman's plans had centered on the Strategic Air Command, and officials had always considered the bomb the equalizer of the land armies of the USSR in the primary European theater. Even as the Truman administration fought the Korean War, it formulated a strategy that first relied on nuclear power.[4] Truman had rejected the ambitious objectives of NSC-68 for the "rollback" of the Soviets in Eastern Europe as soon as Korea became a protracted conflict. Eisenhower was even less enamored of such "liberation" than many Democrats in the preceding administration. Budget concerns as well as a return to less millennial thinking almost immediately compromised Nitze's high hopes. After Eisenhower's election, Nitze, who briefly worked for the GOP as a consultant, attempted to keep the spirit of NSC-68 alive in the form of a buildup of conventional forces, but he had less success with the Republicans than he had had with Democrats after 1950, the year in which the North Koreans had invaded.[5]

On the other hand, the Republicans recognized that in many venues nuclear force alone might be inappropriate. The Eisenhower administration realized that the enemy might not believe the threat of H-bombs in a tangential confrontation. Thus, nuclear weapons might encourage conflict if they were the only option. Almost from the time Dulles announced massive retaliation in 1954, Republicans introduced caveats to the doctrine, and Dulles himself was ambiguous about its meaning—deliberately so if one gives him credit for any intelligence.[6]

Nonetheless, Eisenhower thought that the United States should not supply major infantry forces for local wars, and argued that the Truman administration had substituted greater military spending for a consistent strategic concept.[7] Dulles's penchant for bombast and Ike's independent conceptions and genuine

[4] See Samuel Wells Jr., "The Origins of Massive Retaliation," *Political Science Quarterly* 96 (1981): 31–52.

[5] Bowie and Immerman, *Waging Peace*, pp. 3, 31, 178, 247.

[6] See Robert Mann's discussion in *A Grand Delusion: America's Descent into Vietnam* (New York: Basic Books, 2001), pp. 116–17.

[7] Bowie and Immerman, *Waging Peace*, pp. 75, 251.

interest in capping defense costs did lend a different inflection to the defense conversation of the middle 1950s. RAND-inspired strategists portrayed Eisenhower's policies as clumsy and unintelligent,[8] and as one of his aides pointed out, Eisenhower had an aversion to the subject of smaller conflicts.[9] The president at different times bemoaned that the United States could not afford to fight every type of war and insisted that he never meant to rely only on nuclear weapons.[10] Still, he was "under the impression that our strategic concept did not adequately take account of the possibility of limited war."[11]

At the same time much of the talk of the civilian strategists and their Democratic allies about the constraints of massive retaliation *was* just talk. No one thought about fighting a big war without recourse to nuclear weapons. The issue of conventional weapons only pertained to minor conflicts. Henry Kissinger, who popularized some of these national security guidelines in the late 1950s, wrote that the ideas of the defense policy scientists were not an alternative to massive retaliation, but their "complement." Students of strategy designed such ideas to make room for "the possibility of limited war."[12]

As much as he could, Eisenhower avoided the civilian strategists. Although the accepted understanding of the New Look did not capture his ideas, the president reckoned that in the near future American nuclear superiority best guaranteed peace and stability. The problems that worried RAND did not bother him in the early and mid-1950s. Many American military and political leaders often thought of preventive war: hit the evil while the United States could do so with some impunity. Although this doctrine never gained preeminence, a milder variant of it did: in the event of increased tension and clear indication of malign intent, Eisenhower judged that the United States should launch an attack first. If the Soviets determined on major aggression, America would appropriately respond with a nuclear strike, and such preemption would spare the West.[13]

---

[8] For a less sympathetic appraisal of the president see H. W. Brands, "The Age of Vulnerability: Eisenhower and the National Insecurity State," *American Historical Review* 94 (1988–89), esp. pp. 965, 985.

[9] NSC Meeting, October 6, 1960, FRUS, 1958–60, vol. 3, *National Security Policy, Arms Control and Disarmament*, p. 481.

[10] NSC Meetings, June 24, December 3, 1954, FRUS, 1952–54, vol. 2, *National Security Affairs* (in two parts), part 1, pp. 690–91, and 804 respectively; Dulles-Eisenhower Conversation, January 1, 1958, FRUS, 1958–60, vol. 3, *National Security Policy, Arms Control and Disarmament*, p. 57.

[11] Quoted in Peter Roman, *Eisenhower and the Missile Gap* (Ithaca: Cornell University Press, 1995), p. 71.

[12] Kissinger, *Nuclear Weapons and Foreign Policy* (New York: Harper and Brothers, 1957), pp. 145, 172, 173.

[13] Marc Trachtenberg, *A Constructed Peace: The Making of the European Settlement, 1945– 1963* (Princeton: Princeton University Press, 1999), pp. 160–65.

Eisenhower also thought positively about arming the Western allies, including Germany, with nuclear weapons of their own. A U.S.-led NATO would coordinate defense strategies, but Ike did not want the United States to be the mainstay of European defense forever, and felt that a united Europe might be strong enough to carry forward the atomic strategy that was now in American hands.[14] Like much of his generation's leadership, Eisenhower did not wish American troops in Europe indefinitely, and in the 1950s he feared the infantilization of the Europeans.

In some ways massive retaliation expressed Eisenhower's caution in foreign affairs. If the options were nuclear war or doing nothing, passivity might have priority. Emphasis on air war did result in lowered defense spending and, more so than Truman and the Democrats after 1950, Ike acknowledged the need for a coherent strategy that balanced resources and threat. The president aimed for a secure America, but, dismissing the civilians, he postulated that security could not be perfect, and came at a price that was only marginally elastic. He also looked to the foreseeable future, and for this middle distance the president relied on America's overwhelming nuclear lead.

There was one remarkable irony in this debate that went unnoticed. The civilian strategists often deplored the fact that policy was being made by a general who thought of the last war. Good or bad, this sort of thinking was not so true of Eisenhower as of his critics. In the context of the Korean War, the defense intellectuals tried to work out how a conventional conflict could be waged more successfully when nuclear weapons existed. The president was less interested in planning with Korea in mind.

RAND COMES OF AGE

In the debate over limited war versus massive retaliation RAND gave arguments and sustenance to the Democrats on the sidelines, but the thinking of the strategists went beyond a mere critique of the existing Republican policy. Looking into a future more distant than that of politicians, the defense strategists worried about trouble that did not currently exist, but which would surely come into being if they were ignored. RAND civilians and their kin in the universities also introduced arcane beliefs into the dialogues about international affairs. Assured of generous funding from the air force, RAND and the men it attracted from the academic world promulgated views linked to high intelligence and quantitative reasoning. Humorous critics dubbed them the theologians of war, who adumbrated ideas of *deterrence, second-strike capacity, vulnerability, tactical* or *theater nuclear weapons, graduated deterrence, flexible* or *controlled response, coercive diplomacy, war-fighting, counterforce/*

[14] Trachtenberg, *A Constructed Peace,* pp. 152–54.

no cities, and *assured destruction*. As one commentator has noted, the emphasis on a priori thinking went hand in hand with rumination over atomic weapons, for which there were precious few empirical anchors.[15]

In a way the appearance of this clerisy on the policy stage was heralded in 1951 when Twentieth Century Fox released a notable movie, *The Day the Earth Stood Still*. In this film a representative of a powerful interstellar confederacy arrived in the United States to warn the planet that while minor violence would be tolerated, the human breakthrough to atomic weapons posed dangers that the confederacy could not accept. The visitor Klaatu was immediately wounded by a nervous soldier, and the earthlings thereafter behaved in reckless and foolish ways that only confirmed Klaatu's fears. By the end of the movie he was clarifying his message to civilian "scientists." The nations of the world needed quickly to curb the selfish sovereignty that had led to a diplomacy of nuclear threat and counterthreat, or Earth faced extinction.

RAND exposed the deficiencies of massive retaliation and elaborated on the turns strategy should take. Its social scientists yearned to have executive power and made a peculiar mark that requires complicated exegesis of notions intertwined with the diplomacy of the 1950s.

BERNARD BRODIE AND SCIENTIFIC STRATEGY

RAND's Bernard Brodie was the greatest influence on men like Nitze searching for an intellectual foothold when policy was altering. Kennan had made the Soviet-American conflict in the mid-1940s transparent to a broad public. Brodie articulated the problems of defense for a much narrower range of foreign policy Democrats out of power in the 1950s, but he concentrated not on Eisenhower so much as on the shortcomings of Brodie's employers in the air force.

Brodie brought to his life work an eclectic mix of interests. He had done an undergraduate degree in philosophy at Chicago, when the influence of John Dewey was still strong, and a doctorate in international relations there in the 1930s. But he avoided the emphasis on international law at Chicago and studied political history and geography. The burgeoning ideas of management economics also attracted him, while in the background of his work was the language of power, interest, and national security. Unique at RAND because of his historical approach, Brodie is in many ways an appealing figure, but he suffered because he so often made clear his contempt for those of lesser intellect.[16]

---

[15] Richard K. Betts, "Should Strategic Studies Survive," *World Politics* 50 (1997–98): 13–15.
[16] This trait is adumbrated in Barry H. Steiner, *Bernard Brodie and the Foundations of American Nuclear Strategy* (Lawrence: University Press of Kansas, 1991), pp. 25–26, 196–99, 228–29.

Figure 2. Bernard Brodie

Brodie had published his dissertation, *Sea Power in the Machine Age* (1941), just after the Japanese attack. He thought that he would make a career in maritime strategy, and during the war wrote propaganda for the navy. Then, after five years at Yale's Institute for International Studies, and a year working for the air force, he went to RAND, where his ideas received their widest dissemination.

Brodie supposed that the bomb made received military thinking irrelevant and that the postwar world required new doctrines. Moreover, he drew an analogy between strategy and the economic analysis of scarce resources—marginal costs and marginal utility. Strategic thought needed calculation of the goals of defense or war making; of the consequences of trying to achieve various goals; and of the costs of achieving them. Via economics Brodie saw how to extend the restricted approach of operations research. He added an old-fashioned sense of what happened when conflicting interests brought a nation close to war, and what it could do to prevent it or win it—especially if nuclear interchange was a danger. Brodie made his initial statements in an edited volume of 1946, *The Absolute Weapon*, and a much-cited essay, "Strategy as a Science," in a new journal, *World Politics*, in 1949.

Brodie's essay bought up to date and emphasized themes in a 1940 effort by an illustrious Princeton political scientist, Edward Meade Earle, "National

Defense and Political Science."[17] Two ideas that dominated the thinking of RAND through the 1960s were apparent in Brodie's definition of a new academic specialty. First, a science of strategic studies, Brodie repeatedly argued, could assist the outdated thinking of the armed services. Preparing for war and waging it in the contemporary world required skills, he said, to which the soldier made no pretension—"a genuine understanding of military strategy." Brodie achieved a reputation at RAND for his dismissal of the military as "conceptually behindhanded."[18] The repetition of this idea—into the 1960s—accounted in large measure for the visceral dislike the soldiers felt for the civilians, a mingling of dislike for the latter's hauteur, abstraction, and lack of experience; and envy of their professorial prestige.[19]

Operations researchers also worried about the importance of their trade and their self-esteem. They felt they must not be regarded as engineers but had to "assume the dignity of scientists."[20] Brodie seized on the putative scientific quality of the enterprise and its claim to a superior method. The United States could no longer base strategy on the narrow, pragmatic comprehension of "the last war" that reflected "the absence of the habit of scientific thinking." A 1954 RAND study to which he contributed allowed that an "almost universal consensus" recognized that nuclear weapons "have transformed out of all recognition with the past not only war itself (at least major war) but also all international political strife." The change was so "completely unprecedented that historical comparisons fail us almost completely." The genuine strategist had to go beyond history and experience to develop a "conceptual framework" that would pit one possible war-making plan against another to see which one was better. Thinking in terms of costs and benefits, the strategist trained in economics could provide a *"genuine analytical method"* that would enable more effective thinking about war than the military afforded.[21]

Another civilian strategist, Alain Enthoven, commented that subsequent to World War II, personal and collective wisdom, on which the military had al-

[17] Earle, "National Defense and Political Science," *Political Science Quarterly* 15 (1940): 481–95. Earle achieved his greatest influence before the end of World War II and was the editor of the well-known *Makers of Modern Strategy: From Machiavelli to Hitler* (Princeton: Princeton University Press, 1943).

[18] See Brodie to Spier, November 23, 1954, and Speier to Brodie, November 30, 1954, Box 4, Washington Office Correspondence, Brodie Papers, UCLA.

[19] This idea is traced in the discussion of C. E. Lindblom's papers on RAND–Air Force relations, Brodie to Lindblom, January 29, 1960, Box 1, L, Brodie Papers, UCLA.

[20] See the expressions of concern in *Proceedings of the First International Conference on Operational Research* (Baltimore: Operations Research Society of America, 1957), esp. pp. 13, 519–20.

[21] Brodie, "Strategy as a Science," *World Politics* 1 (1948–49): 473, 475, 478, 484. And for other early expressions of the same ideas see Trachtenberg, *Strategic Thought*, pt. 2: Brodie from *The Absolute Weapon*, p. 81; from "New Techniques of War and National Policies," p. 146; *Strategic Thought*, pt. 3, vol. 1: Brodie from "Nuclear Weapons: Strategic or Tactical?" p. 219. And

ways relied, had become irrelevant to strategy. Since the war, science and technology had gone through a "takeoff" period, and the "new analytical approach" was more important than "the experience and judgment of the military." In a remarkable lecture to the brass that was widely thought to be condescending, Enthoven argued that the soldiers must learn to replace experience and history with "scientific method."[22]

Despite the dismissal of history and experience, the theorists did work in the shadow of Korea and did rely on standard tropes in thinking about war. This is the second point that stands out in Brodie's work. One way that nations got into war was by accident. At work here was an interpretation of the origins of World War I that received expression in the best-seller by Barbara Tuchman, *The Guns of August* (1962), but that RAND widely shared.[23] No one had wanted World War I, according to Tuchman, but lack of thoughtfulness and resourcefulness, rigidities of planning, and mistakes that went unrectified had brought it on. No one at RAND gave much attention to the conflict as the culmination of Germany's grasp at world power, or Britain's long-term patronizing attitude towards its opponent—two interpretations that came to the fore after Tuchman's; or the expanding great power rivalry between Britain and Germany—the accepted historical explanation at the time. All of these views involved tensions that had been brewing for a generation and entailed a historical perspective.[24] For Tuchman and RAND, on the contrary, understanding the war depended on learning to avoid accidents.

Nations could also launch war through aggressive, clandestine attack. Here again RAND discarded political jousting and the evolution of antagonisms, unremarkable variables of diplomatic history. Unexpected wrongdoing replaced them. In this respect the common experience of World War II and the Japanese attack on Pearl Harbor made RAND's thinking as simple as that of the man on the street. The context of war was not past politics but malevolent surprise. In atomic war, wrote Brodie, we had to worry about "blatant aggressions by powerful states." The imagined devastation of nuclear holocaust might be for such states "a stimulus to evil acts."[25]

---

from *Strategic Thought*, pt. 3, vol. 2: Brodie, C. J. Hitch, and A. W. Marshall, "The Next Ten Years" (RAND study), p. 1.

[22] Alain C. Enthoven, "Choosing Strategies and Selecting Weapon Systems," in *A Modern Design for Defense Decision: A McNamara-Hitch-Enthoven Anthology*, ed. Samuel A. Tucker (Washington, D.C.: Industrial College of the Armed Forces, 1966), pp. 134, 138.

[23] For an example, see Bowles-Dobrynin conversation, October 13, 1962, FRUS, 1961–63, vol. 11, *Cuban Missile Crisis and Aftermath*, p. 27.

[24] The conventional ideas may be found in Sidney B. Fay, *The Origins of the World War*, 2 vols. (New York: Macmillan, 1928, 1930; 1956, 1958); the newer ones in Fritz Fischer, *Germany's Aims in the First World War* (London: Chatto and Windus, 1967); and Niall Ferguson, *The Pity of War* (New York: Basic Books, 1999).

[25] Brodie, "Nuclear Weapons," *Strategic Thought*, pt. 3, vol. 1, p. 228.

When they dwelt on a wicked bolt from the blue, another book swayed the strategists. Roberta Wohlstetter's manuscript, "Signals and Decisions at Pearl Harbor" was available at RAND in the 1950s. Roberta Wohlstetter was the wife of Albert Wohlstetter, who would succeed Brodie as the most influential RAND strategist, and her manuscript applied some of RAND's theoretical ideas to the Japanese attack. Roberta Wohlstetter concentrated on why Pearl Harbor surprised the United States, on how the defense establishment missed the signs that it was coming. The attack itself limited her concern. In the over four hundred pages of the published book, *Pearl Harbor: Warning and Decision,* only three or four took up the international rivalry in the Far East in the late 1930s—one paragraph on Japanese expansion in Asia—that prompted the United States to pressure the Japanese and put them into a position where the attack on Pearl Harbor made sense.[26] Roberta Wohlstetter's interpretation of World War II was equivalent to Tuchman's of World War I. In neither case need the scholar take up the history of political antagonism.

Though Brodie was an exception, the dismissal of history and politics characteristic of RAND complemented a view of the onset of war. Historical disciplines could not assist policymakers in grasping the realization of harmful intent that came without warning or reason. The emphasis on surprise may also have implicitly edged the civilians away from sustained interest in analysis of trends in current politics and in preparation for the near future. Instead they were programmed to worry about the unpredictable far future, or to deal with the immediate—unanticipated assault, unexpected crises, and the accidental.

At the same time that Brodie reflected two of RAND's typical themes—that the military was obtuse and that accident and veiled malignity caused war—he wrote about nuclear weapons with thoughtful intelligence. He scorned the air force belief that superior American air power and nuclear weapons would destroy the enemy. The trick, for Brodie, was to make the threat of war so fearful that the likely combatants would avoid it. Thus, he devised a theory of *deterrence*: the United States must employ its nuclear arsenal to make an enemy afraid to strike in the first place. From this idea naturally flowed what

[26] The manuscript was published as *Pearl Harbor: Warning and Decision* (Palo Alto: Stanford University Press, 1962). The historical comments on the coming of the war occur on pp. 353–57. Another theorist, Thomas Schelling, contributed a "Foreword" to this book, possibly because Wohlstetter made use of notions of signaling that Schelling was propounding at that time in respect to foreign policy in the 1960s. But Wohlstetter's grasp of signaling was confused. She presumed that the Japanese were in some way signaling America about the attack, when what they were doing was the opposite. See pp. 1–2, 5, 386–87, 389, 396. Wohlstetter hoped to exemplify Schelling's view that war was about signals—that the actors are trying to convey intents through signs that must be properly read. This was, however, a debatable theory, and Wohlstetter's use of the word *signal* suggested that she did not understand either the meaning of the word, or the theory in which it was embedded. See the discussion of Schelling below. Wohlstetter did better in "Cuba and Pearl Harbor: Hindsight and Foresight," *Foreign Affairs* 44 (1965), esp. p. 690.

was called *second-strike capability*: American forces had to be so strong that even if the enemy struck first, they would have enough left in reserve to assure that the violence would not be worth it. Having enough in reserve was how nuclear weapons could deter. Brodie also considered the *vulnerability* of the nuclear delivery system. To prevent a first strike, Americans had to convince the USSR that its initial attack would be unsuccessful in a critical way. The United States might not need to have a large number of weapons but rather must position the forces it did have so that they would be relatively impervious to any first attack. After it was over, the Americans would still be able to destroy the enemy in their own second strike.

With the test of the much more potent thermonuclear H-bomb in late 1952 and the Soviet response less than a year later, Brodie's arguments became more complex. The "Super" was so powerful that even the successful launching of a few of them would be ghastly. Deterrence would not be easily secured, since even a thwarted first strike would do enough damage to make a second-strike victory Pyrrhic. Moreover, if Americans wanted to have even minimal control of such weapons, they should not think simply of an all-out battle but of a series of scenarios in which different sorts of nuclear weapons were used, and different degrees of damage embraced. The military might employ *tactical* or *theater* nuclear bombs—usually but not inevitably meaning smaller—without a full-scale war breaking out. The air force might direct targeting so that hydrogen bombs did not hit major cities. A state could fight varying kinds of nuclear war of lesser or greater severity, and strategy might involve gradations of destructiveness.[27] Brodie's complicated sense of nuclear combat was of a piece with other civilian proposals about conceiving less-than-nuclear wars. Korea showed that atomic conflict was not the only option, at least in a nonessential theater. Led by Brodie, the strategy scientists envisioned how diplomats might regulate or retard such escalation, or how they might employ lesser atomic bombs without the climb to a superbomb war.

ALBERT WOHLSTETTER AND PERMANENT VULNERABILITY

In Brodie's work strategies that other RAND theorists later spelled out and popularized all received some elaboration, although Brodie never associated himself with a single position. Despite his preeminence, however, this work fit uncomfortably into the quantifying emphasis that dominated RAND by the

---

[27] For Brodie's developing ideas see Trachtenberg, *Strategic Thought*, pt. 2: from *Absolute Weapon*, pp. 76–77; "New Techniques," p. 167; *Strategic Thought*, pt. 3, vol. 1, "Nuclear Weapons," pp. 217–29; *Strategic Thought*, pt. 3, vol. 2, "Unlimited Weapons and Limited War," pp. 16–21; "Next Ten Years," esp. pp. 16ff, 38–39; and "Some Strategic Implications of the Nuclear Revolution," pp. 1–20.

Figure 3. Albert Wohlstetter

mid-1950s. Although the ideas he promulgated remained the conventional wisdom, his mode of presentation was believed to be belletristic and even outmoded.[28] While Brodie antagonized the military with his disdain for their intellect, he dismissed his civilian peers with derision for their methods and practical judgment. Mathematically oriented policy scientists showed "an astonishing lack of political sense." Chief among these was Albert Wohlstetter, who had been a protégé but who had, in embracing the quantifiable, cut off and embittered Brodie.[29]

Wohlstetter was like Brodie, but unembittered.[30] Wohlstetter had studied philosophy of science with Morris Cohen and Ernest Nagel in New York City's institutions of higher learning, and was friendly with the most successful young Turks who were redefining philosophical instrumentalism in logical terms.[31] He spent World War II employed on quality control for the War Production

[28] See Kaplan, *The Wizards of Armageddon*, p. 121.

[29] Brodie to Archibald, May 7, 1966, A, Box 1, Brodie Papers, UCLA. For a good sense of Wohlstetter's sensibility see his "Theory and Opposed System Design," in *New Approaches to International Relations*, ed. Morton Kaplan (New York: St. Martin's, 1968), esp. pp. 19–21.

[30] A comparison of the two is in Michael Howard, "Brodie, Wohlstetter and American Nuclear Strategy," *Survival* 34 (1992): 108–12.

[31] See W. V. Quine, *The Time of My Life: An Autobiography* (Cambridge: MIT Press, 1985), pp. 124, 147, 184, 198, 217.

Board. Before he arrived at RAND in 1951, he ran a prefabricated housing company. At RAND Wohlstetter had detractors who mocked what they saw as his foppish style of living. Nonetheless, Wohlstetter was never isolated like Brodie and gathered around him talented acolytes who appreciated his intelligence.[32] Plato's notion that the harmonious state impersonated the harmonious soul of the statesman received a new twist in the 1950s. As one of Wohlstetter's group put it, the successful strategists of nuclear war must "appreciate different cultures and good art," "find nourishment in things that are beautiful," and be "sophisticated epicures."[33]

By the late 1940s RAND had become critical of the air force's deployment of and reliance on bombers, and reacted negatively to the airmen's view that the civilians ought to support the military.[34] Then, in 1954 and 1956, respectively, Wohlstetter produced two studies for RAND, "The Selection and Use of Strategic Air Bases," and "Protecting U.S. Power to Strike Back," which evaluated air force doctrines harshly but also gained the positive attention of the service.[35] Although each study argued the same sort of point, the earlier paper, known as "The Basing Study," made Wohlstetter's reputation and illustrated the reasoning for which RAND was best known.

Wohlstetter explored where to position American air force bases to respond effectively to a surprise attack. He first did empirical research, learning about the costs of maintaining bases, the manner in which they carried out repairs, the relative merits and demerits of refueling, and such matters. Wohlstetter asked if it were better to locate the forces at home rather than overseas. In one scenario, the military would need refueling bases abroad, and would incur additional costs to protect the strike force in hardened silos at home. Wohlstetter made various educated estimates but persuasively argued that it was cheaper and more efficient to have bases in the United States than abroad. Every reasonable projection of what was likely to happen in the event of a (Soviet) first strike on bombers stationed in allied countries suggested their susceptibility to destruction. Rationality demanded their relocation to the continental United States even though this entailed greater refueling costs and more hazards en route to target. This conclusion held if one started by trying to obtain the best defense at a fixed cost, or by appraising the cost to mount a certain kind of defense.

[32] See Brodie to Gray, n.d., ca. July 1975, G, Box 8, Brodie Papers, UCLA.

[33] Quote from Fred Charles Iklé, "The Role of Character and Intellect in Strategy," in *On Not Confusing Ourselves: Essays on National Security Strategy in Honor of Albert and Roberta Wohlstetter*, ed. Andrew W. Marshall et al. (Boulder, Colo.: Westview Press, 1991), p. 315, but the prefaces to the other essays in this collection are also instructive.

[34] David R. Jardini, "Out of the Blue Yonder: The RAND Corporation's Diversification into Social Welfare Research, 1964–68," Ph.D. diss., Department of History, Carnegie Mellon University, 1997, pp. 60–64.

[35] Both are reprinted in Trachtenberg, *Strategic Thought*, "The Basing Study" in pt. 3, vol. 1; and "Protecting," in pt. 3, vol. 2.

Wohlstetter's next study again emphasized the vulnerability of America's strategic air forces. He had finished the initial one before factoring in the impact of thermonuclear weapons, and only later did Wohlstetter grasp the practicality of nuclear-tipped rockets—known most famously as intercontinental ballistic missiles or ICBMs. In the postwar world, missiles were considered an expensive and untried military technology. The air force also feared that other services might challenge its dominance of American defense if missiles were emphasized over the manned bomber. Indeed, the air force ignored RAND studies of the late 1940s and early 1950s, to which John von Neumann crucially contributed, intimating the importance of rocketry. By the mid-1950s Soviet interest in this new technology forced the United States and the air force to rethink the role of missiles. Eisenhower ordered an augmented program of development and building in the summer of 1955.[36]

To critics, the failure to act promptly was a good example of the sloth and even stupidity of the generals and a cause of the brief Soviet lead in missile technology in the late 1950s, for which Eisenhower received most of the public blame. The foot-dragging also exemplified the inefficacy of RAND's ideas in the face of hostile air force policy.[37]

Wohlstetter worried that both missiles and thermonuclear weapons undermined the presuppositions of his "Basing Study." Missiles could entail the irrelevance of the manned bomber. The enormously greater firepower of the H-bomb might mean that issues of targeting became tangential. In a larger sense Wohlstetter recognized that advanced technology would persistently place each successive American defense system at risk. Studies of vulnerability had to take a permanent place in strategic thought. "Protecting U.S. Power to Strike Back" made this point in its examination of possible Soviet weapons. Wohlstetter reiterated that a deterrent could deter only if one could protect it from a first strike. The problem was continuously to devise ways to shelter one's own ever more complex weapons (for use in a second strike) from a surprise first strike by the enemy's ever more complex weapons.

Contrary to RAND, the air force assumed that diplomatic warning or political tension would precede any war. But Wohlstetter received a high accolade when his studies encouraged the air force to worry about alternative modes of bomber deployment before the era when missiles were practical, and RAND conventionally cited his writing to show its influence.[38] RAND-generated theory rarely intruded into air force strategies, except when the service could use it to justify greater military spending on air power, to assist the air force in its

---

[36] Edmund Beard, *Developing the ICBM: A Study in Bureaucratic Politics* (New York: Columbia University Press, 1976), pp. 95–97, 105, 130, 161–62, 229–30, 240–41.

[37] Air force hostility to missiles is apparent even in official histories. See Jacob Neufeld, *The Development of Ballistic Missiles in the United States Air Force, 1945–1960* (Washington, D.C.: Office of Air Force History, 1989), pp. 57–64, 68–69, 142–43, 241–42.

[38] Kaplan, *The Wizards of Armageddon*, pp. 106–7; Herken, *Counsels of War*, pp. 96–97.

rivalries with other services. Wohlstetter's "The Selection and Use of Strategic Air Bases" showed that the civilians were not merely kept men.[39]

Yet even this triumph was circumscribed. From the late summer of 1953 on—before even Wohlstetter's earlier study—Eisenhower and Dulles had worried about the reliability of foreign bases, which the enemy could easily destroy, or the host government subject to political pressure. By the summer of 1954 Eisenhower was stressing "self-sufficiency" for the manned bombers.[40] Wohlstetter's work was an intellectual addition to a political movement to alter the location of the American deterrent and, later, to diversify this deterrent through rockets.

ON THE ATTACK

The president got little credit from students of strategy. The theorists were not interested in a constriction of defense expenditures, in a static obsession with the H-bomb, or in the stewardship of an army man. By the mid-1950s the shared conviction that Dulles was crude and massive retaliation dangerous, each endangering the security of the United States, unified scholar-experts. Despite the fact that Eisenhower had upheld air force doctrine, he had little time for men such as Brodie, who suggested that defense in the 1950s exemplified exactly the drawbacks he had written about.[41] By the mid-1950s in the Council on Foreign Relations, the New York group that produced *Foreign Affairs*, Paul Nitze introduced RAND ideas. After he left government, he taught at his institute in Washington and established there a Center for Foreign Policy Research. Republicans suspected him "of trying to create a Policy Planning Staff in exile," and the Rockefeller Foundation, led by Dean Rusk, who had helped Nitze with NSC-68 as assistant secretary of state under Truman, supported the Center.[42] At the Council on Foreign Relations Nitze advocated tactical nuclear weapons in crises that were categorized between conventional fighting and all-out nuclear conflict. This was a form of *graduated deterrence*, warding off war by the threat of indefinitely escalating violence.[43] The 1956

[39] See Robert J. Leonard, "War as a 'Simple Economic Problem': The Rise of an Economics of Defense," in *Economics and National Security: A History of Their Interaction*, ed. Crawford Goodwin (Durham, N.C.: Duke University Press, 1991), pp. 276–77.

[40] See Dulles Memo, September 6, 1953, FRUS, 1952–54, vol. 2, *National Security Affairs* (in two parts), part 1, p. 458. The discussion of the issue can be traced in the same volume, pp. 495, 546, 591, 718. An earlier version of "The Basing Study" was completed in March 1953, but it is unclear what effect it had.

[41] Brodie, *Strategy in the Missile Age* (Princeton: Princeton University Press, 1959), p. 250.

[42] Tammi L. Gutner, *The Story of SAIS* (Washington, D.C.: SAIS, 1987), pp. 43–44.

[43] See Nitze's remarks at the Council on Foreign Relations Study Group on Nuclear Weapons and Foreign Policy: Corrections to December 15, 1954 Meeting, n.p.; Third Meeting, January 12,

presidential campaign raised some of RAND's fears, when Democratic candidate Adlai Stevenson denounced Ike for trifling with American security and for being unwilling to fight in limited wars. The electorate would have none of this, but in the aftermath of the lost election, policy intellectuals stepped up their negative review.

While disdainful of these social scientists, Eisenhower had a great respect for many practitioners of the natural sciences, and he gave them an entrée into the counsels of state in a way that would make many problems for him. He appointed two "scientific" panels to examine defense, but it is difficult to believe the president thought much about their composition or watched carefully over their deliberations.[44] James Killian, president of MIT and an advisor of the president's, headed the first. But the report it issued in 1955, "Meeting the Threat of Surprise Attack," did not just deal with the surprise that technological advance might bring, but also bore the marks of Wohlstetter's vulnerability. In truth, the natural scientists shared many of the view of the civilian strategists and hired them to consult in the executive.

The effect of the Killian panel was complex. Its arguments justified pursuing technological innovations in military spending that were likely to come anyway—for new sorts of atomic weaponry that the air force was likely to control and that the Republicans were unlikely to resist. The air force continued to provide for the strategists just because of such findings as those of the Killian panel. Perhaps of greater importance, the panel may have weakened Eisenhower's sense of expertise in the area of national security and guided him to appoint a special assistant for science and technology who was effectively concerned with defense.

In 1957 a committee headed nominally by H. Rowan Gaither of the Ford Foundation but actually led by Robert C. Sprague, a businessman with a commitment to a strong defense, completed a second report, "Deterrence and Survival in the Nuclear Age." These two leaders engaged men who had been involved in the earlier study as well as some RAND strategists—Gaither had had a long and close relation with RAND.[45] The committee was in many ways contemptuous of the president. It looked at the administration as lazy and sleepy, and wanted the GOP not just to wake up but also to spend more money. The committee embraced a more forceful program to insure an ample second-strike force and to protect this American deterrent. Again, Nitze was a prominent critic. Employed as a consultant by the Gaither panel, he took a command-

---

1955, pp. 2–11, Box 248, Vol. 60, CFR Papers, Mudd Library, Princeton University; and Walter Isaacson, *Kissinger: A Biography* (New York: Simon and Schuster, 1992), pp. 84–87.

[44] I have relied here on Snead, *The Gaither Committee*, and Roman, *Eisenhower and the Missile Gap*.

[45] These connections are detailed in S. M. Amadae, *Rationalizing Capitalist Democracy: The Cold War Origins of Rational Choice Liberalism* (Chicago: University of Chicago Press, 2003), esp. pp. 83–132.

ing role behind the scenes in writing the report, which stated the "maximum danger" that the United States faced without the caveats and qualifications that many members of the committee noted.[46] Nitze never gave up on the themes of NSC-68. It is evidence of the correctness of his ideas about the administration's indolence that he was given a platform to express his views.

Although Eisenhower and Dulles and their critics agreed on the primacy of nuclear bombs and, thus, on deterrence by massive retaliation, the critics wanted more leeway. In addition to arguing that the United States should upgrade and make its weapons more secure, Nitze and his peers pleaded that the United States had to have more options and, thus, more conventional armaments and more tactical nuclear weapons—a *flexible response*. This reform would require higher taxes, a larger debt, and economies elsewhere.[47]

IKE LOSES CONTROL

The launching of the Soviet satellite *Sputnik* in October 1957, just as the Gaither committee was wrapping up its work, underscored in public what seemed like the president's shortcomings. More important to foreign-policy thinkers, the government had revealed about a month earlier that the USSR was testing intercontinental ballistic missiles. If the Russians successfully completed these tests, they could conceivably launch first strikes against which American bombers would be defenseless. Missiles gave minimal warning time, and compared to them the airplane was a technologically primitive method of bomb delivery. This anxiety contributed to the force of Gaither's leaked recommendations. Eisenhower did not like them. He considered that the RAND scenarios envisioned destruction that made talk of victory empty. The president also resisted reallocation of resources and the expense that, he thought, would upend the economy or turn the United States into a garrison state. A strong economy that leadership could quickly switch over to war best insured the defense of America. The Gaither report was "far-fetched." The president told Dulles that "this experience had proved . . . definitively, the unwisdom of calling in outside groups."[48]

But the Eisenhower administration did not seem to follow developments in technology—for example, the use of guided missiles with atomic warheads—that gave credence to the possibility of surprise attack. Eisenhower seemed befuddled by the thought that, unlike World War II, the executive might have

---

[46] Kaplan, *The Wizards of Armageddon*, pp. 136–37.

[47] The Gaither report is reprinted in Trachtenberg, *Strategic Thought*, pt. 1, where the Killian report can also be found.

[48] Dulles-Eisenhower Conversations, November 7, 1956, and December 26, 1956, FRUS, 1955–57, vol. 19, *National Security Policy*, pp. 638, 712.

no time to convert the United States to a wartime footing. Nuclear rockets could destroy an economy immediately. Nor did he face the projections that in five years or so—the early sixties—near parity between the United States and the USSR would exist. When that occurred, massive retaliation would no longer permit the United States to escape war, and American statesmen would have to take seriously the dilemmas of deterrence that thinkers such as Brodie and Wohlstetter had adumbrated and that middlemen such as Nitze had pushed in Eisenhower's face.

One result of the administration's protective position was a "Surprise Attack Conference" between the Western powers and the Soviet bloc held in Geneva, Switzerland, in 1958. RAND staffed this six-week "conference of experts," and officials from the two sides negotiated about arms control. American diplomats had their views about Pearl Harbor reinforced—the danger was unjustified and unsuspected violence. The Americans hoped that by trading information about numbers of weapons, launch sites, and capabilities they could construct a framework to insure the failure of any secret aggression.[49] To the extent that America persuaded the Russians to think in these terms, of course, they focused on surprise on the ground, in the style of the June 1941 assault on the Soviet Union by Hitler's Germany. But the Russians felt that both sides could prevent this sort of strike only if they could make deals to resolve the political issues between them. The Americans, on the contrary, argued that science could transform such conflicts. For the United States the conference was "technical," its approach "scientific" and "objective." The Americans had a "methodology" and desired to make "quantitative judgments." If the Russians thought that United States' "hypotheses [were] false," they needed "to submit a technical demonstration of their belief."[50] The conference failed to reach any significant agreements.

Ike did adopt the Gaither committee's recommendation that he reorganize the Defense Department. Money had to be rationally allocated and bargaining among the services damped down. The Pentagon must not have a manager, but a command-post staff that would look systematically at security. The Defense Reorganization Act of 1958 embodied these ideas but had little immediate impact. The president suggested more openly that the United States give Europeans their own atomic bombs.[51] It is hard not to get the sense that the president was tired, hoping that the English, French, and Germans might somehow mount their own defense, allowing the United States to escape some of the problems of nuclear politics.

[49] See Jeremi Suri, "America's Solution for a Technological Solution to the Arms Race: The Surprise Attack Conference of 1958 and a Challenge for Eisenhower Revisionists," *Diplomatic History* 21 (1997): 440–42, 450.

[50] United States Department of State, *Documents on Disarmament 1945–1959*, 2 vols., vol. 2, 1957–59 (Washington, D.C.: USGPO, 1960), pp. 1271, 1306, 1317, 1319, 1321,1324, 1325–26.

[51] Trachtenberg, *A Constructed Peace*, pp. 193–200.

Yet in spite of the truth of the complaint that the Republican administration—and in particular Eisenhower himself—was rudderless in the late 1950s, the president's strategic sense, in the short term, had much to be said for it.

The imperfections of American intelligence, the weakness of the warning system against an attack by the Russians, and the constant strategic bluff of the USSR complicated the situation the Gaither committee investigated. Moreover, although Eisenhower had secret information from various overflights that the Soviet Union had only a limited number of missiles, this information too was limited. While no "missile gap" existed, unless it favored the United States, both sides in this American debate might score legitimate points.[52] But a successful Soviet blow would occur only in the event of "a well-planned sneak attack," "a perfectly coordinated surprise attack," "during periods of low international tension."[53] The Gaither report worried about the vulnerability of American forces "to surprise attack during a period of lessened world tension." American defenses were fine if the assault occurred in a period of tension—if "strategic warning" occurred.[54] In short the report's recommendations only made sense if the USSR was a malevolent enemy, meaning to destroy the United States by a clandestine raid for no reason. A surprise attack might succeed if the Russians decided on it when they had no issues with the United States.

Ike rightly judged that a deficit in a certain sort of missile did not mean a deterrence deficit. Nuclear weapons were so powerful that a credible deterrent required only that a small number survive an enemy first strike and be deliverable. More was not necessarily better and, more to the point, Eisenhower was convinced that the United States still had decisively more. The period of parity had not yet arrived. In addition, he still deprecated the belief that additional money would provide a better defense yet not weaken other aspects of the nation's well-being.

The Soviets' breakthrough in missile technology was only a momentary triumph, and not in the production of actual missiles of war but only in some of the know-how that led to them. Soon, America had an overwhelming lead in missile hardware.[55] But the Eisenhower administration looked weak and was not immune to honest criticism, and Ike might not have energized the American program without the complaints about falling behind in rocket know-how. Eager to believe in surprise attack and vulnerability, RAND—effectively but fallaciously—urged that the Soviet Union had outdistanced the United States

---

[52] Robert S. Hopkins III, "An Expanded Understanding of Eisenhower, American Policy and Overflights," *Intelligence and National Security* 11 (1996): 332–44.

[53] Roman, *Eisenhower and the Missile Gap*, pp. 48, 54, 58.

[54] Kaplan, *The Wizards of Armageddon*, pp. 142, 150–51; and Gaither in Trachtenberg, *Strategic Thought*, pt. 1, pp. 16, 21.

[55] See James C. Dick's essay "The Strategic Arms Race, 1957–61: Who Opened a Missile Gap?" *Journal of Politics* 34 (1972): 1062–1110.

in the equipment necessary to launch missiles that had nuclear warheads. RAND estimated that the Russians outstripped America in production and had put at risk the bomber defense. Assimilating these ideas, Henry Kissinger asserted that there was "no dispute" about a missile gap from 1961 to 1964.[56]

Wohlstetter added to the worries in a much discussed essay in *Foreign Affairs* in 1959, "The Delicate Balance of Terror," which, even more than Brodie's writing, directed the educated public to the RAND style of analysis.[57] Wohlstetter erected his arguments on the premise that the rational thing for an aggressor to do was to launch a surprise attack, and urged that a presumed second-strike capacity did not automatically guarantee deterrence. Identified with vulnerability, Wohlstetter became fixated on it. Like Kennan's "The Sources of Soviet Conduct," "The Delicate Balance of Terror" was designed to rouse a torpid America about the dangers that the United States would face in the 1960s. As in Kennan's earlier piece and in Nitze's NSC-68, Wohlstetter's distillation of his secret work prophesied that Americans would have to "sacrifice" and take "hard" countermeasures to preserve their safety. Wohlstetter limned a world of ever-present threat in which the United States might not measure up.[58] Again and again the civilian strategists evinced their distrust of democratic polity and their commitment to a select management that would lead by exaggeration.

Although he had much in common with Brodie, Wohlstetter stressed what he and no one else had demonstrated as a matter of quantitative reasoning—the vulnerability of the American forces. His essay, like Kennan's, contributed to a heightened fear of a Soviet Union that might deliver a devastating blow to the United States, for no reason except its own dark wickedness. Wohlstetter finally argued for greater defense expenditures to secure a second-strike capability against such an enemy.

Despite his irritation and dislike for his critics, Eisenhower had his National Security Council especially examine the Gaither committee's findings. Toward the end of his second term he shifted some of his priorities, certainly accelerating missile development and massively increasing the number of nuclear weapons. Additionally, at the end of his years in office, floundering, the president turned to a series of peace initiatives, and pursued efforts at disarmament, ventures that came to little. When the Russians shot down the American U-2 spy plane, the event disrupted Eisenhower's last-ditch attempts to halt Soviet-American nuclear rivalry and added to the loss of focus in 1960.

[56] Kissinger, *The Necessity for Choice*, pp. 15, 35.

[57] I have used the version in Trachtenberg, *Strategic Thought*, pt. 3, vol. 3, which also has a brief history of the composition of the essay.

[58] "Delicate Balance," in Trachtenberg, *Strategic Thought*, pt. 3, vol. 3, p. 1.

That year the perceived paralysis of the administration led the civilian strategists to support the Democrat John Kennedy in his quest for the presidency against Republican vice president Richard Nixon, tainted by his association with the weary Eisenhower. Kennedy's speech making itself was synergistically involved with the ideas of the civilian strategists and assisted their expectations for more expensive foreign policies to move the United States through the 1960s.[59]

Historians have argued that foreign policy issues partly produced Nixon's loss to Kennedy. The charges that the Eisenhower administration had a flabby security policy damaged the vice president. Nonetheless, in commissioning the Killian and Gaither reports, Eisenhower had introduced into executive-branch politics the strategists who had done what they could to embarrass him and to defeat Nixon. On their side, the theorists of war found in the victor the leader whom they could support. Kennedy had disclosed his astuteness in reliance on a brain trust of defense intellectuals. Because he had won the election, they would have a more secure role in government, and, they hoped, their models of decision making would get a purchase on policy. They foresaw an era in which they would construct a rational program for the defense of the United States founded on their knowledge. The statesman in charge would show his intelligence in the execution of the program.

Eisenhower's farewell address of early 1961 commented on these issues. He left the presidency with "a definite sense of disappointment" because of his restricted achievements in nuclear diplomacy. He wished he could say "that a lasting peace is in sight," though he could not, but at least "war has been avoided." The president urged Americans to weigh diplomatic strategy in a broad light. They must try to balance the private and public economies, the necessary and the desirable, patriotic responsibilities and individual duties, and the needs of the present and those of the future. The address warned against two threats to striking such balances. "The military-industrial complex" endangered "liberties or democratic processes." Here the worry was to see how security and freedom might prosper together. The second threat was that "public policy could itself become the captive of a scientific-technological elite." Here the worry was to see how the public could make democracy consistent with the scientific expertise that commanded federal money.[60] Eisenhower was troubled that soldiers would enfeeble the political freedoms of civil society, and that scientists and social scientists would replace democracy with the rule of the expert.

---

[59] Kaplan, *The Wizards of Armageddon*, pp. 249–50.

[60] "Farewell Radio and Television Address to the American People," January 17, 1961, *Public Papers of the Presidents of the United States: Dwight D. Eisenhower, 1960–61* (Washington, D.C.: USGPO, 1961), pp. 1035–40.

Soon after the address, a new administration came to power with an accurate sense of Republican lassitude. The Democrats wanted to have greater room for maneuver in defense arrangements and to spend more money, especially to upgrade the missile system. The theorists would accompany them to Washington.

CHAPTER 4

Accented and Unaccented Realism, 1946–1961

THE RISE OF REALISM

Before World War II, Woodrow Wilson's lost system of collective security dominated the thinking of the foreign policy elite. Wilson had supporters, but even in the 1920s and 1930s, some decision makers and thinkers about policy dismissed him. I use the generic term realist to describe those men who in some cases called themselves realists but who in any case emphasized interest in diplomacy or its study. Realism could easily be identified by its deprecation of Wilson and, somewhat less regularly, by its praise of Theodore Roosevelt, whose calculation of the United States' entry into European international affairs defined American foreign policy at the turn of the century, before Wilson arrived on the scene. After World War II, when the Cold War shaped international affairs, this perspective became conventional and commonly contrasted with the "naive," "moralistic" "idealism" of Wilson. We have already seen realist themes at work in Kennan, who was much identified with them. Ultimately they suffused the ideas of the men of RAND and the more scientific policy scientists, and by the 1960s had become part of the constellation of ideas defining defense intellectuals. Nonetheless, we must begin with the leading realist thinker, Hans Morgenthau, an anomalous ally who barely walked in the corridors of power but who had a pervasive influence.

HANS MORGENTHAU

An émigré educated in interwar Europe, Morgenthau had studied traditional philosophy, politics, and law, and he brought together a set of competing strands predictable in the weltanschauung of his teachers. The doctrines of Augustinian Christianity and the cultural pessimism of Oswald Spengler tinged their thought. European philosophical conservatives were committed to a Hobbesian view of man and the state, but their teacher was the antirationalist Friedrich Nietzsche and not Hobbes. They also professed skepticism about what sort of knowledge we could have of politics. Believers in *Lebensphiloso-phie*—the notion that we were all thrown into mysterious forms of life over which we had little control—the Continental professoriate important to Morgenthau had an unhappy view of politics but also sometimes expressed a belief that we just affirmed our hungering wills in social life with no further final justification. These ideas arose out of the horrors of World War I, and the collapse of the Versailles system in the 1930s confirmed them.

Morgenthau began teaching at the University of Chicago in the early 1940s. Social science for him was *Wissenschaft*—a form of knowledge of the human condition conceptually distinct from that embodied in the natural sciences. At Chicago Morgenthau had good relations with Robert Hutchins, the famous traditionalist president of the university, who also had misgivings about the modern world. But Morgenthau distrusted reformist impulses, including Hutchins's creation of a Committee to Frame a World Constitution in the aftermath of World War II. Finding some common ground with the realism of some of Chicago's political scientists, he nonetheless argued against their espousal of John Dewey's creed, which Morgenthau called "scientism." After he lectured on the illusion of substituting technical administration for politics,[1] scholars of public administration would have little to do with him. Morgenthau was very much a fish out of water in any American environment, and his critics charged that his insecurity and vanity exacerbated this circumstance.[2]

A stream of books and essays flowed from Morgenthau's pen from the 1940s through the 1970s, but three volumes written from 1946 to 1951 made his reputation: *Scientific Man vs. Power Politics; Politics Among Nations;* and *In Defense of the National Interest.*[3] Two repeated themes delineated his position.

First, Morgenthau spun out the realist vocabulary in which he would describe international politics. Statesmen had to look to the enduring national interests of their own states and those of their competitors. Geography, natural resources, national character, and political tradition and history grounded this interest, but it was never given, though it altered only slowly. The diplomatist's percipient attention to the behavior of sovereign states discovered the interest. The statesman breathed an atmosphere of power politics and reckoned with the balance of power. In this thinking moralistic abstractions gave way to calculated prudence. Leaders could not exorcise the conflict intrinsic to human society, and national security guided them. In the hands of many Americans, realism always called for combative activism. Morgenthau (like Kennan) differed. Realism meant a cautious assessment of what it was necessary to do and

---

[1] "A Tribute to Hans J. Morgenthau," in *Power and Policy in Transition,* ed. Vojtech Mastney (Bridgeport, Conn.: Greenwood Press, 1984), p. 2.

[2] The reader needs to consult Christoph Frei, *Hans J. Morgenthau: An Intellectual Biography* (Baton Rouge: Louisiana State University Press, 2001). Frei's treatment is exhaustive but not synthetic; it is also hagiographic. Morgenthau's *Science: Servant or Master?* (New York: New American Library, 1972) prints a previously unpublished manuscript from the mid-1930s that displays his early views.

[3] *Scientific Man* (Chicago: University of Chicago Press, 1946); *Politics* (New York: Knopf, 1948); and *Defense* (New York: Knopf, 1951).

of the limits on action. The virtues of restraint and a sense of the precariousness of national well-being were also part of Morgenthau's formula.[4]

Diplomats could not afford to combat evil, but first of all had to protect well-defined advantages. In foreign affairs *raison d'état* overshadowed ethical attitudes appropriate to private life. The politician of international life chose between lesser evils; between making a decision that, as an individual, would be morally indefensible but that, made in diplomacy, avoided an even greater injustice. No policymaker, said Morgenthau, could escape the problem of "dirty hands," but the foundation of his realism, he maintained, allowed people to distinguish a Hitler from a Napoleon, metaphysical wickedness from perhaps overly bloody statesmanship. The morality associated with world policy differed from that of private life but had its own logic. Morgenthau even urged that the power-political ethic was higher than personal ethics. Although ambiguity compromised the decisions of political leaders, their corruption confronted the tragic presence of evil as a permanent part of human existence. But Morgenthau offered no criterion to discriminate between the rule of a Napoleon and the unacceptable malignity of a Hitler.[5]

According to Morgenthau, the United States, especially in the twentieth century, had strayed from realism. He almost said that all American diplomats negligently tended to their state. A self-righteousness that undercut prudence and projected onto the world a U.S. moral code saturated even the beliefs associated with tough-minded Americans. Dean Acheson did not differ from Woodrow Wilson, Harry Truman from John Foster Dulles. The primary culprit for Morgenthau was an optimistic "liberalism" that guided presidents and secretaries of state regardless of party.

Morgenthau combined several ideas in this view of liberalism: that human beings were benign, that problems of foreign affairs could be solved once and for all, and that sovereign states could act on ideals of justice. Perhaps most important, the liberal mind comfortably believed in the goodness of the United States and the badness of its adversaries. The liberal assumed that Americans could universalize their private precepts as a set of principles for diplomacy.

The villain for Morgenthau might have been democracy itself, and he was hard put to justify his commitment to American politics. In republican regimes elected officials and their appointees predictably appealed to the electorate on the basis of individual ethics. But these ideals inevitably undercut decision making. American democracy, complained Morgenthau, incapacitated a commitment to a viable realism.[6]

---

[4] The different possibilities inherent in realism were early pointed out in Robert Tucker's "Professor Morgenthau's Theory of Political Realism," *American Political Science Review* 46 (1952), esp. p. 224.

[5] *Scientific Man*, pp. 176–90, 196, 202–3.

[6] See *Defense*, passim, but esp. pp. 4, 39, 200, 221.

For Morgenthau, Americans might always win the war but lose the peace. Wilson was silly, and his League of Nations a chimera. The United States in the interwar period was culpable for creating the conditions for the rise of the international Fascist terror. While American policy toward Europe from 1945 to 1950 had been wise, its public justification had undermined its strengths. Morgenthau discouraged the anti-Communist crusade, which the Truman administration had embraced, and which Morgenthau said it took seriously, in favor of temperate opposition to inimical Soviet interests. In Asia, where the United States based policy on anti-Communism rather than a determination of interests, the prospects for disaster were great. The future of the 1950s and 1960s looked bleak, demanding diplomacy that could not exist in the United States.

Belligerence did not make for realism, nor did military might. A globalism based on a combination of nuclear weapons and threatening talk might be just as unrealistic as Wilson's. In one passage Morgenthau wrote that the United States was "a political desert whose intellectual barrenness and aridity was [*sic*] relieved only by sparse and neglected oases of insight and wisdom."[7]

Morgenthau's definition of realism seemed to imply that the social science students of international relations might be closet idealists, liberals, or Wilsonians. The second theme prominent in his writing—the "scientistic" mentality of Americans—argued just this point. *Scientific Man Vs. Power Politics* examined the faulty axioms of social science when applied to politics. Morgenthau pitted his own realism against the false realism of many American academics. Liberalism characteristically erred because it believed Enlightenment reason to be supreme in man. What he called "rationalism" led in the nineteenth century to a misplaced confidence in the power of intellect to solve problems, and the assumption that the social world was susceptible to control. In the twentieth century, wrote Morgenthau, as the role of the social sciences grew, they became central to liberalism. He more dramatically expounded themes from Kennan's writing. Morgenthau bewailed the great error of twentieth-century rationalism—its conception that the social sciences, like the natural sciences, purveyed objective and universally applicable conclusions. For his intellectual opponents conflict among nations resulted from miscalculation. Politics was a curable disease or an administrative conundrum in need of clever stage-management. The social sciences only needed their Newton to codify the laws and mastermind their employment in contemporary life.[8]

Morgenthau astutely quoted the most unguarded statements of liberals about the possibilities inherent in a science of politics. For the twentieth century he cited John Dewey to his advantage.[9] But except for narrow technical problems,

[7] *Defense*, p. 4.
[8] *Scientific Man*, pp. 71, 108–9.
[9] *Scientific Man*, esp. pp. 27–29.

social scientists were no more competent than laymen to treat social ills, and Americans foolishly sought more social scientific knowledge to assist them.[10] Some American social science practitioners acknowledged Morgenthau's more conventional criticisms. Thus, he wrote that the social world was more complex than the physical, and experimentation, predictions, and comprehension more difficult.[11] Moreover, when experts came close to power, their analyses might degenerate into justification of existing policy.[12] More centrally, Morgenthau unconventionally depicted the use human beings could make of knowledge of the social world. An elemental biological and spiritual environment enveloped the reason that liberals cherished. Social and personal interests, as well as emotional preferences, colored reason, a weak and fragile dimension of the human psyche. In addition, the milieu and the values of the investigators determined their knowledge of the social order.[13] Truths about

---

[10] *Scientific Man*, pp. 210–13. His distaste increased in the 1960s: see Morgenthau, *A New Foreign Policy for the United States* (New York: Praeger, 1969), esp. pp. 140–44.

[11] *Scientific Man*, pp. 130–31.

[12] *A New Foreign Policy*, pp. 154–55; and *Truth and Power: Essays of a Decade, 1960–1970* (New York: Praeger, 1970), pp. 16–17.

[13] Morgenthau's *Science: Servant or Master?* showed his indebtedness to Karl Mannheim, a German thinker in the sociology of knowledge. One relevant and important theme is contained in a core essay of 1929, "The Prospects of Scientific Politics." (See Karl Mannheim, *Ideology and Utopia: An Introduction to the Sociology of Knowledge*, trans. and ed. Louis Wirth and Edward Shils [New York: Harcourt-Brace, 1936], esp. pp. 126–27, 147–57, 162–64, 189–91.) Influenced by Marxism, Mannheim argued that political and historical knowledge was "relational," dependent on the knowers whose role in the social and cultural matrix out of which they came determined their views. The sort of knowledge connected to politics was also used to direct action, and thus was limited to guiding people in the pursuit of their class interests.

From these premises Mannheim drew two conclusions. First, he urged that this relationalism did not make knowledge subjective, although it was partial and perspectival rather than definitive or certain. The second and more important conclusion turned standard arguments on their heads. Suppose we wanted a political outlook that synthesized conflicting interests in a broad and conciliatory fashion. What would be the social locus of the group that would have such an outlook? If knowledge were socially determined, what class would be constructed so that it would be caused to grasp the world in a way that would look to a coherent synthesis of competing interests? What social circumstances best promoted this synthesis?

Mannheim's famous answer was the class of "the free floating intelligentsia." It was composed of university-based thinkers who indeed had a social locus but who were not bound by class distinctions, birth, status, wealth, or even profession; this class had less a firm social footing than others, and instead was molded by learning, intelligence, and scholarship —a common educational heritage. Mannheim, I believe, underestimated the grounding of his intelligentsia in bourgeois society, although he was not so naive to think that these people escaped bias. Rather, he hoped that such an intelligentsia would train leaders, not in the substance of decisions but in the way decision making was a function of limited perspectives and interests. Structural relations were teachable; judgments themselves were not. An elite trained in such a way would make policies that would indefinitely allow societies to free themselves from the most harmful causes of their political behavior, from blind adherence to some opinions.

Mannheim's ideas might well justify the existence of experts on domestic issues if what one wanted was a view that might synthesize competing positions. It is less clear that such an expert

the social world were relative to culture and emotion. Now, said Morgenthau, social understanding only arose when we acknowledged the shallow grasp reason had on the world. The trick was to accept our limitations, and thus arrive at least at a glimpse of how we stood. "Whoever seeks more will get less," he wrote.[14]

An intelligent appraisal of the issues at work in international politics was all the knowledge a politician needed to make a decision. Social science of the American sort could not aid him. What was necessary, Morgenthau said, was political will—the ability to perceive which limited interests could be circumvented, which overridden, which accepted. The qualities that distinguished the American politician from the true statesman had to do with the wisdom and insight Morgenthau often spoke of, and not the technical application of a scientific solution. Even wisdom and insight were partial, and the most effective statesman had only an incomplete view.[15]

In consequence of this vision, Morgenthau had a different idea about the job of the student of politics. Political understanding blended knowledge and action, grounded both in personal experience and in the practitioner's sense of his own place in a national tradition and in the history of international politics. Diplomacy was a craft, and the scholar a detached commentator on the process. The scholar studied the history of political life, but was in no special position to offer advice or instruction. He might lament, but only from afar. One could not "speak truth to power." This model contrasted with American political science, which postulated that the best students of politics should show statesmen how to apply middle-range generalizations—putative laws of behavior. The true role of the scholar was more distant appreciation or critique, said Morgenthau. The learned ought not to yearn to advise the statesman.[16]

Morgenthau contrasted what he called the moral strength of the statesman to the rationality of the engineer, the diplomat influenced by liberalism, rationalism, and American social science. At other times he identified this strength with the Christian awareness of the tragic element at the heart of human existence. In any event, his conception of a permanently dangerous politics was antithetical to the assumptions of many of the experts who lusted after what he dismissed—obtaining a seat at the policymaking table.[17]

---

would exist for international affairs, where in any event the need to amalgamate alternative positions might be less desirable.

[14] *Scientific Man*, pp. 155–67.

[15] Morgenthau, *Science: Servant or Master?* pp. 39–44. The first part of this book, from which I have taken my discussion, consists of the lectures written in the 1930s.

[16] In the 1960s when Morgenthau joined the movement that opposed the war in Vietnam, he attempted to change policy and influence officialdom, rather than merely to comment on policy, and took a different stance. He later said that in "speaking truth to power" during this era, he was indulging in an "illusion" about the relation of knowledge to politics that he had denounced earlier as a form of liberalism. Hans Morgenthau, "Prologue," in *Truth and Power*, p. 5.

[17] *Scientific Man*, pp. 5–10, 202–3.

Thinkers who shared Morgenthau's doubts about political science and his conception of social knowledge were rare in the United States. While he castigated American social scientists for the analogy they made between the natural and social sciences and for their positivistic universalism, Morgenthau himself sought "laws" that were just as encompassing and based in Augustinian Christianity. The true political philosopher, he said, looked for "the eternal laws by which man moves in the social world." Aside from mathematics, there were "no other eternal laws." Morgenthau searched for "the general causes of which particular events are but the outward manifestation," and hoped to locate "in the contingencies of the social world the concretizations of eternal laws."[18] Perhaps expanding on his view that mathematics and politics provided the only spheres of law, he wrote that to disbelieve the laws of power politics was "like a scientist not believing in the law of gravity." Both were laws "for whose validity nobody is to blame," "iron law[s]."[19] To negotiate the political, Morgenthau's statesman elevated his own experience into "the universal laws of human nature" and represented "true reason." The social scientist, engineer, or technocrat—the "nothing-but-scientific man"—universalized cognitive principles of limited validity and attempted to apply them to inaccessible realms.[20] The American social scientist was "the true dogmatist."

Morgenthau spent his career blaming American policymakers for doing what they should not have been able to do—violating the iron laws of politics. In the end he claimed for his own ideas just the absolute truth he asserted his opponents foolishly demanded for theirs. Morgenthau's absolutism was appropriately grounded in religion. But, on the other side, it is hard to argue with a scholar whose vision is supernatural. The certainties of his opponents, grounded in naturalistic biases, were at least subject to a critique of their empirical moorings.

THE INSTITUTIONAL MATRIX OF REALISM

The scholars of politics in the United States whom Morgenthau chastised took from him the language of realism. They simply ignored, however, his complaints that their sometimes-technocratic commitment to the Cold War meant that they were at heart Wilsonians. At a number of universities new policy centers sprang up, replacing older and pokier organizations of minor importance. The novel organizations gave institutional support to fresh fields of in-

[18] *Scientific Man*, pp. v, 220.
[19] *Defense*, pp. 33, 144. Morgenthau wrote that this particular "iron law"—"that legal obligations must yield to the national interest"—was one from which no nation has been "completely immune" (144). One would think that nations could not be incompletely immune to an iron law.
[20] *Scientific Man*, p. 221.

quiry—international relations or strategic studies—and to American realists who wanted to be regarded as prudent hands-on specialists, knowledgeable about the grim causes of World War II and experts in the battle against the Soviet Union. Chicago, Columbia, Johns Hopkins, the Massachusetts Institute of Technology, Princeton, and Yale jockeyed to win their spurs in this endeavor in the late 1940s and early 1950s. In classrooms in these schools a new respect was shown to Machiavelli and Hobbes. Earlier realists such as Carl von Clausewitz, Alfred Thayer Mahan, and Halford Mackinder gained readers, as did Morgenthau himself.[21]

In critical ways these innovative scholarly enterprises were all modeled on RAND, where the "application of scientific methods to the study of military choice" went along with "the fluid interchange between universities, private research organizations, government, industry, and the armed forces."[22] But, in a unique development in an intellectual world that higher education dominated, none of these schools duplicated RAND's influence in the 1950s. Rather, they mimicked RAND, and the organization established close cooperative relations with leading universities that generated "consultants." Simultaneously, the histories of the institutes at premier institutions illustrated a single generalization that Morgenthau sensed. Voicing a scientific politics, the schools indulged in increasingly politicized scholarship that shrank the acceptable range of scholarly opinion.

Government officials often established these institutions and created ties to international business. By the late 1940s the School of Advanced International Studies (SAIS), which Paul Nitze and Christian Herter had founded in 1943, promoted "overseas investment strategies." It had a board of prominent businessmen and diplomats, including Joseph Grew, William McChesney Martin, Allen Dulles, William L. Clayton, and Edward Burling. A variety of American corporations made substantial donations under the slogan, "a contribution . . . is an insurance premium on America's leadership in tomorrow's world." In addition to its own masters degree, SAIS had a corporate program for executives, who could hold off-the-record talks with Washington policymakers and academics. Nonetheless, it had no permanent funding, and the Carnegie Foundation advised that if SAIS affiliated itself with a major university, a large grant would be forthcoming. Before Nitze became the driving force at SAIS, Herter's last act before he took the governor's chair in Massachusetts was to arrange a deal whereby the school would join Johns Hopkins University.[23]

---

[21] David Baldwin has a good overview of these developments in "Security Studies and the End of the Cold War," *World Politics* 48 (1996): 119–24.

[22] Roberta Wohlstetter and Albert Wohlstetter, "The State of Strategic Studies in Europe, September 1963" (November 14, 1963) in Box 20, Neustadt Papers, JFK Library.

[23] Gutner, *The Story of SAIS*, pp. 15, 16; 1952 Support Program, Minutes May 10, 1950–June 28, 1955, Records of the Foreign Service Educational Foundation, Johns Hopkins University.

The situation was similar at Columbia, where a School of International Affairs was vivified in the mid-1940s, after a long quiescent period. It received a burst of energy when Dwight Eisenhower became president of the university in 1948 and called for an institute within the school that would investigate what was his favorite idea even then—the balance between military preparedness and sound economic principles. Eisenhower left for the presidency of the United States before his plans could take effect, but soon after his departure private donors who were admirers of the general—such as Clarence Dillon, Henry Luce, and Armand Hammer—provided the funds for an Institute of War and Peace Studies.[24]

At MIT nonscientific areas of inquiry were barely represented, but in 1950 the Department of State commissioned Project Troy, a study of how the United States might get radio propaganda into the USSR. The work entailed problems of engineering, for which the institute was incomparably the leader, and those of communication, which galvanized MIT's fledgling social science centers.[25] The bond that grew up between the government and the institute was like that at RAND, stressing the quantitative elements of social science. The next year Max Millikan, a professor of economics at MIT, and his colleague, Walt Whitman Rostow, established CENIS—the Center for International Studies, which began where Troy had left off. After becoming the head of CENIS, Millikan took a year off to be assistant director of the Central Intelligence Agency, the national security organization that had recently been established. James Killian, then president of MIT, personally approved the leave of absence. In the 1950s, the CIA and the Ford Foundation, headed by Rowan Gaither, who would lead the Gaither committee, provided the center with most of its funding.[26]

Traditionally minded academics criticized the connection between scholarship and public affairs that these centers stressed. Through the first half of 1950, in Baltimore and Washington, Herter negotiated a three-hundred-thousand-dollar award from Carnegie agreeable to both SAIS and Hopkins. Hopkins wanted the school, which would continue to exist in Washington, to become a "research" institution, with high standards. But SAIS's trustees

[24] See for example, Krout to Goldschmidt, December 7, 1951, Institute of War and Peace Studies, Subject Files, Columbiana, Low Library, Columbia University.

[25] Alan A. Needell has an exposition in "Project Troy and the Cold War Annexation of the Social Sciences," in *Universities and Empire: Money and Politics in the Social Sciences during the Cold War*, ed. Christopher Simpson (New York: New Press, 1998), pp. 3–38.

[26] See Bruce Cumings, "Boundary Displacement: Area Studies and International Studies during and after the Cold War," Bulletin of Concerned Asian Scholars: http://csf.edu/bcas/sympos/sycuming.htm, whose footnote (p. 13) cites a 1959 CENIS document to which I could not gain access. The funding story is told in AC 20, Dean of Humanities Papers, Folders 68 and 69, Box 2, MIT Archives, and there is a useful set of figures in Donald L. M. Blackmer, *The M. I. T. Center for International Studies: The Founding Years 1951–1969* (Cambridge: MIT Center for International Studies, 2002), p. 225.

feared being put "on a purely academic basis" because they insisted on "a program which would satisfy their [corporate] needs." Hopkins also argued that SAIS should be separate from, and should not duplicate, its existing Walter Hines Page School of International Relations, "primarily a research institute," located in Baltimore. In July 1950 SAIS and Hopkins compromised. SAIS would carry out its "original objectives and broaden such objectives in the field of research and scholarship" and would join Hopkins with an allocation of Carnegie money.[27]

In the 1950s, when he was out of government and teaching at his school, Nitze developed an eclectic political philosophy. Although he relied on quantification and the style of reasoning dominant at RAND, Nitze—like Kennan and Morgenthau—dismissed positivism and the quest for a scientific politics. He also distrusted what he saw as *self-interested* realism. Instead, Nitze argued that the learned could appraise some systems of political values as better than others, and on this basis credibly justify some policies as based on altruism and a quest for the general good. Decision makers who shared the better systems of values could thus, like Plato's guardians, implement policies based on realpolitik without worrying that they were merely engaged in national aggrandizement.

Nitze's writings on these matters were not systematic, but he believed that "his focus, if rigorously pursued, can open up new vistas of illumination."[28] He formulated three concerns. First, he elaborated on the "tension between opposites"—the general and the concrete; change versus order; the individual against society; and so on. Second, Nitze claimed that statesmen attended to four "elements" in decision making: the actual political structures of the world, the extant value systems, the factual situation, and the viewpoint of the actors. Third, diplomats had to master the twin concepts of "crisis stability" and "crisis instability."

Nitze thought that he had explored these twin concepts "for the first time," and thus this last concern is worth unpacking. Like many of his peers, he believed that World War I had come about because of the "competitive mobilization" that gave the advantage to the side that could strike first. This was a situation of crisis instability, and diplomats seeking to avoid unnecessary conflict should establish the opposite situation. It is best to let Nitze speak for himself about crisis stability:

[27] Minutes February 10, March 1, May 10, and July 20, 1950, Minutes May 10, 1950–June 28, 1955, Records of the Foreign Service Educational Foundation; James H. Bready, "SAIS," *Johns Hopkins University Magazine*, December 1951; Carnegie Corporation, 1946–52, Box 1, Page School Papers, Johns Hopkins University.

[28] "Necessary and Sufficient Elements of a General Theory of International Relations" (1959) in Nitze, *Paul H. Nitze on Foreign Policy*, ed. Kenneth W. Thompson and Steven L. Rearden (Lanham, Md.: University Press of America, 1989), p. 40.

It explain[s] stability in terms of a ball and a cup. If one puts a ball in a cup and shakes the cup from side to side, the ball will climb up one side and then the other but will tend to return to the bottom of the cup once the shaking has ceased. If on the other hand the ball is put on the top of a cup that is turned upside down, then given a shake, the ball will fly off into space or fall to the ground. The ball in the upright position is in a position of inherent stability; if disturbed it tends to return to its former position. The ball on the top of the overturned cup is in a position of inherent instability; if disturbed it reacts in a radical and uncontrolled way.[29]

Nitze was an intelligent tactician of foreign affairs, and a forceful writer on real policy matters. Yet, like Forrestal, he was not an able theoretician. Moreover, his thoughts were obscurely related to his practice of diplomacy, which was straightforwardly vigorous and self-righteous. Through the 1950s, as the in-house history of SAIS put it, "lack of scholars kept SAIS from achieving status as a first-rate academic institution," but its close connection with business and government made it well known for its "power-political" viewpoint.[30]

In Massachusetts, CENIS defined its task as mobilizing Harvard and MIT "around certain problems of the cold war" and saw its mandate as solving "the problem of relating knowledge to action." Especially with CIA money, MIT's social scientists fussed for fifteen years about what might be their compromised impartiality, but never so much as to question their efforts in any fundamental way.[31] Its leaders believed CENIS could "evaluate government operations objectively and without bias" but asked its members to avoid situations "which are embarrassing to the government or to the Institute." This attitude prompted MIT's provost to criticize CENIS for the "dubious quality of [its] scholarly neutrality,"[32] but MIT's dean also agreed that he might not be able to examine CENIS's secret work.[33] Somewhat later, administrators fended off a proposal that would offer an MIT masters degree for up to sixty people a year whose scholarship would be a year of work in the Department of Defense in Washington.[34]

At Columbia criticism was less open because policy study directly involved the university's leaders. After Eisenhower went on leave from Columbia for

[29] I have drawn this analysis from Nitze, *Tension between Opposites*, pp. 1–57; and the essays in *Nitze and Foreign Policy*. The quote is from *Tension between Opposites*, p. 29, and in "Necessary and Sufficient Elements," there are three elements and not four; see p. 29.

[30] Gutner, *The Story of SAIS*, pp. 45–47.

[31] This is a constant theme in Blackmer's in-house history, *M. I. T. Center*, pp. 69–70, 95–96, 122–23, 162–72, 177–79, 187, 212–13.

[32] Folder 68; Stratton to Burchard, August 6, 1953, Folder 69; Memo for Robert Lovett, October 30, 1957, Folder 72, Box 2, AC 20, Dean of Humanities Papers, MIT Archives.

[33] Burchard-Stratton, May 19, 1952, Burchard-Stratton, June 5, 1952, and Millikan-Burchard, June 10, 1952, Folder 92, Coordinating Committee, 1952, Box 3, Millikan Papers, MC 188, MIT Archives.

[34] Kaufmann proposal, Folder 30, Box 5, CIS Files, AC 235, MIT Archives.

NATO, the organizing genius for its institute was Grayson Kirk, another student of international politics who put diplomats and businessmen on the board of the institute. Kirk claimed that the enterprise would not "propagandize," but would narrow the gap between "basic research" and "policy making" through the "the solution of practical questions of public importance."[35] Kirk took over at Columbia when Eisenhower left for good, and later Andrew Cordier, a prominent diplomat, became dean of the School of International Affairs and still later president of the university.

These organizations put viewpoints at odds with realism on the defensive. For some twenty years the University of Chicago had led in the study of international politics. Chicago's Quincy Wright, an influential student of international law, trained many of the realists, who were typically younger academics on the make. Wright was a generous and productive scholar, and by no means a stereotypical Wilsonian. He did, however, take a complex view of the origins of the Cold War, and believed that strengthening the United Nations was a smarter policy than containing Soviet power, which would lead to a bipolar world, an arms race, and war.[36]

Wright's realist students respectfully discounted his work, despite his "paternal" interest in them and his desire to have them return to Chicago.[37] Outside evaluators denigrated his program, and at Chicago itself, beginning in 1945, he tried unsuccessfully to create an "Institute on World Affairs" in the manner of Columbia (and Princeton and Yale). Chicago's president, Robert Hutchins, was interested in world federalism but put Wright off.[38] Then in 1950 Hutchins gave his blessing to a Center for the Study of American Foreign Policy, led by Morgenthau. Morgenthau had almost no connection to Wright and got his funding from the Lilly Endowment.[39] A year later Hutchins again rebuffed Wright's attempt to form an "Institute of International Relations."[40] Hutchins was well known for dismissing practical study of the contemporary world, but apparently was willing to have it if he did not have to pay.

At Johns Hopkins the Cold War directly intruded into the conflict between old and new students of policy. Its Page School of International Relations was

---

[35] Krout to Goldschmidt, December 7, 1951, Institute of War and Peace Studies, 1952–53; Krout to Meany, December 18, 1953, Institute of War and Peace Studies, Subject Files, Columbiana, Low Library, Columbia University.

[36] For Wright's ideas at this time see Wright to Poole, October 27, 1947, Folder 6, Box 15; Wright to Eichelberger, January 12, 1950, Folder 2, Box 6; and Wright to Willits, February 9, 1951, Folder 18, Box 13, Wright Papers, University of Chicago.

[37] Wright to Willits, February 9, 1951, Folder 18, Box 13, Wright Papers, University of Chicago.

[38] Wright to Hutchins, August 27, 1945; Hutchins to Wright, September 7, 1945, Presidents Papers, 1940–46, University of Chicago.

[39] Morgenthau, Box 20, Addendum 1, Wright Papers, University of Chicago.

[40] Wright to Tyler, February 21, 1951; Hutchins to Wright, April 16, 1951, University of Chicago, Box 28, Addendum 1, Wright Papers, University of Chicago.

lethargic and marginally funded. In conjunction with academic departments, however, it did award a doctoral degree, and its long-serving director was Owen Lattimore, a noted scholar of China and Central Asia. But in March 1950, at the same time that Hopkins's president, Detlev Bronk, was parleying with SAIS, anti-Communist senator Joseph McCarthy "named" Lattimore as a leading subversive, and the "Lattimore case" was headline news for almost the next three years. While not a Communist, Lattimore had publicized his erratic opinions about world politics in the 1930s and 1940s. More important his connection with the Page School assured that it was more than a scholarly organization. Lattimore had consulted for the government and liked advising on current events, especially on the thorny issue of China. Like many other intellectuals attacked by the Republican Right, he had voiced displeasure over American support of the recently defeated Chinese Nationalists.[41]

While agreeing to fund SAIS, in 1952 Carnegie refused to renew a grant to the Page School that had kept it solvent, and at the end of 1952 Hopkins gave Lattimore leave of absence to defend himself against the charges made against him. Five months after he left, Detlev Bronk abolished the Page School in a reorganization of the university.[42]

The linked stories of Yale and Princeton dramatically illustrated how acceptable opinion shriveled and how the connection of scholarship to current politics grew. Yale's Institute for International Studies, which had been founded in 1935, received most of its money from the Rockefeller Foundation but some also from Carnegie, and later from the federal government for a mysterious "special purpose." Along with the institute, Yale established graduate and undergraduate programs in international relations, and attracted an able group of scholars—Nicholas Spykman, Arnold Wolfers, Jacob Viner, and their realist organizational leader, Frederick Dunn. The institute published a number of prominent books under its auspices, including A. Whitney Griswold's *Far Eastern Policy of the United States* (1938) and Samuel Flagg Bemis's *Latin American Policy of the United States* (1943). In 1948 it gave birth to the journal *World Politics*. A number of younger scholars became associated with institute projects, among them Gabriel Almond, Bernard Brodie, William T. R. Fox (all students of Quincy Wright), and William Kaufmann.

The purpose of the institute was "to clarify the fundamental problems of American foreign policy." During World War II and its aftermath, however, the academics seized on opportunities to make names for themselves in Washington. The Yale men stressed their special skills and mentorship of those who

[41] This story is told in Boxes 2–6 of the papers of the Page School, Johns Hopkins University.

[42] The fullest source is Robert P. Newman, *Owen Lattimore and the "Loss" of China* (Berkeley and Los Angeles: University of California Press, 1992). I have also used Boxes 2–6 of the papers of the Page School, Johns Hopkins University.

could move into government positions in foreign affairs. By the late 1940s, the institute had informally joined up with RAND, testifying to its novel slant.

This orientation got the institute into trouble with Yale's new president in 1950. The institute had published a book of A. Whitney Griswold's, but even though a member of the foreign-policy opinion elite, Griswold was an academic conservative. The institute, he complained, should become more scholarly and philosophical and less captivated by "short books addressed to timely, ad hoc situations." He wanted history stressed in its studies, and favored old-fashioned individual research as opposed to what he saw as the politicized teamwork of social scientists. Griswold feared that the institute would try to replace institutions like the Council on Foreign Relations in New York, and not do what it should be doing—making detached analyses. Despite his close relations to many policymakers—Henry Stimson, who had wound up his extraordinary career as secretary of war under Franklin Roosevelt, was an important Yale alumnus, as was Secretary of State Dean Acheson and Republican leader Robert Taft—Griswold distinguished Yale's role from policymaking.[43]

At Princeton forces were also opposed. On the one side, Edward Meade Earle, who held a position in the School of Economics and Politics at the Institute for Advanced Study, led the cause of policy-oriented realism. Earle consulted with agencies interested in military affairs. During World War II he worked in operations research for the air force and advocated strategic bombing. We have already met him as a precursor to Bernard Brodie. As the war in Europe ended, Earle tried to endow a military studies group at the institute at James Forrestal's instigation. In 1946, just as Kennan was reaching the brief height of his fame among Washington insiders, Earle worked to get him a "senior academic position" in a variety of Princeton departments. In the late 1940s, in a report to the University of Chicago, Earle assisted in diminishing Quincy Wright's power.[44]

On the other side, Princeton president Harold Dodds supported Wilsonian objectives. In 1948 Princeton's modest School of Public and International Affairs was renamed the Woodrow Wilson School of Public and International

---

[43] The history of the institute can be constructed from its papers in the Yale University Archives, Boxes 1–8, YRG 37 U/RU 482; and in the Seymour Papers, Yale University, Institute and Political Science Folders, Boxes 86–89, and 128. Quotes from General Statement (n.d.), Folder 765, Box 89; and Griswold to Provost, January 9, 1951, Folder 1153, Box 128. See also Paulo J. B. Ramos, "The Role of the Yale Institute of International Studies in the Construction of United States National Security Ideology, 1935–1951," Ph.D. diss., Department of Government, University of Manchester, 2003, pp. 132–44, 372–73.

[44] On Operations Research and strategic bombing see the Earle Papers, Boxes 29, 30; on Forrestal, Folder F, Forrestal, June 1, 1945, Box 16; on Kennan, Earle to Dodds, November 18, 1946, K-4, Box 18; on Wright, Earle to Dunn, August 16, 1949, Box 15; and Earle to Hutchins, March 23, 1949, Professional Activities: Harris Foundation, 1948–49, Box 29, Mudd Library, Princeton University. See also Inderjeet Parmar, "Edward Meade Earle and the Rise of Realism in the United States Academy," *Manchester Papers in Politics* (University of Manchester, 2001), pp. 1–24.

Affairs. Dodds broke ground for a Woodrow Wilson Hall and announced the enlargement of the school as a "living Memorial" to the martyred president. In 1950, within the school, the Compton family of Princeton alumni created a new Center for Research in World Political Institutions as a "constructive" tribute to a son who had been killed in World War II. This center pledged "to minimize the risk of war by substituting [for war] the rule of law among nations." International politics must "expand . . . community" and achieve "progress toward a decisively stronger United Nations." In addition to the money the Comptons gave, Dodds announced at the end of 1950 that the Milbank Foundation would fund a professorship in the new center for someone committed to the study of global legal organizations.

Less then six months later, in the spring of 1951, Dodds made a U-turn, when his flexible leadership took advantage of the falling out between Yale's institute and Yale president Griswold. Seven people left Yale for Princeton, while William T. R. Fox went to Columbia. The policy scientists brought with them various foundation grants and the journal *World Politics*. Becoming more "masculine,"[45] Princeton could scarcely contain its glee at Yale's discomfiture. The Milbank Foundation money, previously reserved for a Wilsonian professor, was awarded to the leader from Yale, Frederick Dunn.[46] A new Center for International Studies elbowed aside the now orphaned Center for Research in World Political Institutions. The latter center closed up shop in the midfifties, and Princeton terminated its director, at one time a candidate for the professorial chair.[47]

Realism commanded the field at Princeton, whose Yale refugees became the university leaders in the fledgling field of security studies. In the early years of Eisenhower's institute, for example, Columbia's academic advisors were almost all drawn from Princeton.[48] Fox at Columbia led the Social Science Research Council's Committee on National Security Research and built up "a network of academics," eclipsing the subfields of international law and organization.[49] But Princeton did not have near the influence of RAND, which dominated strategic studies. Indeed, Princeton's significance lay in forging links between RAND and the professoriate. The university assisted in making

[45] Van Wagenen to Wright, February 19, 1951, 17, Box 12, Wright Papers, University of Chicago.

[46] "The Social Sciences at Princeton University," reprinted from *Princeton Alumni Weekly*, May 4, 1951, Historical Subject Files, Box 328, CIS; Woodrow Wilson School, Misc., Folders: 1931–49; 1951–59, Box 330, Mudd Library, Princeton University.

[47] Woodrow Wilson Center, 1945–48, 1948–51; Center for Research on World Political Institutions, Dodds Papers, Mudd Library, Princeton University. The fired head of the defunct center, Richard Van Wagenen, was not a strong scholar, but he became dean of the Graduate School and professor of international relations at American University.

[48] Institute of War and Peace Studies, Newspaper Clipping Files, Columbiana, Low Library, Columbia University.

[49] Betts, "Should Strategic Studies Survive," p. 13.

RAND-style security studies respectable in the more traditional academic world. Scholars at Princeton and other schools consulted for RAND, and freely went to and from it and university positions. Moreover, the professorial realists camouflaged the technocratic reformism of RAND. They disguised its utopian dimension and gave it a patina of circumspect sobriety. The universities gave RAND the lexicon of realism.

The study of international politics in these centers reflected the mounting influence of the norms of the political world over the academic world. Politics had always influenced scholars of foreign policy, but observations were diverse. Now opinion was narrower in range than it had previously been in the older and less worldly institutes of international affairs. Explicit Wilsonian sentiment was downgraded, and all ideas outside of the political mainstream were discounted. The rhetoric of social science was used to legitimate requests for the ear of policymakers, but after the "scientific revolution" in post–World War II political science, scholarship was less detached and more partisan than it had been. The nonempirical basis of RAND's ideas often came to connote realism, and over time RAND's students flavored realism with their reformism.

REALISM'S PROBLEMS

Realism brought to the field of security studies conceptual problems that scholars never solved. As a more-or-less factual thesis realism argued that in examining the interactions among states, the student should look to interests, power relations, and economics as independent variables. Scholars should downplay statements of principle or morality and their causal efficacy. A realist studying history might argue that an adequate narrative of the course of international politics over a certain period would demonstrate that interest drove the interactions of states, no matter what individual diplomats said about the purity of their motives or the demands of principle.

As a linguistic net thrown over international politics, realism defined foreign affairs as the realm of the balance of power, *raison d'état*, and realpolitik. Such a vision had the virtues and vices that characterized most such positions in the human sciences, in which the notion of *theory* has more the force of my belief, sense of things, or viewpoint, and not the force of Newtonian paradigm, quantum physics, or evolutionary biology. Realists were programmed to look for certain things and to overlook others. For example, what one might assume were impulses to moral decision making were ignored, or interpreted to mean something else. Theodore Roosevelt might bluster about the obligations of civilization, but according to realists always acted prudently, aware of the sinews of power. Stalin's claims to being peace-loving were automatically translated into calculations of advantage or disadvantage, for statesmen did not act on the basis of moral ideas.

More important was that realism was not clearly taken up as a factual thesis. Rather, in addition to depicting the political arena as one governed by competing interests, the realist implicitly argued that other factors might be causally relevant but, in the past, had led to disaster. In the present statesmen should shun them. Wilson's legalism about the settlement of World War I had had bad consequences, and the prudent contemporary diplomat would avoid such a posture. That is, realism blended a factual view of how diplomacy had operated on some occasions with prescriptions about how it ought to operate. But this explication prejudices matters in favor of realism, for an evaluative construal of certain kinds of diplomacy was part and parcel of the history that realists elaborated. Realist language would categorize diplomatic endeavor of which realists approved. They might then imply that had another dynamic been at work, the results would have been worse. Henry Kissinger liked the strategy of diplomats in early-nineteenth-century Europe and made it a central example of realism. He dismissed arguments that nonrealist precepts might have guided the strategy. Wilson's views were disliked and thought to be disastrous, and thus for some realists Wilson was to be taken at his word—ideals and not self-interest drove his policies. Examining the present, realists urged that their precepts would be beneficial. Other precepts—usually Wilsonian—would be counterproductive.

More dubiously realists thought that something in the international system compelled it to operate on principles associated with the balance of power—this was essential to Morgenthau's realism. Yet foolish human beings were somehow able to disregard the order in the system and seek impossible solutions to intractable problems. For the realist, the idealist was the enemy, but if realism were correct, the idealist should not have been able to get a grip on decisions in the first place.[50]

Realism was, then, not entirely an empirical thesis. It was, rather, an outlook presuming that diplomats were more likely to reach international stability by looking to the security need of their state than whatever ethical ideal they had imbibed from their culture. One could find politicians who acted contrary to realist prescriptions but would also find that realists would deprecate the policies of these politicians. Realism was a mode of thinking that wove together an interpretation of the past and guidance for the present. The view spoke to the need of leadership not to be soft, to foreswear the reckless but to exhibit resolve—especially when called upon to make dangerous decisions that might send others to their death. Realism was designed more for engaged actors than for aloof scholars.

---

[50] Marc Trachtenberg has brought together these two elements. The calculation of interest that drives international politics, he argues, is "palpable" to the historian (interview, January 21, 2003), yet he also intimates that the peace constructed in the period he wrote about was not "given" but in some way subject to human choice. This book relies heavily on his *A Constructed Peace*.

Finally, to put this analysis more pointedly, realism directed many "tough" policymakers to necessities inherent in the political system but also afforded a comfortable warrior code that endorsed the willful exercise of power. Often using abstract nouns as subjects, or verbs in the passive voice, realists rhetorically bowed to the inevitable but also congratulated themselves on their nobility. In "The Sources of Soviet Conduct," George Kennan gave thanks to Providence for forcing Americans to accept "the responsibilities of moral and political leadership that history plainly intended them to bear."[51] Lesser realists of the RAND sort related that in the 1930s America "attempted to withdraw from its responsibilities" but later was willing "to shoulder its responsibilities." As the Cold War unfolded, the United States "was forced to assume the largely unanticipated role of the dominant superpower." "The shift of power" after World War II "put the burden of leadership" on the United States.[52] The nature of the international system, said NSC-68, "imposes on us, in our own interests, the responsibility of world leadership."[53] And Henry Kissinger wrote in 1960 that "history will not excuse our failure."[54] This was the old American Calvinist idea of self-abnegation and assertiveness translated into twentieth-century diplomacy.

RICHARD NEUSTADT

At the same time that political scientists courted a burly realism in foreign affairs, some idealist preconceptions survived in the writings of scholars concerned with the improvement of domestic institutions. Administrative science, as an area of political science, had some roots in the study of international law and drew on the same reformism. Nonetheless, in the institutional setting of the university, administrative scientists often avoided the discomfiture that (diplomatic) idealism suffered. These administrative scientists confined their theorizing to domestic politics and covered their progressivism with a certain cynicism. The most significant such figure in the postwar period was Richard Neustadt.

Neustadt grew up in Washington, D.C., the son of a Democratic Social Security administrator during the New Deal active in the passage of domestic welfare legislation. In the late 1940s, still under thirty, the son served Harry Tru-

---

[51] Kennan, as reprinted in *American Diplomacy*, expanded ed. (Chicago: University of Chicago Press, 1984), p. 128.

[52] George E. Pickett, James G. Roche, and Barry D. Watts, "Net Assessment: A Historical Review," and Paul D. Wolfowitz, "Present Trends and Future Consequences in the Asia-Pacific Region," in Marshall et al., *On Not Confusing Ourselves*, pp. 159–61, 239–40, respectively.

[53] In May, *American Cold War Strategy*, p. 29.

[54] Kissinger, "Limited War: Nuclear or Conventional?" *Daedalus*, 1960, in Trachtenberg, *Strategic Thought*, pt. 3, vol. 3, p. 817.

man as a junior member of the White House staff and concentrated on domestic issues. Before the Democrats went out of office in 1953 and still at work for the president, Neustadt completed his Harvard graduate education, which had been interrupted by the war, with a thesis that blended his practical experience and his interest in political administration.[55] In 1960, holding an associate professorship in Columbia's Department of Government, he published *Presidential Power*, a book about the "politics of leadership."[56]

Presidential Power consisted of case studies that evaluated how the presidencies of Roosevelt, Truman, and Eisenhower achieved their goals. Neustadt sorted out those strategies most likely to bring a president success and concluded that the power of the modern presidents resided in their ability to persuade. The president was, in Neustadt's scheme, the leader of a collective bargaining committee, and his capacity to function in such a role measured his victories in office. Neustadt moreover developed some low-level "rules of conduct" that might increase the effectiveness of the holder of the office. On the eve of Kennedy's election, Neustadt ended his book by saying that the 1960s would require "presidential expertise of the peculiar sort this book has stressed" and "a presidential expert" in the new administration.[57]

In many ways *Presidential Power* was traditional political science. The book studied the presidency and how it might be made more effective. In an era when political scientists proclaimed their scientific neutrality, Neustadt only nodded in that direction. He dismissed presidential forecasting that might become "a science practiced with the aid of mathematics" as ignoring "the complexity of the real world." And even with the aid of experts, presidential politics was more likely to be akin to negotiating a contract than "a reasoned argument among philosopher kings."[58] Although his only point was "to clarify the nature of the search for personal power," the book showed his liberal Democratic commitments, which he asserted throughout his life.[59] His model of leadership presumed the sort of vigor that FDR had illustrated, and Neustadt ranked the presidents: Roosevelt, Truman a close second, and Eisenhower, an amateur, not a politician, a distant third.[60]

Although Neustadt was old-fashioned in his faltering belief in objective social science, he took a new tack in assessing policymaking as successful or unsuccessful, rather than as good or bad. Early commentators criticized the book because it lacked any exploration of the Roman virtue of public officials,

---

[55] The most extended treatment is Charles O. Jones, "Richard E. Neustadt: Public Servant as Scholar," *Annual Review of Political Science* (2003): 1–22.

[56] Richard Neustadt, *Presidential Power: The Politics of Leadership* (New York: John Wiley, 1960).

[57] Neustadt, *Presidential Power*, pp. 154, 186, 191.

[58] Neustadt, *Presidential Power*, pp. 46, 60–61.

[59] Neustadt, interview, October 8, 2001.

[60] Neustadt, *Presidential Power*, pp. ix, 185.

virtù, in the presidency. Neustadt did not examine whether the work of the president was admirable. The argument focused on how the president might augment his power—that was success—and Neustadt was accused of being a Machiavellian, of being concerned only with political effectiveness. Neustadt allowed, however, that he had presupposed virtù.[61] The president oversaw American politics, and Neustadt was here a conventional small-d democrat. The politics of democracy was virtuous, and the outcome of the process was good by definition. *Presidential Power* only examined how the president increased his power because the book presumed that good decisions emanated from the system itself.

At the same time Neustadt hinted at issues prominent in his later writing. Policy was not about rational planning and the outcome of such plans. The democratic process was more chaotic, less subject to linear construal. As did RAND, Neustadt wanted to make policy more subject to control but was less certain that it had even the rudiments of rationality. *Presidential Power* intimated that large bureaucracies did not look much like those postulated by Herbert Simon in *Administrative Behavior*. Nor could they be transformed into such a system as RAND had implied. Like political leaders, Neustadt despaired of the power of bureaucrats, the public, and the media to thwart policy initiatives, but he intimated that only less technocratic methods than those RAND presumed could nudge matters into a more productive course.

Neustadt looked backward at the presidency instead of forward. The president's chief job had been in domestic affairs, where the president, the legislature, the public, and various interest groups negotiated policy. The executive's own orientation was muted. He steered the process. None of this was wrong, but as Neustadt extended his analysis to foreign affairs, he missed the growth of the national security state in the 1940s and 1950s and what would be the significance of international politics for the United States in the 1960s and 1970s. Here, following the precedents FDR, Truman, and Eisenhower had set, the executive in the next two decades would often operate clandestinely, more independently of Congress or the public. There would be more scope for executive decision-making and less room for the bargaining that defined domestic politics. Other factors than lawmakers or the electorate might constrain policy choices.

The new administration would move in this direction, as Kennedy shied away from presidential leadership at home. The president instead gravitated to foreign policy, in which the conciliation Neustadt believed to be essential would less compromise the executive himself. More important, even before he started his term in office, Kennedy made Neustadt into a house intellectual. The president-elect had read *Presidential Power* and stated that in the transi-

---

[61] Neustadt conversations, 1978–79.

tion he would rely on the professor's ideas. Suddenly Neustadt was thrust into the limelight.[62]

Commentators read the book for a key to Kennedy's thinking and touted its author as the brand of expert that the White House sought. Neustadt represented the youthfulness of the Kennedy White House—he was forty-one in 1960—and *Presidential Power* was modern in its emphasis on the effective use of power and on the active executive. Neustadt set forth an academic vision consonant with the self-image of the new administration. The absence of moralizing and the concentration on the rule of prudence also set Neustadt apart from his more quantitatively oriented peers, who might theorize about what government should accomplish. With his practical stance and experience in government, Neustadt exemplified the "cool" style of Washington in the early 1960s, and the reputation of *Presidential Power* boosted his career.

It should not be a surprise that in selecting those who would work for him Kennedy brought together contradictory impulses. The RAND people who came to Washington had views that existed in textbooks on management. They thought they could base politics on reason, while Neustadt assumed that policymakers must accept something less. RAND realists thought they could make foreign affairs rational. The less-than-realist Neustadt eschewed moralistic attempts to impose realism. Both groups were unconcerned about goals. Neustadt attended to process, while the RAND theoreticians thought that the fiat of leaders established the ends.

LEARNING FROM HISTORY

During the early 1960s, teaching in New York and consulting in Washington, Neustadt began to look to history for help and to work out an intricate design to improve national politics.

Two suppositions, not entirely consistent, elaborated on his early work. First, Neustadt took as elements of debate separate, individual events. Scholars might look at a set of events outside of historical circumstance. Second, to improve policy, Neustadt sponsored a form of study of the past. He devised a model for grasping "contemporary history" that would prompt politicians to act more perspicaciously. Neustadt asserted that a "traditional claim made for the use of history was that we learn from it." More nuanced and circumspect, his message strengthened that claim. If policymakers wanted better decisions, they should try to see how a present problem had arisen. Neustadt recommended a series of "mini-methods" that included learning the story that culminated in the problem and avoiding easy comparisons that prescribed decisions to resolve it. The historically minded decision-maker found out about the per-

---

[62] The story is best told in Neustadt's recollections of the September 1960–February 1961 period in his "oral history" at Columbia University taped in January and February 1961.

spective of the other personalities and institutions involved in the issue, checked for similarities and dissimilarities in past situations, and finally weighed the value of options by imaging various sorts of outcomes.[63]

A book by one of Neustadt's collaborators lobbied for the use of historical experts in government, on a par with economists and other specialists. *"Lessons" of the Past: The Use and Misuse of History in American Foreign Policy* by Ernest May showed that the decisions of policymakers rose from their historical sense, even if it was faulty or superficial. This effort, while uncontroversial, showed the formalist presumptions of many scholars in politics, for it was inconceivable that policy could not emanate from being situated in time, and peculiar that someone had to prove this idea. *"Lessons" of the Past* argued that the state might give special treatment to appropriate historians of the recent past, who might function to remind policymakers of the most appropriate historical analogies, the ones most conducive to correct action. Politicians used history badly, and if they were to do better, "nothing is more important than that professional historians discover means of addressing directly, succinctly, and promptly the needs of people who govern."[64]

Neustadt admitted that his formulas might often be reduced to a plea for caution, and consciously did not claim overmuch. In an era dominated by quantification-smitten thinkers, he had modest hopes, and reservations about the success one could achieve. Those who followed him wanted to improve policymaking "at the margins." They also did not claim to be historians, but social scientists who exploited funded experience to decide what to do today "about the prospect for tomorrow." At the same time they could not resist the dominant instrumentalism in the social sciences. "The future has no place to come from but the past," they said; "hence the past has predictive value."[65] And they could not resist hinting that they would increase the mathematical probability of achieving one's ends in making decisions, beyond that achieved without their methods.[66]

This approach had a basic, recurring problem, which became even more apparent later in the decade. Neustadt and his associates took individual decisions out of context in order to compare decision making across time. They looked for the common structures that might exist in certain kinds of problematic circumstances. Then scholars might learn what behavior was most appropriate in these circumstances. Analogical reasoning was paramount. Neustadt hoped to "dodge" poor analogies that would produce questionable decisions. Korea in

---

[63] Richard E. Neustadt and Ernest R. May, *Thinking in Time: The Use of History for Decision Makers* (New York: Free Press, 1986), pp. 232–44.

[64] Ernest R. May, *"Lessons" of the Past: The Use and Misuse of History in American Foreign Policy* (New York: Oxford University Press, 1973), quote at p. 190.

[65] Neustadt and May, *Thinking in Time*, pp. xiv, xxii, 251. This reasoning is an example of the logical fallacy of affirming the consequent: it does not follow from the fact that the future entails the past that the past entails the future.

[66] Neustadt and May, *Thinking in Time*, pp. 105, 165.

1950, for example, was not like Munich in 1938, and Truman might have avoided trouble had someone at the time decoupled the two in the collective mind of the administration. But history was a venue for learning only if some analogies were legitimate and others illegitimate. That is, scholars must be able to outline the criteria specifying the common structures that events must have to count as appropriately analogous or disanalogous. The conventional idea was that at the Munich conference Neville Chamberlain made a weak decision, encouraging Hitler to take Germany to war. For Neustadt, however, the Korean peninsula was more like the Balkans in 1914, which led all the great powers into a terrible war. Korea required circumspection more than pugnacity.

It is clear, for example in 1950, that policymakers used analogical reasoning to justify their decisions: Truman and Acheson said that Korea was like Munich. One question was whether such reasoning actually explained the decisions that were taken. Did Truman and Acheson respond in Korea because they feared another Munich? (Or because both were thoughtlessly forceful or afraid not to act because of domestic repercussions; or because they appreciated the Asian balance of power?) But a more crucial question concerns the cogency of the analogies themselves.

We could learn how to behave in the future from the July crisis of 1914, which took the Europeans into World War I, or the Munich crisis of 1938 only because embodied in the events that made up each crisis was a constellation of structural features in which we could see the connection between these events, certain human action, and further events. In a bullying situation, further bullying would follow weakness. The bully's retreat would follow standing up for one's rights. Historically minded policy scientists were seeking the characteristics possessed by different events that permitted categorization based on genuine similarities. Was North Korea's invasion of the South a case of bullying? Or should it be classified differently? Theorists like Neustadt, however, had no way of showing that Munich and Korea, or the Balkans and Korea, were relevantly similar or dissimilar. They could not show that treating North Korea as if it were Hitler's Germany produced bad consequences, worse than would have occurred had diplomats, say, moved with the far greater sensitivity befitting a Balkan powder keg. Neustadt did not outline why some analogies were better or worse than others. Henry Kissinger, who was for a long time on the fringes of the people I have been describing, recognized the ambiguities at work when he wrote that history taught the consequences of certain actions in certain situations, but left to each generation to determine the character of the situation it faced.[67]

Neustadt and his colleagues sought to anchor policy in scholarship that fell short of what they needed. But the weakness of this approach was different from that of the RAND strategists who wanted to realize a vision that the world would break.

---

[67] Kissinger, *Nuclear Weapons*, p. 21.

CHAPTER 5

RAND and the Kennedy Administration, 1961–1962

EISENHOWER'S MANAGEMENT REFORMS

By the late 1950s, reality had dashed the hope of the National Security Act of 1947, the first such act: that a secretary of defense would coordinate the activities of the army, the air force, and the navy. Politicians had believed that within a single department a properly chosen secretary would make the military behave more like a well-run business and spend money more wisely. At various times Louis Johnson (under Truman) and then Charles Wilson (under Eisenhower) made this the focus of the secretary of defense, but to no avail. A member of each of the independent services did sit on the Joint Chiefs of Staff, and reported to the secretary of defense, but successive secretaries had not formulated a unified policy. The size and organizational complexity of the military and its squabbling were still an issue.

Eisenhower had kept a lid on military spending. He allocated to defense a fair percentage of a total government budget that he wanted minimized. National security expenditure for Eisenhower resulted, equally, from what he thought was the least that he could get away with and from what he thought were the actual security needs of the United States. Because of his prestige, Eisenhower staved off requests for greater spending, and among American military leaders uniquely disapproved of such spending. Within the defense establishment there was no such distaste. Interservice rivalry for the limited resources continued. Competing service heads not only disagreed on security requirements, but also acted to justify their own claims on the budget. Intelligence estimates of enemy capabilities bolstered the requests of the service that presented the estimate. The secretary of defense, who supposedly integrated defense planning, behaved like a politician and adjudicated the antagonistic interests.

In this contest the air force had been most successful, because it controlled the nuclear and thermonuclear weapon of choice in the 1950s and 1960s. But the RAND scholars who clarified air force policy were aware of the selfishness of their client, and although the air force and its advisors often shared a desire to overcome Eisenhower's aversion to spend, the civilians had their own ideas about management that pulled them away from the air force. The airmen liked bombers. But by the late 1950s, when it became possible as a practical matter to deliver nuclear warheads by missiles, it was uncertain whether the army or the air force should have charge of them. Moreover, missiles launched from submarines—the effective Polaris system—would seem to be in the purview of the navy. Technology was driving a wedge between the air force and its social scientists, who might now find that rational security did not favor their employer. The civilians saw their mission as devising a scientifically objective defense for the United States. The air force compromised their impartiality and gave RAND, they thought, the reputation of being biased. The air force believed that RAND employees should defend its priorities, and tried to bring the think tank to heel.[1] The Defense Reorganization Act of 1958 underscored this emerging diversity of interest.

The act harkened back to recommendations of a commission led by Herbert Hoover in 1947 for a "performance budget." Leadership should not just allocate money among the services but spend it to accomplish an overall objective. The 1958 act called for greater centralization in the Department of Defense, more adequate planning, minimization of competition, and elimination of duplicate projects. One immediate consequence of the act came in the last years of the Eisenhower administration, with the development of a Single Integrated Operational Plan (SIOP), to unify the air war of the various services. Created by Eisenhower's last secretary of defense, Thomas Gates, the SIOP gained military approval by adding together the plans of the services. The SIOP revealed the interest of Gates and the president in the integration of defense but also a tenacious and carping military. An effective secretary, Gates had a short reign at the end of a tired administration, and left office with the Defense Department oriented to the intent of the 1958 act, yet far from its operational goal. The Defense Department still awaited reform.

RAND civilians had their own ideas about a new structure, and publicly criticized the act. But the social scientists also explained how a new administration, which would take office in 1961, might reconceive defense problems. In a significant primer, *The Economics of Defense in the Nuclear Age*, C. J. Hitch and his RAND associates expounded their views as "a way of looking at military problems." They were all essentially "economic problems in the efficient allocation of resources." To treat defense as such would reconcile the differences between the politicians responsible for raising money and the soldiers for strategy. RAND thinkers positioned themselves as the experts who could offer a method to assist civilian authorities.[2]

---

[1] See Jardini's excellent but mistitled "Out of the Blue Yonder," pp. 170–71, 189, 239–40.

[2] Charles J. Hitch and Roland N. McKean, eds., *The Economics of Defense in the Nuclear Age* (Cambridge: Harvard University Press, 1963), p. v; on RAND's criticism of the Reorganization Act, pp. 256ff.

SCIENTIFIC DEFENSE A REALITY

When John Kennedy took office in 1961, he brought into the government academic advisors like Neustadt. But he also placed experts in policymaking positions—men such as his assistant for national security, former Harvard political scientist and dean, McGeorge Bundy; and Secretary of State Dean Rusk, who had been a Rhodes scholar and had begun his career as a professor of international politics. His secretary of defense, Robert McNamara, had studied economics at Berkeley before taking an M.B.A. at the Harvard Business School. During World War II, McNamara was a member of a statistical control group in the Army Air Corps. Using the techniques of operations research, it calculated—first in the European theater and then in the Pacific—the logistical requirements and schedules for the bombings. McNamara coordinated the men, equipment, and fuel to mount the most effective campaign. After the war the Ford Motor Company lured him away from a Harvard Business School professorship to consult, with several others, in reorganizing the automobile company. A drowsy business, Ford bounced back in the postwar period under the direction of McNamara's group and Henry Ford II, grandson of the founder. McNamara had risen rapidly, and Ford had named him president of the company a month before Kennedy made him secretary of defense.

McNamara's appointment gave new meaning to the German aphorism that Americanism was Taylorism plus Fordism. More than that, although McNamara's career path had been different, his mind-set was identical to that of RAND. He read Hitch's edited book, *The Economics of Defense*, and offered Hitch the job of comptroller in the Department of Defense. Hitch was the first of a group of civilians with RAND connections, "the Whiz Kids," to join McNamara. As the most knowledgeable authority has written, the relation between the new secretary and RAND was "love at first sight."[3] Almost all the prestigious strategists, most with RAND backgrounds and in Wohlstetter's circle, hooked up with the Department of Defense in the 1960s. Elated that the "vast wasteland of the Eisenhower years" was over, they thought that their "perceptible actions" would alter "the unsatisfactory organization of the Defense Department." Men like Eisenhower and Dulles would no longer ignore RAND management studies, and they would now reform the American government.[4] Radical folksinger Pete Seeger celebrated with a 1961 piece of music, "The RAND Hymn."

A popular novel of the period, *Fail-Safe* (1962), written by Eugene Burdick and Harvey Wheeler, also recorded RAND's ascent to power and aped the

[3] Kaplan, *The Wizards of Armageddon*, p. 251.

[4] Paul Warnke, Oral History (January 1969), tape 1, p. 3; Alain C. Enthoven, Oral History (December 1968), pp. 1–2, LBJ Library. A more modest RAND program is put forward in Enthoven and Henry Rowen, "Defense Planning and Organization," P-1640 (1959).

earlier whimsy, Edward House's *Philip Dru*. Set in a 1967 future, *Fail-Safe*'s leading character was national security consultant Walter Groteschele, author of the acclaimed book *Counter-Escalation*. This sinister professor, who argued for a preemptive strike on the USSR, was played by Walter Matthau in the later movie of the same name, and was a pastiche of Henry Kissinger and the civilian theorist Herman Kahn. The lunatic Dr. Strangelove actually preceded Groteschele in the 1964 film *Dr. Strangelove or: How I Stopped Worrying and Learned to Love the Bomb*. Although Strangelove was more the mad scientist type, he speaks of the "BLAND Corporation." Peter Sellers, who played Strangelove, modeled himself on Henry Kissinger.[5]

McNamara's men restructured the defense budget and showed their true colors, as the air force believed, by turning on their former client. The civilians would use systems analysis to understand national security, military strategy, and weapons systems. With Bundy's approval policy initiatives often came out of McNamara's Department of Defense, while the less favored Department of State, under Dean Rusk, was ignored.[6] Three issues of organization and management illustrated the tone of the Defense Department in the early 1960s and the impact of scientific management on it.

Changes occurred in what might be called housekeeping, although they had been in the works since the late 1950s.[7] A new Defense Supply Agency centralized the thousands of purchases the services required and tried to prevent the government from being overcharged. McNamara closed military bases that he thought were wasteful, and opposed "pork barrel" projects of the Congress that involved allocating money to the Pentagon. The secretary also eliminated the military reserve units composed of congressmen and their employees in the House and Senate.[8] This was straightforward economizing that many secretaries had advocated and worried about. McNamara was more zealous and more precise in analysis of the savings, although he was not above conventional horse-trading and politicking with Congress, and did not eliminate exorbitant prices.

More systematic but along the same line was the implementation of a new budget system. Soon after they arrived, the Whiz Kids set up the Planning-Programming-Budgeting System (PPBS). Under the old guidelines, adminis-

---

[5] Eugene Burdick and Harvey Wheeler, *Fail-Safe* (New York: McGraw Hill, 1962). See also Jack G. Shaheen, ed., *Nuclear War Films* (Carbondale: Southern Illinois University Press, 1978); and Fred Kaplan, "Truth Stranger than 'Strangelove,'" *New York Times*, October 10, 2004, AR, p. 21.

[6] For an analysis of the administration's style see Matthew Jones, "'Calling three meetings in five days is foolish—and putting them off for six weeks at a time is just as bad': Organizing the New Frontier's Foreign Policy," *Diplomacy and Statecraft* 15 (2004): 413–25.

[7] See Stephen Enke, "An Economist Looks at Air Force Logistics," *Review of Economics and Statistics* 40 (1958): 230–39.

[8] Henry L. Trewhitt, *McNamara* (New York: Harper and Row, 1971), pp. 85, 125.

trations had imposed a ceiling on military expenditures, and the services split the pie amongst themselves. With little attention to overlap or lack of coordination, the services organized expenditure as if each spearheaded a different mission. The new program theoretically enabled the United States to determine the security needs of the nation, and to figure out how to meet them economically. This was hyperbole, for spending limits always existed, and so did service rivalry. McNamara nonetheless promised that although more would be spent on defense, systematic priorities would come to the fore, and that there would be no business-as-usual.[9]

PPBS conceived defense spending according to mission, for example research and development, and cut across the separate branches. The 1958 Defense Reorganization Act had contemplated such a formula, and the unified war strategy developed by Thomas Gates moved in this direction, even though it aggregated individual army, navy, and air force ideas. The civilians now compared air force bombers, missiles launched from the ground, and navy missiles launched from submarines. The administrators would come up with a strategy and budget that was cost effective and that guaranteed security without respect to which service was favored or injured. An ideal of overall priorities measured each weapon system.

The Defense Department finally searched for projects common to the services, and the paradigmatic instance was the secretary's quest for a plane to serve both the air force and the navy. Progress in engines and aerodynamics, including a movable wing, McNamara thought, made it possible to meet the requirements of both services with one aircraft. The TFX—Tactical Fighter, Experimental or, later, the F-111—resulted.[10]

The story of the TFX had begun in the early 1950s as the air force struggled to keep abreast of advancing technology. The development of missiles, which were less vulnerable, challenged the war plan based on the bombers of the Strategic Air Command. The air force had proposed a new plane that would launch missiles. When this project got to McNamara's desk, he rejected it on the grounds that the plane had the weaknesses of a bomber and a missile, and no additional advantages. At the same time the secretary smiled on a further air force need for a new fighter-bomber that could fly nonstop across the Atlantic and also criss-cross small, unfinished airfields in Europe. Planners were to design an aircraft that could fly both high and slow, and low and fast.

During the same period the navy was requesting a plane with a sophisticated missile system that would guard its ships from aerial attack. When the secretary's assistants recommended a "multiservice" fighter-bomber, the prospect of saving money and of integrating military operations animated McNamara. The crucial technological advance was a wing that could move in flight. It

[9] Trewhitt, *McNamara*, pp. 110–11.
[10] Trewhitt, *McNamara*, pp. 24–25.

made possible a fighter-bomber that, when the wings were extended, could fly slowly at high altitudes, a desideratum of the navy. For the supersonic, low-level flight that the air force wanted, the wings could be swept back. In late 1961 the secretary ordered the air force to build such a plane, which would blend the conflicting requirements of each service—the TFX. After fights about which contractor would get the contract, the project went forward, and in October 1964 McNamara greeted the first production model of an aircraft that would meet the mandate of the two services, the F-111.

The services had had this plane forced on them, and were not unhappy when the F-111 displayed problems that were not resolved through 1965. By the time McNamara left government in early 1968, the F-111 had proven a disaster. The navy version was unsuccessful. The air force version had done a moderate job (in Vietnam) but was thought to have a limited role for the 1970s. Not only had commonality failed, but the Defense Department had also poured money out for an ineffectual plane. Later commentators pointed out that the notion of a common defense had so infatuated civilians that they had not studied the F-111 in their own terms of cost-benefit analysis. McNamara jumped at the idea because it represented rational unity. For seven years, critics urged, the debate and allocations for the plane paid tribute to the secretary's lack of political acumen.[11]

The pluses and minuses of the budgeting system are still debated,[12] but the terms were set by the early 1960s. In 1961, in *The Common Defense*, political scientist and theorist Samuel Huntington argued that Eisenhower did not "rationally determine" defense. Instead, strategic programs resulted from "controversy, negotiations, and bargaining among officials and groups with different interests and perspectives."[13] For Huntington this demanded change. One of McNamara's critics wrote that Huntington saw democratic dialogue as a weakness. According to the critic, RAND and the armed services struggled not exactly as civilians and the military, nor as scientists and nonscientists. Two other matters were at issue: the scientific pretensions of "cost effectiveness" as opposed to "methodological pluralism" in coping with national security; and the fact that the secretary of defense had rejected "the political process."[14]

McNamara himself openly gloried in these contrasts. His duty, he said, was to care for the national interest, as distinct from "the parochial interests of

---

[11] The standard, though narrow, study is Robert F. Coulam, *Illusions of Choice: The F-111 and the Problem of Weapons Acquisition Reform* (Princeton: Princeton University Press, 1977).

[12] For an assessment see Harvey Sapolsky, "The Science and Politics of Defense Analysis," in *The Social Sciences Go to Washington*, ed. Hamilton Cravens (New Brunswick, N.J.: Rutgers University Press, 2004), esp. pp. 71–73.

[13] Samuel Huntington, *The Common Defense: Strategic Programs in National Politics* (New York: Columbia University Press, 1961), p. 146.

[14] James Roherty, *Decisions of Robert S. McNamara: A Study of the Role of the Secretary of Defense* (Coral Gables: University of Miami Press, 1970), pp. 101, 151.

particular industries, individual services, or local areas." The main problem was undermanaging reality, and allowing some other force than reason—emotion, greed, aggressiveness, hatred, ignorance, inertia—to shape human life. If reason did not rule man, man fell short of his potential. The "mechanism" of scientific management exercised human reason.[15] But leadership had to run such a management system from the top down, so that the bureaucracy carried out its orders promptly. McNamara's system established "a rational foundation as opposed to an emotional foundation for . . . decisions." He could "la[y] out on paper" such a "rational structure" or "intellectual foundation." Not surprisingly, McNamara conceded that he could not quantify everything. But individuals could reason about all reality, and not to quantify what they could quantify was to be content with "less than the full range of reason." Arguments against the new calculational technology associated with the computer argued "against reason itself." The machine was not in question, McNamara concluded. Americans should rather question whether "Dr. Strangelove is sitting at the console."[16]

The Impact of RAND

Although Republicans and Democrats agreed that nuclear weapons were the heart of American defense, Eisenhower had worried that his focus and budgetary limitations foreclosed for him a strategy for limited wars. Despite the publicity about flexible response, the Democrats did not stray much from this commitment. Conventional forces were not enlarged, although the soldiers got more modern weapons. The budget grew even though the administration learned that the "missile gap" on which it had campaigned no longer existed, if it ever had, and that the United States had a compelling advantage in nuclear weaponry. A key change was McNamara's acceleration of the rocket program, especially the sea-launched Polaris, to insure that the American deterrent would not become obsolete and vulnerable.[17] In the minds of some commentators strategic realities were overridden by the continued sense of threat, politics, and the ideology of vigorous leadership that Kennedy promoted.

The manned bombers of the social scientists' old employer, the air force, were pushed aside. Increases in spending brought the end of polite relations between the services and the academics. The air force's intellectuals had al-

---

[15] Robert S. McNamara, *The Essence of Security: Reflections in Office* (New York: Harper and Row, 1968), pp. 103–4, 110, 115–16.

[16] Roherty, *Decisions of McNamara*, quoting McNamara, p. 69.

[17] The Department of Defense's opposition to increasing conventional weapons is a theme of FRUS 1961–63, vol. 8, *National Security Policy*, pp. 61–63, 80, 191, 194n, 209f., 219, 221, 448ff., as well as of Frank Gavin, "The Myth of Flexible Response: United States Strategy in Europe during the 1960s," *International History Review* 23 (2001): 847–75.

ways trickily connected to their former military bosses. Now, the airmen believed that civilian authority was stabbing them in the back when it took a less partisan view of defense needs. McNamara's heavy-handed leadership brought the military in line but added to the distrust. The services were paying for years of self-interested rivalry, and an unwillingness or inability to overcome individual stances to obtain a broad view of their nation's security. The strategists who had been in the pay of the air force for years brusquely reorganized the operation of the services. In the early 1960s a group the air force especially had come to dislike imposed civilian "rationality," although the soldiers slowly imbibed the cutting-edge management techniques.[18] As one historian-observer wrote, RAND communicated "a widespread appreciation" of its style in the air force—but not to reach impartial conclusions. Rather, competing service staffs summoned rosters of doctorates to combat proposals they did not like. In "the battle of the doctors," opposing Ph.D.s supplied suppressing fire for their side of an issue.[19] At the same time, although the military did not surmount the prejudices of its individual fiefdoms, it did come together in hatred of a common academic opponent and put its requests in the language of strategic science. The leadership of the Department of Defense accomplished the impossible with the generals and admirals. It gave them more money but also increased their anger at nonuniformed officialdom.

"On balance," one observer wrote, "the principles of civilian administration . . . were more firmly implanted . . . [and] the armed services were more of a unified institution."[20] Yet if civilian control and greater order are considered positive accomplishments, they must be weighed against the hostility between the soldiers and the politicians that would pervade the next decade.

The Republican stress on massive retaliation had reflected American nuclear superiority, and policymakers were a long time giving up the idea, even while the Soviet nuclear arsenal grew. Truman, Eisenhower, and Kennedy believed that they could only solve outstanding problems and negotiate with their adversaries from a position of strength. Thus, in the 1950s, disarmament could only become a real possibility after the United States had secured a commanding lead in weapons. But because the other side never allowed such a commanding lead to emerge, disarmament receded into the indefinite distance. By the early 1960s RAND-stimulated officials in the Kennedy administration initially reflected that by avoiding nuclear parity with the USSR, they might still find a smaller comparative advantage useful for *coercive diplomacy*, if not for massive retaliation. The basic idea was that the United States would dominate the

[18] See the primer edited by Tucker, *Modern Design*.

[19] I. B. Holley Jr., "The Evolution of Operations Research. . . ," in *Science, Technology, and War: The Proceedings of the Third Military History Symposium, United States Air Force Academy 8–9 May 1969*, ed. Monte D. Wright and Lawrence J. Paszek (Washington, D.C.: USGPO, 1969), p. 96.

[20] Trewhitt, *McNamara*, p. 281.

Soviet Union by contrasting the entire destruction of the USSR to the partial destruction of the United States. Kennedy came into office a bit infatuated with how international politics might benefit from skilled management and creative thinking about matters as far apart as guerrilla warfare and nuclear intimidation. The language of flexible response blended with gradual escalation. America could face crises with an array of options deployed to insure the least destructive military hardware for the job at hand but with the threat of using greater and different sorts of atomic force if necessary. At the same time and more important, strategic theories were put into play to legitimate political decisions that were made about pressing policy matters.[21]

Nuclear Strategy, Germany, and the USSR

The civilians in the 1960s did not just intend to make foreign policy rational but also to meet fresh challenges. While their most open criticism of Eisenhower about the missile gap turned out to be wrong, they did face an issue that defined their low estimate of the security policies of the late 1950s.

The central problem of Soviet-American relations was not a surprise attack but the Russian fear that the Germans would have an independent nuclear force and the related American inability to manage the Western proliferation of nuclear weapons. Two spheres of influence based on the distribution of troops had emerged at the end of World War II. Unable to decide cooperatively what to do about Germany, Russia and the United States had divided that nation along the lines of occupation. With the division of Germany went the division of Europe, an accomplished fact by the late 1940s and early 1950s. With good reason the Eisenhower administration assumed that the United States had settled the major issues with the Soviets. Eisenhower shored up established allies and avoided commitment to dubious and high-risk areas, such as those in Asia where, he thought, the Democrats had maladroitly mired themselves in Korea. Yet ideological hostility coalesced with the new and ever changing atomic technology to destabilize again and again the postwar claims of the Iron Curtain in Eastern Europe and the NATO alliance in Western Europe. The abundance of nuclear weapons combined with the growth of the power of West Germany meant that the Germans might obtain nonconventional armaments in the context of an intense fight about rival ways of life.

---

[21] On these issues still remarkable is Desmond Ball, *Politics and Force Levels: The Strategic Missile Program of the Kennedy Administration* (Berkeley and Los Angeles: University of California Press, 1980), esp. p. 211. On the ambiguity in the White House see FRUS, 1961–63, vol. 8, *National Security Policy*, pp. 1, 74, 82, 103, 196, 209.

For the Russians any permanent settlement had to deny atomic weapons to West Germany. A nuclear-armed Germany presented a threat to the USSR that invited confrontation with the United States and the likelihood of war.[22]

As I have suggested, while thermonuclear stockpiles got bigger and technology complicated methods of delivery, it was plausible if not compelling to argue that the second Eisenhower administration lost its way. The president stumbled in appraising the effect of his nuclear policies on the USSR and never grasped Russian anxiety. In the late 1950s, the ghastly complexities of the bomb and the arms race frustrated Eisenhower, who sought to get the United States out of Europe. Western Europe might achieve security, he thought, if his allies acted collectively and responsibly, without U.S. interference at all times. Their joint strength would match the Soviet Union, and the American occupation of Germany might end. The president worried that continued American domination of the alliance might make the Europeans incapable, and professed to trust them. Thus, Eisenhower considered nuclear arms for NATO and for West Germany. He was old-fashioned enough to believe that the United States might leave Europe and return to some pre–World War II state. At any rate, the emphasis on nuclear weapons made them a prestige item in Europe, and Ike's speculations about giving them to Germany increased Soviet suspicions about the commitment of the West to peaceful coexistence.[23]

The victors in World War II had divided the German capital of Berlin into occupation zones, like Germany itself. But located within the Soviet zone, western Berlin became a separate entity itself as the two Germanys became a factual reality. In 1948 a currency reform in the Western zones implying the formation of an independent West German state prompted the USSR to deny the Western powers access by ground to western Berlin. This first "Berlin Crisis" lasted for almost a year, while the Western powers supplied "West Berlin" using their formal air rights. Russia was warning the West of its fear of independent German power, but the Soviets were not strong enough to sustain their position, and the crisis petered out in 1949. The troubles of the Berlin airlift presaged a standard set of moves. To signal the Americans of its security interest, the USSR would threaten West Berlin when the United States seemed to grant Germany too much leeway, though the Russians never felt powerful enough to move much beyond bluff. The more they threatened West Berlin, the more it symbolized American commitment to the status quo. A free West Berlin was essential to make the world safe for America. Nikita Khrushchev, the new Soviet leader in the middle 1950s, recognized this fact, which he colorfully expressed. West Berlin, he said, was the testicles of the West; every

---

[22] On this view see Trachtenberg, *A Constructed Peace*, especially his summation, pp. 352–402.
[23] Trachtenberg, *A Constructed Peace*, pp. 193–200.

time he wanted a reaction, he gave them a yank. But he also said the city was a "thorn," a "cancer," a "bone in my throat."[24]

When West Germany joined NATO in 1955, the USSR constructed a counter-NATO, the Warsaw Pact. The missiles placed in West Germany at the end of 1957 threatened the Russians more, even if the rockets were under American purview, and even if the USSR had its own weapons to retaliate. Some West German politicians wanted nuclear weapons for their country, and the Americans bruited various plans for sharing, whose outcome was ambiguous. Secretary of State Dulles, for example, wrote in *Foreign Affairs* that tactical nuclear weapons could be made available to NATO.[25] In these speculations Dulles was not clear about whose finger would be on the trigger. The Russians at first intimated that diplomats should keep atomic weaponry out of central Europe. In October 1957 the Polish foreign minister, Adam Rapacki, presented a plan to the United Nations that would recognize two German states and create a nuclear-free zone. The United States rejected this and a revised "Rapacki plan" of a year later, in November 1958. The Russians expressed their frustration and hostility in the first act of another prolonged "crisis" over Berlin.[26] German weapons alarmed them.

Over the next two years Khrushchev threatened to give East Germany sovereignty (and thus power over all of Berlin) or to make West Berlin a "free city." The Communists hoped to extract some settlement that would preclude a West German nuclear force but were unforthcoming about what they wanted. The Soviets were too weak to push their grievances about the atomic status of Germany, and the Republican era of "crisis" faded way. Eisenhower had a nonconventional superiority that restrained the USSR, but he did not comprehend that a Germany with atomic rockets might convince the Russians to go to war despite the imbalance of forces. Although the fear of surprise attack that guided RAND did not blind Eisenhower, he was unable to focus on Russian dread of a contest with an atomic Germany.[27]

As the administration took up the idea of nuclear sharing in the late 1950s, it backed away from the most simplistic statements of massive retaliation. But the shift caused the civilian strategic community to have new doubts about Ike. Wohlstetter urged that European nuclear weapons would be vulnerable,

[24] Thompson to State Department, December 13, 1958, FRUS 1958–60, vol. 8, *Berlin Crisis 1958–1959*, pp. 149–51.

[25] The basic national security directives are reprinted in Trachtenberg, *Strategic Thought*, pt. 1. For the speculations about who would have access to atomic weaponry see pp. 169, 199, and 235–36, which cover the years 1957, 1958, and 1959 respectively. Dulles's statement is in "Challenge and Response in United States Policy," *Foreign Affairs* 36 (1957): 33.

[26] On the complexities and ambiguities of American policy see Jan Melissen, "Nuclearizing NATO, 1957–1959: The 'Anglo-Saxons,' Nuclear Sharing and the Fourth Country Problem," *Review of International Studies* 20 (1994): 253–75.

[27] See Suri, "America's Solution," 440–42.

and opposed their proliferation. He also worried about controlling a graded array of weaponry that at its upper limits would include atomic bombs and about placing such weapons in NATO.[28] The Republicans had not thought through this problem, and when Eisenhower walked into it, he stirred up concerns not only among the Russians, but also among American strategists. The problems confused the retiring president. Worried about the Defense Department's development of new weapons and increased costs, Eisenhower said that "if he were in charge he felt that he could take $5 billion out of the Defense budget."[29]

While Eisenhower had faltered over the German issue—and witnessed his authority in international politics erode in the face of allied squabbling and Soviet invective—Kennedy and his new secretary of state, Dean Rusk, saw the crux of European security. In charge of the negotiations with the Russians, Rusk repeatedly recalled that German nuclear weapons were for them a casus belli.[30] The Soviet intent was not always transparent, but the Kennedy administration understood that an independent West Germany preoccupied the USSR. From his inauguration Kennedy's priority was to limit the proliferation of nuclear weapons, and secure superpower control of them. But the problem was daunting, for both the Soviet Union and "nuclear plenty" tested the United States. The New Frontiersmen wanted to increase but also control defense spending. Conventionally anti-Communist, Kennedy still thought seriously about the human prospect that nuclear weapons threatened. In encouraging the Germans to look to their own defense and hinting that they would have the tools to do it, Ike had disturbed the Soviets. In seeking to reduce the risk of nuclear confrontation with the USSR, Kennedy had to persuade (or coerce) an ever-stronger Germany to continue to place its defense with the United States, when both Britain and France wanted more freedom from the restraining American hand. The USSR repeatedly damned proposals for a "multilateral force"—the MLF—designed to be less than nuclear sharing but still satisfactory to the Europeans.

Early in Kennedy's term in 1961 at a summit meeting in Vienna, Khrushchev threatened yet another "Berlin Crisis." The Russians would give East Germany its sovereignty and turn over West Berlin to their client state. Part of the problem was that Khrushchev took ill-thought-out actions. Eager to test the new administration, he also wanted to convince it of Soviet might. But the Soviets additionally responded to their fading prestige in East Germany. The East Germans were voting with their feet by emigrating to the West via Berlin, and later that year Khrushchev built a wall around West Berlin. Although this move

[28] Kaplan, *The Wizards of Armageddon*, pp. 202–3, 337–38.

[29] Memorandum, Eisenhower and National Security Advisor Gray, December 8, 1958, FRUS, 1958–60, vol. 3, *National Security Policy, Arms Control and Disarmament*, p. 170.

[30] Dean Rusk, *As I Saw It* (New York: Norton, 1990), pp. 265, 341.

measured Russian weakness, it further isolated West Berlin and heightened its value for the United States. Although there was not much for Kennedy to do, the lack of an American response may also have emboldened the Soviets.

WILLIAM KAUFMANN AND THE MANIPULATION OF RISK

To generate a policy, the administration turned to the latest wrinkle at RAND. In the middle and late 1950s a group of Wohlstetter's acolytes—Daniel Ellsberg, Alain Enthoven, Herman Kahn, and Harry Rowen—rose in prominence. Chief among them was William Kaufmann, who had had an uneventful time in World War II but later trained in international politics at Yale. He spent the first half of the 1950s as a Princeton professor of political science. At RAND, working with Wohlstetter, he criticized massive retaliation in a book he edited, *Military Policy and National Security* (1956). Drawing on the ideas of other RAND thinkers, Kaufmann urged *war-fighting*, an attempt to structure conflict in favor of the United States by maintaining a dominant military capability, no matter what the costs. In the contest with the USSR Americans no longer had the only atomic force, but if they had a significant edge, it could shape crises in favor of the United States. This strategy required massive conventional forces, as well as a nuclear arsenal. There might then be a punctuated or graded escalation into nuclear conflict. Vital for Kaufmann was a doctrine called *counter-force* or *no cities*.

Suppose the side with an offensive advantage targeted an enemy's weapons and not its industry or population. That side could use the advantage to mount a disabling and disarming first strike. Planners could imagine a numerically superior nuclear force eliminating the threat of retaliation by combining the preemptive destruction of most of the other side's forces with the hostage taking of its people. In such a scenario statesmen might initially only go after military installations and hold the cities of the opponent captive. Or perhaps they would pick off one city, signaling that devastation was avoidable if agreements could be reached. Counterforce outlined a situation conducive not to reaching a plateau between strategic arsenals, but to building to obtain a lead that many thought would be America's.

Critics attacked counterforce as exemplifying how the strategists foolishly thought they could tame nuclear war. But RAND was aware of the problems. Its thinkers had rather concluded that a nuclear cataclysm was unacceptable as the nation's only general war option. The no-cities concept was an alternative.[31]

Kaufmann left RAND on Kennedy's election. He spent half his time teaching at MIT, half consulting for the Pentagon. He wrote some of McNamara's

---

[31] See Marc Trachtenberg, "Strategic Thought in America, 1952–1966," in *History and Strategy* (Princeton: Princeton University Press, 1991), pp. 26, 32, 34–35.

speeches and then edited a "potboiler" in which they were quoted as testimony to the secretary's astute judgment, *The McNamara Strategy*.[32] Searching for a way to ensure that nuclear weapons did not get into German hands, McNamara, throughout 1962, fabricated a new United States policy that used Kaufmann's ideas as its rationale. Before the NATO ministers in Athens and then at the University of Michigan for an audience at home, McNamara argued that the Europeans, especially the Germans, had to expand their conventional forces, beefing them up to provide a first line of defense against the Soviets. At the same time the United States would centralize nuclear weapons in its hands.

An American trigger would insure that if war started, the West would be better able to manage what might occur, and a more unified strategy would be possible. Instead of an all-out nuclear war with many nations fighting on several fronts, a crisis that a single executive oversaw might eventuate in less damaging graduated escalation. By 1962 this notion and an emphasis on European conventional weaponry were standard in theoretical conversations. McNamara publicly baptized the notion as counterforce, and stressed that in ascending a ladder of escalation, centralization would best spare urban life in Europe.[33] This was Kaufmann's thinking, joining the gradation of war, selective urban targeting, and American control of nonconventional weapons.

McNamara had argued that everyone who had a defense role in Washington should, by constitutional requirement, pass a one-hundred-hour course in nuclear issues,[34] and in the first two years of the Kennedy administration the secretary's assistants advocated various types of controlled response. Yet what McNamara's immersion in these doctrines gave him was a fund of ideas that rationalized decisions made on other grounds—in this case the administration's desire to meet the acceptable demands of the Soviet Union to keep atomic bombs from the Germans.

To cap defense costs—another favorite theme—McNamara believed at the same time that downgrading conventional weaponry and maintaining a mere second-strike capacity were appropriate. This old-fashioned idea of deterrence demanded less of an arms race than war-fighting, which was indefinitely expensive and more dangerous. Promoting counterforce–no cities, McNamara simultaneously promoted its alternative, second-strike capability, which was eventually named *assured destruction*.[35]

---

[32] William W. Kaufmann, *The McNamara Strategy* (New York: Harper and Row, 1964). It is unclear if Kaufmann meant his work on this book to be taken ironically, or whether he was actually trying to disguise his role in the writing of the speeches that he cites as indicative of McNamara's intelligence. "Potboiler" is his own characterization, from Kaufmann to Brodie, February 17, 1964, K, Box 2, Brodie Papers, UCLA.

[33] McNamara's proposals—"Remarks at the NATO's Ministers Meeting," May 5, 1962; Michigan "Address," June 16, 1962; and New York "Address," November 18, 1963, are all reprinted in Trachtenberg, *Strategic Thought*, pt. 1. See esp. pp. 580–81, 586, 591–92, 600.

[34] Cited in Herken, *Counsels of War*, p. 304.

[35] Kaplan, *The Wizards of Armageddon*, pp. 300–319.

One of McNamara's assistants recalled that counterforce was never adopted. Speechifying about it had to do with "Pentagon politics."[36] By 1963 the administration had implicitly repudiated war-fighting. In July of that year, Kennedy himself asked McNamara and Bundy what had happened to the McNamara doctrine of counterforce propounded the year before, but then the president recalled it as a legitimating device they no longer needed. Counterforce–no cities, said Bundy, "was only good for about a year." McNamara continued: "we're running out of them [theories needed to justify policy], Mr. President."[37] Years later in one of his most astute essays Wohlstetter himself noted that in respect to nuclear weapons official "doctrines" and "operational policies" often diverged. He lamented that during McNamara's tenure, particularly, the secretary allowed politics to debase a strategy that could have been more discriminating.[38] Wohlstetter rightly suggested that the problems of nuclear weapons were of especial moral and intellectual difficulty, and that they merited adherence to the most careful thinking. For Kennedy, McNamara, and Bundy to joke about strategic theories was in some ways grotesque. Yet Wohlstetter was minimally aware of what a crude tool politics was.

In 1962 the administration had employed the ideas of the academic strategists like Wohlstetter and Kaufmann to justify the denial of nuclear weapons to the Germans. This policy did not change in 1963. What led the Americans to abandon the rationale?

---

[36] Adam Yarmolinsky to Richard Smoke, February 4, 1971, Institute of Politics, Box 116, Yarmolinsky Papers, JFK Library.

[37] For this conversation and its interpretation see Trachtenberg, *A Constructed Peace*, p. 319n. Assured destruction itself was inconsistent with the basic plan for general war, which McNamara did not revise. See Trachtenberg, *History and Strategy*, p. 249 n. 37.

[38] Wohlstetter, "Bishops, Statesmen, and Other Strategists on the Bombing of Innocents," *Commentary*, June 1983, esp. pp. 25–26.

CHAPTER 6

Cuba and Nassau, 1962

TWO EVENTS OF 1962 illuminated U.S. foreign policy and how experts associated with the Kennedy administration conceived it. The missile crisis of October pitted the Americans against the Soviet Union when it attempted to install
nuclear-tipped missiles in Cuba and brought the world close to atomic war. At
the end of that year a public rupture occurred between England and the United
States over American cancellation of a joint rocket program, "Skybolt." The
United States then patched matters up at a 1962 Christmas conference held
at Nassau in the British West Indies. The missile crisis became a sustaining
intellectual bone of civilian strategists. All pointed to it as a "classic" success
story, and Graham Allison, a student of Richard Neustadt's, brought the interest
to a high point in his book of 1971, *The Essence of Decision*.[1] The lesser
but still wrenching trials of the Skybolt missile prompted another publication.
Kennedy agreed to Neustadt's offer to examine what had gone wrong in the
diplomacy surrounding Skybolt,[2] and Neustadt delivered a report, "Skybolt
and Nassau," to the president in November 1963, a little less than a year after
the original fracas. In those circles in which Washington politicians overlapped
with political thinkers, this piece of writing came to have greater importance
than the event it was about. The conflict over Skybolt was minor, but the report
exemplified what knowledge could add to public life.

NUCLEAR WEAPONS AND THE GERMAN PROBLEM

Soviet-American dilemmas in the late 1950s and early 1960s revolved around
the Russian fear that the Germans would acquire an independent atomic force
and the related American inability to control the proliferation of nuclear weapons in the West.[3]

The Soviet triumphs of the late 1950s surrounding the launching of *Sputnik*
gave credence to Soviet leader Nikita Khrushchev's bragging about USSR
rockets, and the "missile gap" for a time convinced Democrats that the West
was in arrears. After the Kennedy administration came to power and recog-

[1] *The Essence of Decision: Explaining the Cuban Missile Crisis* (Boston: Little, Brown, 1971).
[2] Neustadt to Bundy, February 25, 1963, White House, General, Box 18, Neustadt Papers,
JFK Library.
[3] On this view see Trachtenberg, *A Constructed Peace*.

nized American superiority, it reassured the electorate. In October 1961 it went further when Deputy Secretary of Defense Roswell Gilpatric spoke to inform the Soviet Union that an American second strike would be more devastating than a USSR first strike. Gilpatric may have intended to suggest that Russian belligerence served no useful purpose, but the Soviets might also have taken the speech as a warning. In any event, the facts reminded the Russians of their strategic deficit.

To demonstrate to the West that the Soviets would stand firm, the Russians had pressured West Berlin in the 1940s and 1950s, and they did so again after Kennedy took office. This was in many ways irresponsible of Khrushchev and attributable in part to an antagonistic makeup. But the United States wanted a strong West Germany and did not appreciate how worried the Soviets were about such strength. The Americans also knew that West Berlin was itself trivial, but it accrued importance because it was the exposed point in the armor of the West. When the Russians menaced West Berlin, its status rose. Berlin symbolized the tensions of nuclear diplomacy. To show fortitude Americans must consider its defense. But would the United States fight a general war over this city, when it was not clear that Soviet assertiveness was a prelude to an invasion of Western Europe? But why would the Russians contest West Berlin except as a preliminary to something else, or as part of a long-term plan to erode the Western alliance? Should not the United States remove the cause of Soviet unease, the possibility of Germany getting nuclear weapons? Should the USSR risk atomic confrontation over this possibility?

Throughout 1962 the Kennedy administration raced against time, struggling to persuade the Europeans, including the Germans, to downgrade their reliance on nuclear weapons. American nuclear superiority had always limited the Soviet response to growing German power. What would happen when Russian rockets could challenge the United States in central Europe? That year the Americans worried that the near future held a crucial face-off over Berlin, and as Secretary of State Rusk negotiated with the USSR, he heard repeated complaints about "the number one problem" of a nuclear Germany.[4]

CUBA

As many historians have noted, in the late 1950s and early 1960s the triumph of revolution in Cuba under the leadership of Fidel Castro obsessed Washington. In early 1961, the United States failed to overthrow him in an invasion by Cubans that it sponsored at the Bay of Pigs. Half listening to vague CIA plans, Kennedy decided at a critical moment not to escalate and provide air protection

---

[4] Rusk-Dobrynin Conversation, August 8, 1962, FRUS 1961–63, vol. 7, *Arms Control and Disarmament*, pp. 544, 546.

for the American-subsidized rebels. The failure embarrassed the administration, enraged the country even more about the regime on its doorstep, and led the Cuban regime to expect another attack. By 1962, the United States found Castro an outspoken Russian ally and had various plans to overthrow him, which the USSR wished to counter. Although outmoded and scheduled for replacement by the Polaris missiles launched from submarines, American missiles in Italy and Turkey were trained on the USSR. Why should the Soviets refrain from using the territories of their allies as missile bases? By the spring and summer of 1962 Khrushchev put into motion a plan to base rockets armed with nuclear weapons in Cuba.

Soviet motivations were complex, but the culmination of the Berlin emergencies occurred in the Caribbean.[5] Perhaps most simply, the Russians were set on trouble until the United States had resolved the German problem in favor of the Soviets. Many commentators have argued that Khrushchev thought Kennedy a weak and untried young man whom he could bully. The Bay of Pigs told the Russian leader that Kennedy was indecisive, and then a few months later, after years of blustering to no effect about Germany and Berlin, the Soviets built the wall and the Americans did not respond, although there was little to be done. Khrushchev was perhaps encouraged to be more assertive.

Partly, the Russians wanted what they later said they wanted in Cuba—to force an American pledge to forswear invasion of the island. Khrushchev may also have hoped to trade the missiles in Cuba for something in Germany or something related to West Berlin. Khrushchev wished Kennedy to be aware of what it was like to have a dangerous ally of one of the two superpowers—such as the Russians considered the West Germans and the Americans the Cubans—close to having control over atomic bombs. The United States contemplated giving West Germany nuclear weapons, the Russian leader seemed to say; this frightened the Soviets. Well, how would the Americans feel if the USSR put the future of West Berlin in the hands of the East Germans, or gave nuclear weapons to the Cubans? Khrushchev told the story of the man who had to live with a goat: he did not like it but got used to the smell. American missiles and West Berlin were Khrushchev's goats. Russian missiles in Cuba were to be America's.[6] Yet a final aspect of Khrushchev's psychology may have been that he felt desperate, especially after Gilpatric's speech rubbed the inferiority of the Soviets in their leaders' faces. The "correlation of forces," as communists liked to say, favored the West, and would become irrevocable if

---

[5] A good treatment is Robert Weisbrot, *Maximum Danger: Kennedy, the Missiles, and the Crisis of American Confidence* (Chicago: Ivan R. Dee, 2001).

[6] The most comprehensive discussion of this dimension of the missile crisis is in Philip Nash, *The Other Missiles of October: Eisenhower, Kennedy, and the Jupiters, 1957–1963* (Chapel Hill: University of North Carolina Press, 1997).

West Germany obtained nuclear weapons. To put missiles in Cuba moved to a more equal correlation.

After American statesmen discovered the missile construction in October 1962, they puzzled over why the Russians had acted so dangerously. But they consistently assumed that the Soviets were maneuvering over Germany, and constantly took Berlin into account in their deliberations. An executive committee—the Ex Comm—that Kennedy had advising him quickly decided that the Soviets would have to do away with the missiles and could only get a minimal quid pro quo for retreating. This fundamental idea of achieving a status quo ante bellum persisted through the American debates. The United States must get the Russians to back down, or else. Indeed, Khrushchev had been counseled that a Soviet move over Cuba would provoke a political firestorm in the United States, which felt a presumptive right to dictate political arrangements in Cuba. The mentality of the Americans was not much different than it had been during the Spanish-American War of 1898. The face Kennedy put upon the American intervention in the defense arrangements of the two states concerned the "deliberately provocative and unjustified change in the status quo." The president did not want nuclear war, and a major theme of the deliberations was how he could reach his goal without a fight, but the documents suggest that an atomic exchange was likely if it were the only way to force the Russians out of Cuba.

The Americans also determined to justify morally a position based on a calculation of the Soviet assault on the balance of power. In terms of reasons of state and realpolitik, the Americans may have had good reason to react to the Soviet move. American prestige was at stake. Yet Kennedy and his advisors cogitated over how to explain the issue in legal and ethical terms. Kennedy's speech to the American people said that "our goal is not the victory of might, but the vindication of right." In all events the Ex Comm worked out how to dilute for the public what Cuba was about—force majeure.

In their conversations the Ex Comm essayed a number of responses to the Russians, each of which was to result in the dismantling of the missiles: negotiations, various sorts of naval "quarantines" of Cuba that would selectively challenge ships taking materiel to the island, a stricter "blockade," a limited air raid—a "surgical strike"—against the missile installations, a more sustained air attack to be followed by invasion of the island, and finally such an attack with a presumption that it would lead to nuclear war. Kennedy again and again expressed his preference for doing what was least provocative. He rejected negotiations only because he thought they would be ineffective, and in his first attempt to coerce the Russians, the president agreed on a loose naval embargo that became more liberal in its enforcement and that many were uncertain would work. Hoping that he could persuade the USSR to bow out, Kennedy also offered assurances that the United States would not invade the island. Then he pledged a further deal, unknown to many members of the Ex

Comm, which remained undisclosed. Through his brother, Attorney General Robert Kennedy, he told the USSR that the United States would later remove the Turkish rockets if the Russians dismantled the Cuban ones. But the arrangement must remain secret and could not look like a trade, nor be revealed as one. Finally, he prepared the most secret plan, which Dean Rusk was to effect. The United States would respond positively to a UN overture to trade Cuban and Turkish missiles.[7]

The last option proved unnecessary, and many commentators have credited Robert Kennedy's negotiations with ending the confrontation. But we now know that Khrushchev, with his missile deficit and perhaps fearing that the president could not control U.S. "hawks," had decided to dismantle the rockets before he got the news of Robert Kennedy's secret proposal.[8] The conclusion of the crisis on the Russian side depended on U.S. nuclear superiority. On the American side, Kennedy's decision to oblige the Russians to remove the missiles yielded an unnecessary concession because he shrank from a fateful atomic exchange. The Russians reckoned that they would be destroyed in a nuclear battle, while the United States would minimally suffer. The Russians had bluffed, and the atomic edge of the United States prevailed. Soviet inferiority had prompted the crisis, and determined its outcome.

For both the president and the men around him, one commentator has argued, the two-week period was life altering.[9] The outcome buoyed up Kennedy's advisors. In their view the USSR had folded immediately—in part because of their leadership. Kennedy, on the contrary, was sobered up. The world had come close to nuclear war, and he felt the near miss more than his Ex Comm. Kennedy stepped up his efforts to get at the root of the problem, to forbid nuclear weapons to the Germans. And he did change tactics. The imbroglio over the Skybolt missile, occurring within weeks of Cuba, at least illustrated and perhaps defined this shift.

Skybolt

In the early 1960s the new administration had tried to treat all the European allies equally and, thus, to pressure them all to let the United States control nuclear weapons. Kennedy reversed Eisenhower's impulse to share atomic power, and McNamara introduced counterforce in order to place all nonconventional weapons in American hands. In 1962, however, one specific arrange-

---

[7] See James G. Blight and David A. Welch, *On the Brink: Americans and Soviets Reexamine the Cuban Missile Crisis* (New York: Hill and Wang, 1989), pp. 113ff., 333 n. 5; and Rusk, *As I Saw It*, pp. 240–41.

[8] See the discussion in May and Zelikow, *The Kennedy Tapes*, pp. 684, 689–90, 694, 699.

[9] James G. Blight, *The Shattered Crystal Ball: Fear and Learning in the Cuban Missile Crisis* (Savage, Md.: Rowman and Littlefield, 1990), esp. p. 145.

ment the Republicans had initiated was still hanging. Ike had hesitatingly gone a little way to cooperate with the English on joint production of a missile launched from aircraft. The new Democratic policy would frustrate this policy because the weapon would continue to provide Britain with an independent nuclear force. Then, the missile crisis prompted urgent recalculation over Skybolt and persuaded Kennedy that he need not bludgeon the other allies and thus sidetrack the British atomic deterrent. The United States might forbid the Germans an executive role in atomic diplomacy without making the other Europeans yield roles that they already had. It was more important to deny the Germans nuclear arms than to preserve their dignity by limiting the nuclear capability of other Europeans. West Germany's only option would be to go along with the American lead. This thinking was inconsistent with the "Europeanist" views of some officials in the State Department who worked for a policy that would treat the Europeans equally and unify their defense, and Dean Rusk did not lead his people to the new purpose. Yet Kennedy, Bundy, and McNamara adumbrated the goal, and Rusk did not resist the direction, although some of his colleagues did.

Skybolt had technical and financial problems that might close off its development, and the Americans could have used the end of the program to discourage English nuclear weapons in the future. But Kennedy was ready to allow the English a desirable alternative—the submarine-launched Polaris missiles. The English would acquire Polaris if they pushed for it, and the negotiations took place under the aegis of the Defense Department so that Rusk would not have to take the heat from his underlings. Through a series of botched public-relations moves, however, the English did not pick up the Kennedy administration's (admittedly obscure) signals in November 1962. McNamara, moreover, was not fully aware of what he was conceding to the English. The Europeanists in the State Department abetted the confusion by pressing standard treatment on the European allies, and insisting on no replacement for Skybolt. The Americans discredited Skybolt, but did not hint at the benefits of Polaris. For internal political reasons the English prime minister, Harold Macmillan, now needed not just the alternative to Skybolt but a victory over the Americans, who were thought in England to have trampled the rights of their oldest ally.

After an initial public dispute over Skybolt, the Americans were not permitted simply to replace it with Polaris. Or, rather, they went along with a complicated English performance in which Macmillan extracted a commitment to Polaris from Kennedy. This drama took place at a heads-of-state conference in Nassau in the Bahamas in December 1962.[10]

[10] My account is based on Skybolt-Memcoms in Box 20A of the Neustadt Papers, especially, that of Neustadt-McNamara, May 30, 1963, JFK Library; and Adam Yarmolinsky, Oral History, 1964, pp. 60–66, JFK Library.

In the aftermath of this embarrassment, events moved to give Kennedy something of a resolution to the German issue and at least a better grip on the distribution of nuclear weapons. Disturbed by the linked problems of a nuclear Germany and an unrestrained arms race, the president pressed for an agreement with the Russians. Now led by Kennedy favorite, Averell Harriman, and not Secretary of State Rusk, diplomats negotiated the nuclear Test Ban Treaty of August 1963. This agreement brought into being the structures that would regulate the production and control of nuclear weapons that the two states could not otherwise prohibit or limit. The treaty ordered an arms race that neither side could end but also finished the effort to shape a common European policy on nonconventional armaments. The Russians made their view "well known," that an "indispensable element" of the treaty was to deny the Germans a nuclear force.[11] The Germans unhappily signed this international obligation, which effectively required them to renounce an atomic capability. Thus was brought to fruition the "NATO solution" that completed the division of Europe after World War II. Germany was kept down—it would not have nuclear bombs. The United States stayed in—American troops would remain in Europe and Germany to protect the Germans and the Russians from one another. And the USSR was kept out—the Russians would accept the status quo that left West Berlin "an island of freedom" behind their lines in Eastern Europe.[12]

The notion of a European multilateral force that would give the Germans a piece of an integrated nuclear capability did not immediately die, however. Moreover, concerns over the balance of payments in the United States—which could be assuaged by a reduction in the American forces stationed in Germany—also assured that the NATO solution was not immediate or perfect. Nonetheless, the missile crisis, Skybolt, and the Test Ban Treaty were jointly a climacteric of the Cold War.

The summer of 1963 was a banner year for Kennedy as a democratic statesman. At the same time as he committed the United States to civil rights before worldwide television audiences in June, he delivered an extraordinary speech at American University. He announced negotiations over the treaty and enunciated a version of détente with the Soviet Union that impressed even Khrushchev.[13] Two weeks later Kennedy made a speech in West Berlin, goading the USSR—"we don't need a wall to keep our people in." He committed the United States in the most outrageous way to the defense of West Berlin—"Ich bin ein Berliner." Six weeks later in exchange for this rhetorical bombast, West Germany gave up nuclear weapons. The country relinquished the

---

[11] Aide Memoire, January 10, 1963, Soviet Government views, no. 159, FRUS 1961–63, vols. 7, 8, 9, *Arms Control, National Security Policy, Foreign Economic Policy*, Microfiche Supplement.

[12] See Geir Lundestad, *The United States and Western Europe since 1945* (Oxford: Oxford University Press, 2003), pp. 7–8, 21 n. 26.

[13] Harriman-Khrushchev Conversation, July 27, 1963, FRUS 1961–63, vol. 7, *Arms Control and Disarmament*, p. 862.

only items that would make it necessary for Kennedy to honor his pledge to fight for Berlin.

THE SCHOLARS' CUBA

How did the scholars of strategic studies look at Cuba and Nassau? How did these events contribute to the analyses that defense intellectuals were developing?

Cuba confirmed the scholars' view that they should explore international politics as segmented events that experts might understand and help to manage. The missile crisis also corroborated the belief that surprise and stealth would bring danger to the United States,[14] reinforcing the tendency not to place foreign policy in historical time. The crisis additionally became an exemplar of good decision-making. In the thrill of victory after the crisis, the participants in postmortems and in their later recollections placed a reasoned gloss on events that scholars absorbed. For Rusk, McNamara, and Bundy, the outcome demonstrated the benign effects on politics of their intelligence and knowledge. Emblematic here was Arthur Schlesinger Jr.'s, account in *A Thousand Days: JFK in the White House* (1965). A Harvard historian on the president's staff, Schlesinger wrote his eloquent and perceptive history after Kennedy's assassination. According to him the missile crisis combined "toughness and restraint, . . . will, nerve, and wisdom, so brilliantly controlled, so matchlessly calibrated . . . [that it] dazzled the world."[15] Testifying to McNamara's leadership, William Kaufmann, McNamara's assistant and speechwriter, claimed that, for the secretary of defense, Cuba was the *experimentum cruces*—the definitive experiment—for avoiding nuclear war and using multiple options.[16] This assessment continued, even as more documents were published. When a full set of Ex Comm transcripts became available in 1997, Neustadt wrote, "Read this and mourn his [Kennedy's] loss."[17] The missile crisis crystallized thought about politics implicit in RAND thinking—the rational-actor model of decision making, which the Ex Comm typified. Good decisions came about when intelligent leaders realized national purposes through the ideas scholar-advisors supplied.

But theory and pride in the proximity of scholars to power overwhelmed evidence. The Ex Comm meetings were extraordinary, but what one might expect when a group of individuals was forced to consider their role in the destruction of the planet. The talk was confused, halting, sometimes unintelli-

---

[14] Wohlstetter, "Cuba and Pearl Harbor."

[15] Schlesinger, *One Thousand Days* (Boston: Houghton, Mifflin, 1965), p. 841.

[16] Kaufmann, *The McNamara Strategy*, pp. 274, 294.

[17] May and Zelikow, *The Kennedy Tapes*, back cover blurb.

gible, at times not rational. The meetings displayed half-formulated ideas, fragmented thoughts, mutual fears, and bravado. A harsh observer, Dean Acheson, said the discussions were "repetitive, leaderless, and a waste of time," undertaken by men "many of whom had little knowledge in the military or diplomatic field."[18] The most authoritative student of the Ex Comm meetings has written that the sessions had "rambling exchanges," "overlapping comments, conversational dead ends and a great deal of repetition."[19]

One can extract from the transcripts an emerging caution about what the disputants might get into and a majority view that they should threaten retaliation with as much watchfulness as possible. Nonetheless, the crisis was seemingly resolved in a way that much of the Ex Comm had deprecated. Many thought no trade of any kind should occur, but Kennedy left the dissenters out of his ruminations and tried to end the impasse by a secret deal to exchange Turkish missiles for Soviet dismantling in Cuba.[20] And then this arrangement, historians have suggested, proved unnecessary when the USSR gave up the game simply because it felt itself outgunned.

It is difficult to see why students of strategy found a textbook example of rationality in this messy story. What went on was not crazy, or even irrational, but it bore little resemblance to the "rationality" that many scholars had been debating for fifteen years. They or people close to them, however, had weathered this crisis, and its outcome had satisfied the United States. The scholars had little trouble reconstructing the decisions as rational. It was not so much a triumph of their theories over less than recalcitrant evidence as the victory of a desire to believe what they wanted about a past event whose meaning in the West they controlled.[21]

RAND'S CUBA

Cuba exemplified two of RAND's theories. First, many saw in the deliberations a virtuous application of flexible response and graduated escalation. The decisions both followed from and confirmed these theories. The Ex Comm had started with a minimal rejoinder, and the threat implicit in the ability to continue induced the Kremlin to give way. There was some truth in this thought.[22]

---

[18] Dean Acheson, "Dean Acheson's Version of Robert Kennedy's Version of the Cuban Missile Affair," *Esquire*, February 1969, pp. 77, 46.

[19] Sheldon M. Stern, *Averting the Final Failure: John F. Kennedy and the Secret Cuban Missile Crisis Meetings* (Stanford: Stanford University Press, 2003), p. xv.

[20] May and Zelikow, *The Kennedy Tapes*, especially the introduction, pp. 1–43.

[21] Richard M. Pious, in "The Cuban Missile Crisis and the Limits of Crisis Management," *Political Science Quarterly* 116 (2001): 31–105, some forty years later, began the reevaluation of the event for those in strategic studies.

[22] See Bernard Brodie's discussion in "What Price Conventional Capabilities in Europe?" *The Reporter*, May 23, 1963, p. 32.

Conceding the rough way that experience might bear out a set of ideas, one could see that the Americans had constructed a "ladder of escalation" and climbed it slowly in the hope that the USSR might surrender at an acceptable rung. Nonetheless, one must factor into the analysis that Kennedy's secret offer had nothing to do with graduated escalation. The principal participant had behaved in a way for which the supposition did not account.

The second theory that Cuba validated was a variant of the first and concerned strategic superiority and the management of risk that had received its fullest exposition in Kaufmann's ideas of war-fighting and counterforce—no cities. A superior power could manipulate and exploit its superiority in favor of itself, even though the superiority was far from absolute. The crisis showed that Americans could monitor the drift to war, and that the adroit threat of force could favorably resolve a standoff. Strategic ascendancy convinced the enemy to yield before the United States suffered unacceptable damage. The United States had crafted a response to the Russians that exhibited ideas of deterrence that many of the scholarly strategists had promoted.[23] Indeed, if the historian can trust their observations after the fact, the civilian theorists had indeed grasped an important truth. From the start of the crisis, those who were in academic offices had asserted that the USSR, possessing a modicum of rationality, would throw down its hand.

Yet their ruminations did not capture the psychological reality of the drama. One astonished military observer at a debriefing after Cuba was "amazed," "given the general intellectual brilliance of this group," that it lacked an understanding of the use of force in international politics.[24] The theorists later expressed surprise that the Ex Comm's meetings had been a draining ordeal. Khrushchev had no other option but to fold. His decision would be made, they predicted, in accord with deterrence theory, and it was, although no one thought the outcome would be "Red surrendering following our first move."[25] At the same time, as many of the Ex Comm members testified, their two weeks of fevered deliberations did not evince the confidence of their superiority that the RAND strategists postulated. Khrushchev had caved in before the Turkish deal. Kennedy made it when he did not have to.[26] The evidence suggests that while Kennedy had been enamored of counterforce ideas when he came into office, experience cured him of the infatuation—one could not manipulate nu-

---

[23] See Thomas Schelling, *Arms and Influence* (New Haven: Yale University Press, 1966), pp. 96–97. Schelling's ideas are further explored in chapter 7.

[24] Lawrence Legere Memo of White House Staff Meeting, October 31, 1963, FRUS 1961–63, vol. 11, *Cuban Missile Crisis and Aftermath*, p. 320.

[25] See, for example, Blight and Welch, *On the Brink*, pp. 153, 170, 200ff. The quotation is taken from Novick to Collbohn, March 10, 1964, Rand Inter Office Memos, Box 2, Bernard Brodie Papers, UCLA.

[26] For discussion and citation, see Blight, *The Shattered Crystal Ball*, p. 158; Blight and Welch, *On the Brink*, pp. 153, 170, 200ff.

clear war.[27] In some ways the crisis corroborated counterforce ideas. Yet in its aftermath the president rejected them as too scary.

An important comment must conclude this discussion. One might rightly argue that the grasp of psychological reality was tangential. A theory was confirmed because behavior that it predicted occurred. But social scientists conceived of their work as enabling human beings, on the basis of social knowledge, to alter their behavior in light of what they knew. The basic idea was to use knowledge to change the behavior of the actors involved in socio-logical generalizations. If a generalization were confirmed, using it in the fu-ture would generate an altered generalization. People acting with knowledge of its truth in the past would act differently and thus require the social scientist to reevaluate the causal elements at work.

For Cuba, the strategists had a model that construed diplomatic activity as a form of bargaining, and they interpreted behavior in such circumstances as the American exploitation of risk. They produced a related model insisting that American diplomats had (successfully) acted in terms of graduated escalation. It could indeed be persuasively if not compellingly argued that American be-havior in the missile crisis verified the models. But what happened if Kennedy and members of the Ex Comm grasped the "truth" of bargaining theories dis-played during the crisis? Then, rational actors might behave in the future on their advanced sense of what was involved in a strategic bargain. They might act differently and do a different job in new circumstances that required negoti-ation and graduated deterrence.[28] The missile crisis may have led a restrained Kennedy to eschew coercive diplomacy, even though he had flourished at it. But the crisis may have empowered his advisors in respect to the stage-man-agement of risk.

NEUSTADT ON CUBA

Neustadt and his colleagues launched the most influential examination of the October discussions. They mined Kennedy's decision to find structures that other leaders might use. Cuba set the standard for good decision-making. But

[27] In July 1961 McGeorge Bundy asserted that Kennedy had been impressed with counterforce reasoning about nuclear war (see FRUS, 1961–62, vol. 14, *Berlin Crisis*, pp. 56n, 170–72); and many documents on national security issues from 1961 and 1962 suggest this interest (see FRUS, 1961–63, vol. 8, *National Security Policy*, pp. 1, 74, 82, 103, 196, 209). Blight's work in *The Shattered Crystal Ball* indicates that the experience of Cuba altered the president's views, and thereafter counterforce does, indeed, cease to be an issue. Compare also the remarks of McNamara in James G. Blight, David A. Welch, and Bruce J. Allyn, *Cuba on the Brink: Castro, the Missile Crisis, and the Soviet Collapse* (New York: Pantheon, 1993), pp. 40, 137.

[28] For an example see Wohlstetter, "Cuba and Pearl Harbor," p. 707.

the analysis went aground on the series of problems that we began to examine in chapter 4.

To argue that decision making was good, the analyst must link the desirable outcome to effects of the decision and argue that some effects were better than others. The actions of the Americans had more attractive consequences than other things they could have done. Neustadt and his colleagues joined consequences to decisions but also prized one set of consequences more than another. By threatening the Russians with a blockade, rather than with an air strike against Cuba, for example, Kennedy gave both sides time to contemplate the risks they were running and allowed them to escape war. Had the Americans struck Cuba by air, the Russians would have had no alternative but to launch some sort of attack against the United States. That sort of decision would have had less desirable consequences. That is, to treat decisions of policymakers as causal elements entailed "counterfactual" reasoning.

In the 1950s explicit counterfactual examination was an accepted academic enterprise, although not among students of strategy.[29] Later they undertook it for its independent interest as a thought experiment, and such reasoning has provoked a frustrated counterargument that scholars must first explore what actually happened—what caused what—and not speculate about what might have happened. More important, the popularity of the enterprise has obscured a critical truth. Ascriptions of causality imply the justifiability of some counterfactuals and the falsity of others. Causal reasoning and counterfactual reasoning cannot be separated. If historians are interested in the causes of what happened, they must be concerned with speculation about what might have happened. If the blockade allowed the Russians and the Americans to circumvent a nuclear exchange, then, for example, without an air strike, the Soviets had insufficient pretext themselves to launch an attack; an air strike would have instigated a war. It is, however, a minor issue to convince scholars that causal and counterfactual analyses are logically involved. The real problem, as anyone who has examined counterfactuals can testify, is the grave difficulty involved in warranting any historical counterfactual against another.[30] That is, scholars attribute causality in explaining historical events, but have little reason to do so, for they rarely can give a convincing counterfactual analysis. Scholars

[29] The work of Nelson Goodman in *Fact, Fiction, and Forecast* (Cambridge: Harvard University Press, 1955) is foundational. Goodman had Harvard connections and indeed taught there from the mid-1960s, but political scientists and policy-minded historians were not aware of his work as a philosopher.

[30] For a recent survey see Philip E. Tetlock and Aaron Belkin, eds., *Counterfactual Thought Experiments in World Politics: Logical, Methodological, and Psychological Perspectives* (Princeton: Princeton University Press, 1996). Tetlock has produced several more recent pieces, but none of them is sensitive to the fact that counterfactuals of the sort under scrutiny are contested. From the other side, see Jonathan Bennett, *A Philosophical Guide to Conditionals* (Oxford: Oxford University Press, 2003), esp. pp. 222–24, 246–51, 302–21.

cannot demonstrate that had Kennedy behaved differently, the results would have been better or worse or different from what resulted when he acted as he did. For this reason history as a form of knowledge is interpretative—meaning contestable—and is epistemologically unable credibly to come up with conclusions that establish causality.

One might argue that had Kennedy reasoned with the hawks, a nuclear war might have broken out, but the United States would have triumphed, and the destruction of the USSR in 1962 might have spared the world twenty-five more years of tyranny. Less chiliastically, one could argue that no specific warning compelled the Soviets to back down. The key American determination was to forbid the missile installation. Any real American threat would have sufficed. To look at Kennedy's lack of hawkishness with favor and to focus on the blockade teach us about the minds of the analysts but not those of the Russians.

Neustadt and his followers ignored this sort of counterexample that reflected the conceptual trouble involved in the scholars' attempt to comprehend historical analogies. Analogical reasoning is a special case of counterfactual analysis. During the crisis General Curtis LeMay told the president that forswearing an air strike to remove the missiles was "like" Chamberlain at Munich. To identify appropriate structural features of an event as evidence of bullying, let us say, implied that standing up to the bully would bring success. But we do not know what would have happened at Munich had Chamberlain been forceful. Similarly, to pigeonhole the attack on Korea as other than bullying meant that caution would have avoided disaster, though we do not know what would have happened in Korea had the Truman administration been less belligerent throughout 1950.

If an event possesses the appropriate structural features, they will credit relevant counterfactuals. For a bullying situation: had Chamberlain been firm at Munich, Hitler would have backed down. For a situation of complexity: had the United States proceeded more cautiously, Truman would have resolved the Korean War more expeditiously. But just as argument is interminable over whether an analogy is apt, so in history we cannot differentiate between counterfactuals that are acceptable and those that are not. Had the English faced down Hitler in 1938, he might have bided his time and become far stronger when he went to war later. Had Truman shown more restraint, the North Koreans might have overrun South Korea and Communist forces might next have looked to Japan. We do not have the resources to toss out (or to embrace) the counterfactuals that some policy scholars like, or to toss out (or embrace) others that they dislike.

In addition to assuming a causal analysis, Neustadt premised that some causal explanations resulted in consequences that were better than others. Kennedy's strategy avoided war, and that was good. It would be wrong to suppose that an air strike would have precluded war, or led to a conflict in which the

United States would have achieved an even greater victory than it did. Neustadt, however, did not have an independent standard of a good outcome.

Scholars wrote that Kennedy's decisions were successful because the participants so regarded them, and so did journalists. "Knowing mostly tales with less happy endings," Neustadt and those who studied the missile crisis with him were "not inclined to apply more rigid criteria" of what constituted a good decision. The consequences of Kennedy's decisions—withdrawal of the missiles and retreat from war—met an immediate need without overriding longer-run concerns. The decision making "appeared sound to most contemporaries and still appeared so in retrospect."[31]

Perhaps the decision making was successful and the consequences may have been better than those that could be associated with some other decisions. But Neustadt's examination did not make the case. When he suggested that the removal of the missiles and the aversion of war were attractive, Neustadt was thinking about the American participants, who were elated by the outcome, as were many Western journalists. But what about the Soviet participants, or the Cubans, or educated observers in Russia or Cuba? In Neustadt's view, the Western scholars on the left who reviled America's swagger were ignored. And so too were the Soviet commentators, disgusted that the Americans were arrogantly throwing their weight around. Should scholars have had some sort of a poll to see if a majority favored the Ex Com? And base their view of success on that poll?

Why an impartial observer would consider the removal of the missiles desirable was hard to say.[32] Might it not be argued that the crisis would not have spilled out of control in the first place had Kennedy not made an issue of two sovereign countries reaching agreement over nuclear weapons, as the United States and its allies had done with Italy and Turkey? Or could a scholar not say that the world might have been better off had circumstances forced the United States early on in the Cold War to accept some sort of parity in terms of vulnerability to nuclear war? Had Kennedy not acted and his party been defeated in the congressional election of 1962 and then again in the election of 1964, do we know that that would have been bad? Or could not the scholar argue that the air strike, which some of Kennedy's associates proposed, would have been a more effective response to Soviet recklessness? That it would have forced the USSR to back down without the Americans having to make a deal?

Perhaps a brief war, or even a nuclear exchange, might have restrained politicians around the world. The alternative to Kennedy's solution need not have

---

[31] Neustadt and May, *Thinking in Time*, p. 2. Their version of the missile crisis occurs on pp. 2ff.

[32] This is the reasoning of Richard K. Betts in *Nuclear Blackmail and Nuclear Balance* (Washington, D.C.: Brookings Institution, 1987), pp. 109–23, but see especially p. 113.

been cataclysmic. Suppose, for various reasons, that in 1945 the successful American test of an atomic device had been delayed for several weeks; that the Russians entered the Pacific war in August and brutally fought the Japanese on the Asian mainland; that the United States unleashed a series of horrific and unremitting conventional bombing attacks on Japan through September and October; and that the Japanese surrendered before an invasion. Then, in the aftermath of the defeat, commentators on World War II learn that the United States had been within weeks of using atomic weapons. Thank God, the consensus is, that nuclear bombs were not dropped: their use would have disastrously altered the postwar world and destroyed American credibility as a moral leader against the Soviets in the looming Cold War. Or perhaps, the argument would go: if only the United States would have used nuclear weapons to end the war, matters would have turned out better. The Russians would never have gotten a hold in China because the display of atomic weaponry would have cowed them. It is a speculative, if appealing, argument that shunning nuclear bombs in the missile crisis was a triumph.

We may put this kind of reasoning pointedly by comparing Cuba and Munich as LeMay did to Kennedy during the crisis. From Neustadt's perspective this false analogy was thoughtlessly oversimplified. Was Kennedy's decision making akin to Chamberlain's? Did it encourage the belligerence of his adversary? Would firmer leadership have resolved the issues between the United States and the Soviet Union more satisfactorily? Kennedy's actions were not an instant victory for the Russians, as some thought Chamberlain's were for the Germans (although many in 1938 congratulated Chamberlain for steering clear of war). The resolution of the crisis humiliated the Russians and may have encouraged them to spend more on the competition with the United States. Had Kennedy behaved more aggressively, the result might have been the destruction of the Soviet system before it had achieved equality with the United States.

Neustadt believed that the United States was better off not applying the Munich analogy. But his belief stemmed not from a grasp of causal connections, but from the sense of appropriate American behavior. The United States should not make a preemptive strike, nor should it display a mailed fist.

These thought experiments point to the problem that recurs in this scholarship. Political scientists might take a state of affairs they liked and assume that good decision-making produced it. They were then obligated to extrapolate from such decisions common factors that might be the core of rational decision-making. How did they grasp such factors? Neustadt emphasized proper communication, historical sensitivity, and the like. But he failed to show that these characteristics were any more part of his good decisions than they were of bad ones.

The best example is the oft-cited contrast between the bad decision to invade Cuba in 1961 and the good decision of October 1962, Cuba I versus Cuba II. According to the usual narrative, planning for the Bay of Pigs was flawed in the way that missile crisis decision-making was not. In the earlier crisis policymakers did not debate—an academic account argued that "groupthink" applied. Substantive deficiencies included ignorance of the history that had led to the covert operation to oust Castro. In addition, minimal understanding of the military dimension of the enterprise existed. There was little honest communication amongst relevant agencies, and opposed views were unexamined or dismissed.

But the facts do not sustain these comparisons, all detrimental to Cuba I. The planning for the Bay of Pigs may have been defective, but was it less rational than the planning over the Soviet missiles—two weeks of marathon talks by overtired and irritated officials? In each case policymakers worried about how it would look if the United States launched a surprise attack against a weaker opponent. In both 1961 and 1962 Kennedy overruled decisive action and emphasized graduated escalation. At the Bay of Pigs he wanted to use the least amount of force. Had he used more, he might have been successful. Had he used more in October 1962, are we certain that the decision would have been considered successful? Scholars faulted the military during the Bay of Pigs because it trimmed its advice to the president, but a year and a half later the military was barely consulted. The president additionally kept his final deliberations secret from everyone who could have disagreed. Was this not groupthink?[33]

Policy scientists did not appraise alternative interpretations of their stock decisions. Nor did they demonstrate that the causal connections among elements of the decisions that were good were as the investigators supposed them to be. Nor did they isolate the structural features necessary to effective decision-making. In understanding the missile crisis, the intellectual historian must conclude that the analysts of the 1960s lacked criteria for what constituted a desirable outcome, and they did not have the tools to distinguish a consequence that came about because policymakers intended it from one that came about through good fortune. Analysts *did* presume that American aims were essentially benign and had to conclude that what the United States accomplished was worth achieving. Though scholars, Neustadt and his colleagues were partisans. They could not see beyond the political culture they were investigating, or beyond the needs and interests of the decision making under study, and so did not press their exploration in an impartial or skeptical direction.

No treatment of the missile crisis warranted the view that doing the minimum was causally efficacious, or that the resolution based on the minimum was good. The reasoning exemplified the post hoc ergo propter hoc fallacy. Dean Acheson made this point, though not many listened. No one, he wrote,

---

[33] The standard work comparing the two cases is Irving L. Janis, *Victims of "Groupthink": A Psychological Study of Foreign Policy Decisions and Fiascoes* (Boston: Houghton Mifflin, 1972).

could show that astute and knowledgeable management contributed to the outcome; it was a matter of "plain dumb luck."[34]

THE SCHOLARS' NASSAU

Neustadt's report to Kennedy, "Skybolt and Nassau," served as a model of what the expert could teach the politician about failure, as opposed to success. Neustadt solicited an invitation to write the report despite the fact that its outcome signaled, for the administration, a positive turn in resolving Russian fears over Germany.[35] In his finished document Neustadt cited material indicating that Kennedy and his associates were aware of the relevance of German nuclear weapons to Skybolt. Neustadt also had access to the confidential documents and immediate recollections of the participants.[36] Yet while the meaning of this crisis was ambiguous, "Skybolt and Nassau" ignored policy and the shift in policy that the deal with Macmillan illustrated. The United States would not try to oust the British from the nuclear club, although Germany was surely not to be admitted into it. Neustadt repeatedly alluded to this aspect of McNamara's diplomacy, but did not see its relevance.[37] Germany did not figure in Neustadt's case study. He said this himself while writing the report: "this is not an inquiry into policy but rather into method."[38] "Skybolt and Nassau" talked about failed communications and bureaucratic mix-ups that occurred when underlings did not get the less-than-clear messages of their chiefs.

The Americans were not happy to replace Skybolt with Polaris, wrote Neustadt, and had they handled their dealings with the English more carefully, with due attention to the sensibilities of their ally, perhaps Skybolt could have been dumped without having to offer Polaris. But this was not vital, and after some embarrassment, Kennedy had made it up to Macmillan. At the last minute, the report concluded, when some minor damage had been done, Kennedy rescued matters by making concessions that preserved the Anglo-American alliance, more important than Polaris.

Neustadt suggested that Kennedy could rectify such problems by better management techniques, a more efficient executive system. There was, too, a touch of the courtier in Neustadt. JFK got the highest marks of American officials, and in saving the situation displayed Western decency.

[34] Acheson, "Dean Acheson's Version," p. 76.

[35] I have no evidence but it may be that Neustadt was asked to request to write a report that would show Rusk as an ineffective leader (as it did), and so give Kennedy ammunition to push or even dismiss the secretary.

[36] See, for example, Neustadt's memos in Box 28 of his papers at the JFK Library.

[37] Richard E. Neustadt, *Report to JFK: The Skybolt Crisis in Perspective* (Ithaca: Cornell University Press, 1999), pp. 36–37, 69, 70, 73, 76, 77, 98.

[38] Neustadt to Bruce, July 11, 1963, Country: Skybolt, Box 28 Neustadt Papers, JFK Library.

The report evidenced how the reasoning of *Presidential Power* had evolved. Skybolt showed that the United States would keep the German finger off the nuclear trigger without a further compromise of the nuclear capabilities of the other Western European allies. But Neustadt's outlook excluded from international politics any concern for understanding the conflicts that defined the Cold War. America's role was given, and American purposes were premises, or unquestioned outcomes of national political negotiation. This assumption carried forward the idea of *Presidential Power*, that the politics of democracy defined good policy.

Neustadt told the president a story and so preserved some role for history. At the same time he gave a secondary priority to the documents to which he had privileged access. He often did not trust them, and policymakers often wrote them with motives other than to state what the authors had thought. Neustadt stressed friendly interrogation of policymakers, which would allow them confidentially to elaborate on what had gone on but subject them to some cross-examination. Finally, the point of the Skybolt story, summarized in the conclusion but implied in the tale, hinted how the United States might have improved its performance. In this case, Kennedy warded off disaster. But Neustadt drew the moral that clearer directives and coordination would better serve the president in the future. The expert did not picture the president as a policymaker who wanted to keep atomic rockets from the Germans. Rather, Kennedy rescued the process. In a more carefully organized political world, last-minute intervention would not have been necessary. At the very least, Neustadt did not discuss the point of the intervention, and gave no attention to the diplomatic outcome.[39]

RAND had a hyperrational idea of what policymakers might achieve, especially when brilliant social scientists joined enlightened leaders. In working out his own views Neustadt had lost a sense of policy as contested goals for which a complex group with varying kinds of power strove. The missile crisis and the Skybolt affair, finally, set in stone the scholarly examination of separate events and weakened the effort to locate them in a historical continuum. RAND promoted Cuba as just what an effective leader could do with properly chosen intellectuals. Neustadt suspected decision making more—though not that over Cuba—but thought that judicious tinkering could enhance it.

In reflection on the experience of 1962, students of strategy and policymakers with intellectual proclivities believed that they had an unusually adequate grasp of how the world worked, and how they might shape events in their favor. But their learning had engendered a distorted if glorified view of the recent past and dubious if assertive lessons for the immediate future.

---

[39] Neustadt's report was classified for many years, though widely available. It was published along with other material as Neustadt, *Report to JFK*. The retrospective essay in this volume did not bring up the problem of Germany.

CHAPTER 7

Intellectuals in Power, 1961–1966

THE RAND analysts in the Department of Defense and the more heteroge-
neous group of political scientists sharing Neustadt's concerns were soon
caught up in the growing commitment to Southeast Asia. Their thought was
often blamed as the cause of the war in Vietnam. But the complex connection
between ideas and the conflict undermines the case for their responsibility,
blameworthy or not.

VIETNAM

Two elements stand out in assessment of the American involvement. On the
one hand, the United States opposed the murderous regimes associated with
the rise of international Communism after World War II. On the other hand,
the United States generally assumed the indivisibility of the menace. Indeed,
the assumption of a unified enemy probably contributed to a commonality of
purpose that otherwise might not have been so clear among the USSR, China,
and the Communist forces in Southeast Asia. Even undiscriminating American
hostility could not hide friction between China and the Soviet Union, whatever
their ideologies. Similar friction existed between the Chinese and the Communists of Vietnam. The Chinese desired a weak Asian client state in their old
enemy, Vietnam, and the Communist Vietnamese bid for hegemony in all of
the French colonial possessions of Indochina—Vietnam, Cambodia, and
Laos—strengthened the desire. The Russians and the Vietnamese directed their
deeper friendship against the Chinese.
  Clarity about these geopolitical facts might have deflected the interest of the
United States in confronting the Communist movement in northern Vietnam
whose triumph over the French in the early 1950s signaled the denouement of
their empire. The Geneva Conference of 1954 removed French power from
Southeast Asia. The Communists got what soon became "North Vietnam,"
which had excellent reason to affirm that Vietnam was one country whose
revolutionary independence northerners sought. Although French colonialism
in the nineteenth century had divided the Vietnamese people differently and
although tensions existed between northerners and southerners, the "South
Vietnam" emerging in the middle 1950s was an artificial entity. The northerners never considered it a separate country, and it remained independent only

because the United States determined to preserve it. One cannot know that China would have offset the North's aspirations to rule not only South Vietnam but also the rest of Indochina—Laos and Cambodia to the west of Vietnam—and unburdened the Americans from action. But the absence of an American sense of the balances within Asia did not help matters.

The Geneva Conference partitioned the north and the south of Vietnam with a demilitarized zone at the seventeenth parallel. Soon after the conference set the boundary, the northerners were circumventing it. They continued the strategy effective against the French, traversed the eastern parts of Laos and Cambodia, and sent fighters into southern Vietnam to assist indigenous rebels. Skirting the DMZ and spreading their ideas to their fearful neighbors, northerners built the Ho Chi Minh Trail, named after the North Vietnamese leader. This portentous development would have evil consequences for American policy. It would take a conflict embracing all of Indochina to defeat the North Vietnamese. Khrushchev's call for wars of national liberation, which suggested that revolutionary fires would burn throughout the undeveloped world, further disturbed American policymakers. They felt beleaguered, as only the most powerful can.

As early as 1959 and 1960 the Eisenhower administration believed that a monolithic enemy was on the move in Southeast Asia and was alarmed that the United States would have to fight in Laos, where the North Vietnamese assisted—perhaps spearheaded—local Communists. In 1962 Kennedy and Khrushchev "neutralized" Laos. This arrangement anticipated keeping the competition among Laotian political factions at the low level that befitted the nation's triviality. Americans feared that Soviet Communism would craft totalitarian regimes throughout the old colonial world, but also realistically reckoned the strategic irrelevance of Laos.

A larger meaning thus impregnated American policymaking in South Vietnam despite its minor significance in the early 1960s. Diplomats wanted to legitimate the South, but preferred to temporize. With military advisors from the United States, South Vietnamese leader Ngo Dinh Diem could indefinitely keep at a distance the insurgents infiltrated from the North and those in his midst.

Kennedy was more ambivalent about the growing American commitment than his successor, Lyndon Johnson.[1] Although one need not conclude from this fact that Kennedy was correct and Johnson more than imprudent, JFK did procrastinate over Vietnam and resisted his more anxious and activist advisors. Despite agonized hesitation, Johnson appeared less able to withstand them. Detached from expertise but easy in using it, Kennedy differed from Johnson, uncomfortably in its thrall. Moreover, the European settlement of the summer

---

[1] The best presentation is David Kaiser, *American Tragedy: Kennedy, Johnson, and the Origins of the Vietnam War* (Cambridge: Harvard University Press, 2000).

of 1963 opened up space for peripheral conflicts. This space was not available for Kennedy, who was dead three months later. To the extent that it did exist, JFK marched into it, as his role in the overthrow of Diem exemplified.[2]

In the summer of 1963 the South Vietnamese leader showed himself inept in dealing with domestic Buddhist opposition to his dictatorial Roman Catholic regime. The Kennedy administration had fretted about Diem's inability to mobilize his country to fight the revolutionaries, as well as his fragility. Yet the United States had no other options, and Diem had been in power for almost ten years. One small group of Kennedy's advisors shared his distaste for Vietnam. Kennedy esteemed the State Department's Averell Harriman, Michael Forrestal, and Roger Hilsman, for their willingness to carry forward his ideas in the face of Dean Rusk's lackluster leadership. The three pondered whether the Americans would be better positioned to leave South Vietnam if it was rid of Diem and seized an opportunity to encourage the generals around Diem to replace him with one of their own. The idea was not the president's and never had his full, attentive approval for the two-month period in which it became a reality in the late summer and early fall of 1963. But he did convene a reconstituted Ex Comm[3] to deliberate about Diem's dilemmas, and the insouciance with which the Americans enabled their ally to fall victim to a coup and to be murdered in November 1963, when they had no alternatives to him, intimated, at least, loose thinking.

Kennedy presided over these events. That Vietnam "doves" led the Americans to overthrow Diem does not speak well for those who believe JFK would have avoided an American commitment, even if one believes that avoidance was reasonable.[4]

With the Soviet Union, Kennedy attended to realpolitik nuance. In South Vietnam, he thought of abstract Communism.[5] In the early 1960s, Americans insisted on embedding themselves in South Vietnam despite the regime's distaste for them. For them Vietnam was a venue. The United States was unconcerned with South Vietnam, its people, its government, or its leadership. Kennedy said to Diem: "in all that it does in its relations with your country, the United States Government gives absolute priority to the defeat of the Commu-

[2] A good account is Kai Bird, *The Color of Truth: McGeorge Bundy and William Bundy: Brothers in Arms, A Biography* (New York: Simon and Schuster, 1998), pp. 261–64.

[3] See FRUS 1961–63, vol. 11, *Cuban Missile Crisis and Aftermath*, p. 739n; and FRUS 1961–63, vol. 4, *Vietnam, August–December, 1963*, p. 27.

[4] See Lawrence Freedman, *Kennedy's Wars: Berlin, Cuba, Laos, and Vietnam* (New York: Oxford University Press, 2000), pp. 367–97.

[5] This theme repeatedly occurs in Howard Jones, *Death of a Generation: How the Assassination of Diem and JFK Prolonged the Vietnam War* (New York: Oxford University Press, 2003), esp. pp. 13–48.

nists." The "central purpose" was that "Communists should be defeated."[6] In a candid letter to his brother, McGeorge Bundy later made the same point. The United States needed to make a stand. "There had to be a war."[7]

Three weeks after Diem's murder, Kennedy himself was dead, and Lyndon Johnson became responsible for American programs when the situation in South Vietnam was worsening. He had to devise a policy that did more than buy time. By early 1964 the president was persuaded that the United States was losing the proxy battle against North Vietnam. He searched to contain the conflict without sacrifice of his priorities, first his election later that year, thereafter his domestic programs. Johnson relied on convinced advisors, although Dean Rusk, McGeorge Bundy, and Robert McNamara were more worried, thoughtful, and tentative than they have been depicted, as was Johnson himself. They modestly believed in the war and the efficacy of the strategies to fight it. Commentators have criticized the war managers for carrying on because they feared that not to do so would compromise their careers. According to this critique, concern about personal preferment and not the nation's interest guided them. The short-term damage to their own prerogatives should they disengage was clearer to them than the long-term consequences of not disengaging. If this critique is legitimate, their short-term calculation about their reputations as high officials was their worst misjudgment, for none of them escaped the disgrace of running the war that many people at the time discredited and that commentators later excoriated.[8] For the many policymakers who themselves came to rue their involvement, the war was "Johnsonian," as McGeorge Bundy again put it. "The conduct of the war—as distinct from the decision . . . [to make war] was so different from what any of the rest of us would have wanted that in the long run it is likely to be a crucial distinguishing factor between our view of history and the President's own." JFK, Bundy thought, would have done the job at lower cost.[9]

Many men with scholarly backgrounds formulated the policies that took the United States into Vietnam, and the ideas they generated have often been urged as the cause of the commitment. How much added value did learning bring to Vietnam? What ideas from the university world did policymakers carry over

---

[6] Kennedy to Diem, September 16, 1963, FRUS, 1961–63, vol. 4, *Vietnam, August–December, 1963*, p. 231.

[7] M. Bundy to W. Bundy, November 14, 1969, Criticism and Comments, Box 5, Additional William Bundy Papers, Mudd Library, Princeton University.

[8] This is the message of Bird, *Color of Truth;* a similar point is made by H. R. McMaster, *Dereliction of Duty: Lyndon Johnson, Robert McNamara, the Joint Chiefs of Staff, and the Lies That Led to Vietnam* (New York: HarperCollins, 1997), p. 297.

[9] M. Bundy to W. Bundy, November 14, 1969, Criticism and Comments, Box 5, Additional William Bundy Papers, Mudd Library, Princeton University.

Figure 4. Secretary Dean Rusk at a cabinet meeting (LBJ Library photo by Yoichi R. Okamoto)

to foreign policy? Did these ideas influence their decision making in ways that distinguished them from officials who did not have academic backgrounds?

Dean Rusk and McGeorge Bundy

The answer to these questions for Secretary of State Rusk and Assistant for National Security Bundy is obvious. The scholar's cloister was not germane to their policymaking. A poor boy from Georgia, Rusk went to Davidson College in North Carolina, where he majored in political science, focused on international law, and graduated in 1931. He spent the next three years at Oxford University as a Rhodes scholar, obtaining a B.A., where again he made a legalist approach to foreign affairs the chief object of study. As important to Rusk's development as his academic efforts was his appraisal of world politics. Like many articulate southerners of his generation, he was devoted to Woodrow Wilson, and found that the collapse of the international system in the 1930s confirmed Wilson's belief that without collective security, Europe would drift toward war. Yet Rusk cannot be categorized as an idealist giving priority to global legal proprieties. He did stress formal constraints in world politics but would never forswear the use of force. Through the 1930s, he lamented that the Western democracies refused to show the teeth in collective security.

From 1934 till 1940 Rusk taught government and international relations at Mills College in California, rising to the deanship. He interpreted the modern European and American past in ways that the educated elite interested in foreign policy and sympathetic to the Roosevelt administration shared. After the defeat of Napoleon, European diplomacy from 1789 to 1914 had created a peaceful balance of power that only World War I had shattered. Although Wilson had expected too much, the retreat of the United States to isolationism and the collapse of the values of the League of Nations had led to totalitarianism in the 1920s and 1930s. At the end of the 1930s Rusk advocated at Mills College that the United States follow a more assertive internationalism than that which engaged the Roosevelt administration. It is reported that he wept in his classes over the passivity of the democracies in the face of Fascism.[10]

Rusk's views were conventional in some American circles. He was an interventionist, perhaps more oriented to legalisms than some of his peers, but not more passive. To describe his standard attitudes, one biographer has designated Rusk "a liberal internationalist."[11]

In 1940, before he completed a law program that he was enrolled in at Berkeley, Rusk joined the army, beginning a career in political-military affairs that would carry him to high office under Truman. A Democrat, he became president of the Rockefeller Foundation after Eisenhower's victory in 1952, and from 1961 to 1969 secretary of state. On retirement he returned to his home as a professor of international law at the University of Georgia from 1970 until 1984. Yet the commentator will unsuccessfully search the evidence for the impact of scholarly knowledge on his actions. Based on his experience as a foundation head and teacher, he commented negatively in his autobiography about academic theories and the foolishness of professorial publishing projects.[12] An intelligent, hardworking administrator, Rusk took safely anti-Communist positions, and like many Democrats of his era was associated with global interventionism. His policymaking flowed from this commitment, shaped by the common American experience of the recent past and immediate political pressures. Biographers have seen in Rusk the mind of a bureaucratic conservative. Kennedy did not think much of him.

More important and self-assured was McGeorge Bundy, national security advisor from 1961 to 1966.[13] Bundy had more an intellectual edge than Rusk, but like him rejected theory in politics. He and his brother William, another

[10] Rusk, *As I Saw It*, p. 90.

[11] Thomas W. Zeiler, *Dean Rusk: Defending the American Mission Abroad* (Wilmington, Del.: Scholarly Resources, 2000), pp. 6–11.

[12] See in Rusk, *As I Saw It*, pp. 85, 189, 533, 553, 598, 607–8.

[13] In this sketch, I have relied on Bird, *The Color of Truth*, pp. 69, 88–93, 104–9, 118–37.

Figure 5. Sketch of McGeorge Bundy made during a 1964 war game (LBJ Library)

defense intellectual prominent in the 1960s, came from a wealthy family with New England and Republican roots. They went to Yale in the 1930s, demonstrating considerable gifts. McGeorge majored in mathematics, but his real interest was international politics. As his biographer has written, Bundy aimed "to move in the world of action while, paradoxically, still preserving his sense of ironic detachment." Rather than study for a doctorate, McGeorge joined the Society of Fellows at Harvard. This new program funded members to study whatever issues fascinated them. Bundy had prominent connections with Harvard and was an obvious choice in Cambridge after his career at Yale. World War II interrupted his stint at Harvard, but his father was a special assistant to Republican secretary of war Henry Stimson, and McGeorge served as an aide to Admiral Alan Kirk. Returning to Harvard after the war, McGeorge combined his fellowship with an illustrious assignment and helped Stimson with his autobiography, *On Active Service in War and Peace* (1948). Bundy is credited with substantial assistance in writing the memoir as well as an important essay of Stimson's of the same period that explained the A-bombing of Japan,

"The Decision to Use the Bomb," published in 1947 in *Harper's* magazine. The GOP internationalism of father, son, and Stimson was stretched in another, thinner, book of 1952, *The Pattern of Responsibility: From the Records of Dean Acheson* (1952). This volume comprised Acheson's public statements and Bundy's refutation of Acheson's bitter Republican critics.

In 1949 Bundy began to lecture on international relations at Harvard, and two years later the Department of Government tenured him. In 1953, thirty-four years old, he became Harvard's dean of arts and sciences. Commentators have recognized Bundy for raising Harvard's standards during the 1950s. He also steered the school through the period in which Joseph McCarthy terrorized universities. The dean sacrificed nonpermanent staff while protecting the tenured faculty, demonstrating an expedient cast of mind. He solved problems without worrying much about principles. This focus on immediate concerns preserved Bundy's sense of detachment.

When Kennedy appointed him, Bundy epitomized the rise of Cambridge academics in the councils of government. Harvard's Littauer School of Public Affairs was a cramped institution, and despite its ability to attract talented thinkers in international politics, Princeton and RAND overshadowed it in the 1950s. Kennedy, a Harvard alumnus, changed the institutional balance as president. Washington called RAND thinkers, but the influx and distinction of Cambridge men was more impressive. Johnson called them "the Harvards," and Bundy was their bureaucratic chief.

This did not mean that Bundy had no ideology. As an instructor in government, and in continuing some teaching in American foreign policy as dean, he purveyed the same ideas as Rusk and carried them forward from the late 1930s through the 1950s. Although he emphasized Stimson's more cautious internationalism over Wilsonianism, Bundy had toyed with studying Wilson, who rightly saw that the United States must throw its weight on the side of stability around the world. Teaching the interwar period, Bundy lamented, with Rusk, isolationism in the United States and argued that Britain and France, and secondarily the United States, ought to have been more assertive in the 1930s.

World War II obligated the United States to exercise global power. Bundy upheld the Cold War against the Soviets, believing it grew out of the World War II settlement and the continuities between German and Russian totalitarianism. He taught that the United States had learned "the lessons of the 1930s." Belligerent conduct, if unchecked, led to war. The appetite of aggression was never satisfied. To withdraw from one battlefield meant only to prepare for the next. In the aftermath of World War II the Americans judged that they could not behave as they had after World War I, and thus from 1945 to 1960, the United States confronted the Soviets. To express these historical formulations Bundy and others spoke of appeasement. The Munich analogy was an emotional weapon that encapsulated thinking about the need to be tough and to make the hard choices.[14]

Like Rusk, Bundy typified the liberal cold warrior. His experience and the conventions of the foreign-policy elite, and not scholarly theory, shaped his teaching. In approaching contemporary history, he stressed—as he did in the dean's office—how the diplomat molded events in responding to urgent demands. The good statesman would be a pragmatic anti-Communist, and the presumptions of this view would shape his decisions. Bundy was "enough of a diplomatic historian," he said, to know that a government would "certainly be in trouble" if it worried about abstract definitions. "Actual policy," said Bundy, articulating a view that he displayed over and over, "was determined by adding up actions that the President had approved . . . or by asking the White House staff how the President felt."[15] Tactics and not philosophy were paramount. In 1964 Bundy participated in one of the many war games that the military had learned to conduct using the tools of the civilian strategists. In this simulation an American attempt to force North Vietnam from the field led to mutual escalation and a stalemate between the two sides at a far higher level of violence than that at which they started—just the result many later said had taken place by 1968. Bundy's brother William, another participant and a high-ranking State Department official, reported that the outcome made no impression on the participants because the game was unrealistic, run by theorists and not by policymakers.[16]

Strategic theorists nonetheless *rationalized* what might be done in Vietnam in 1964 and 1965. To assist in this process, almost on cue, Thomas Schelling arrived on the scene.

Tom Schelling and Deterrence

Schelling, a Harvard professor of economics and a man of luminous intelligence, had started out as a trade negotiator and in the 1950s had made his academic career working on international economics, trade policy, and tariffs. He was an outstanding writer with a flair for the apt phrase and pungent example. His reputation as a strategist rested on essays collected in *The Strategy of Conflict* (1960) and *Arms and Influence* (1966), and his theories won acclaim

---

[14] Bruce Kuklick, "History as a Way of Learning," *American Quarterly* 22 (1970): 614–19, has many examples of this set of interpretations.

[15] White House Staff Meeting, November 4, 1963, FRUS, 1961–63, vol. 4, *Vietnam, August–December, 1963*, p. 555; Editorial Note, FRUS, 1961–63, vol. 8, *National Security Matters*, p. 197.

[16] On Sigma II-64 see National Security File, Agency Files, War Games, vol. II [1], Box 30; and on William Bundy's analysis, Bundy Papers, Mss. on Vietnam, Chapter 15-a, pp. 2–3, LBJ Library.

that was coterminous with Kennedy's accession to power.[17] The president had appointed Paul Nitze as an assistant secretary for defense, and Nitze offered a job to Schelling in the Defense Department. Schelling instead recommended his Harvard friend and professor of law, John McNaughton, who became McNamara's general counsel and close associate. In McNamara's estimation McNaughton rose while he received tutorials from Schelling, who thus brought his ideas to the Department of Defense.[18]

Schelling had RAND connections, and in some ways popularized Kaufmann's writing. Like the noted Herman Kahn, who cannibalized the ideas of other theorists and wrote a Kaufmann-inspired book, *On Escalation*,[19] Schelling too was concerned with signaling and limiting conflict.[20] But rooted perhaps more in mathematical than economic analysis, he concentrated not so much on vulnerability as on the game-theoretic aspects of bargaining, and formulated more active strategies than had Albert Wohlstetter. Less evident in Schelling's work than in that of Wohlstetter was the paradigm of Soviet surprise attack, although Schelling could write in 1966 that there was "a difficulty" with "our being an unaggressive nation . . . whose announced aim has been to contain rather than roll back."[21] At the same time, the belief that the military required civilian, academic help reached its high point in Schelling. Defense studies needed "a general theory of strategy" that would unify the structure of a concept like deterrence in different fields. Such a theory would mix "game theory, organization theory, communications theory, theory of evidence, theory of choice, and theory of collective decision." Civilians were now just creating such a theory because, in contrast to all other professionals—say economists or educators—the military had no "identifiable academic counterpart." The service academies were undergraduate institutions (and thus had no graduate students or research programs). The "war colleges" were not very good. The military did not have the "intellectual skills."[22]

Drawing on material from the social psychology, group dynamics, and personality studies of the 1950s, Schelling argued that varied situations exhibited a structure that game theory could illuminate. His version of it was thus a logical form that modeled real predicaments. Put the other way, the predicaments illustrated the theory. While he deprecated his theory in comparison to the complexity of the issues, Schelling drew on daily life, the theater, the novel,

[17] A book-length study is Robert Ayson, *Thomas Schelling and the Nuclear Age: Strategy as Social Science* (London: Frank Cass, 2004).

[18] Kaplan, *The Wizards of Armageddon*, pp. 332–33.

[19] New York: Frederick A. Praeger, 1965.

[20] Herken, *Counsels of War*, p. 119.

[21] Schelling, *Arms and Influence*, p. 71.

[22] Schelling, *The Strategy of Conflict* (Cambridge: Harvard University Press, 1960), pp. iii–iv, 8–9, 14–15. For the precursors to the book see Trachtenberg, *Strategic Thought,* pt. 3, vol. 1, pp. 161–212, 213–36, 326–49.

parenthood, and history from the Greeks to the present. All bargainers, for example, estimated what the other guy would do, judged what threats might be effective and what retaliation might occur and what it might cost, and evaluated how deliberate ambiguity—"the threat that leaves something to chance"— might assist the achievement of goals.[23] *The Strategy of Conflict*, which had a marked stylistic grace, revealed the flavor of his outlook. Schelling recognized that the international world was dangerous, yet assumed diplomatic risk was manageable. "The philosophy of the book," he said, was that similarities existed "between, say, maneuvering in limited war and jockeying in a traffic jam, between deterring the Russians and deterring one's children."[24] Jockeying in traffic was something millions of people did every day, and the penalty for failure was a smashed fender. In 1960 the one "limited war" that had concerned America had driven the Truman administration from office. To compare child-rearing—common, after all—and the conflict with the Soviets—its nuclear dimension unique in human history—was arresting. Schelling literally *patronized* the Russians, as his proclivity to speak about how "to teach the Soviets" to "behave" and how to punish "misbehavior" also revealed.[25] Moreover, he intimated that raising children was a less complicated and dubious business than it is. Either massive retaliation or graduated escalation, for example, is a response to offspring that fails as often as it works, and each is fraught with unintended consequences.

Schelling was best known for his conception of limited war as a form of signaling. In this view strategists might anticipate a graduated escalation between the protagonists in a dispute that was comparatively minor:

> War is always a bargaining process, one in which threats and proposals, counterproposals and counterthreats, offers and assurances, concessions and demonstrations, take the form of actions rather than words, or actions accompanied by words. It is in the wars that we have come to call "limited wars" that the bargaining appears most vividly and is conducted most consciously. The critical targets in such a war are in the mind of the enemy as much as on the battlefield; the state of the enemy's expectations is as important as the state of his troops; the threat of violence in reserve is more important than the commitment of force in the field.[26]

After the missile crisis, Schelling grasped the *structure* of crises the Department of Defense faced. Berlin in 1958 and 1961 and both incidents in Cuba

---

[23] For the use of social science see Schelling, *The Strategy of Conflict*, pp. 85–86, 108, 116; for self-deprecation, *Strategy,* pp. 117, 162–63, 166–67n, and *Arms and Influence*, p. 9; and for ambiguous threats, *Arms and Influence*, pp. 121–22.

[24] Schelling, *The Strategy of Conflict*, p. v.

[25] Schelling, *Arms and Influence*, p. 173; "Nuclear Strategy in Europe," *World Politics* 14 (1961–62): 429; and "Managing the Arms Race" in *National Security: Political Military, and Economic Strategies in the Decade Ahead*, ed. David M. Abshire and Richard V. Allen (New York: Praeger, 1963), p. 613.

[26] Schelling, *Arms and Influence*, pp. 142–43.

displayed a pattern of dare and double-dare, where a weak reply encouraged the enemy but a strong one rebuffed him. Now, diplomacy would work more surely if theory enriched it. In October 1962 the Americans had seen a malign enemy employ deceit to threaten the planet. But graduated incrementalism had warded off a real battle. Simultaneously McNamara and his staff self-consciously came to see themselves as "crisis managers," and soon as managing crises in the style of Schelling's bargainer.

In 1964 Schelling added an incident in the Gulf of Tonkin off the northern coast of Vietnam to the roster that displayed how strategic thought related to real problems and how policy might embody strategic ideas. The United States believed, with equal parts of realism and unrealism, that infiltration and support from the North propelled the guerillas in the South. To convince the North Vietnamese to yield, the United States had harassed the North in the early 1960s. These activities were covert. Even later, President Johnson said that Asian boys were to fight the war, but the South Vietnamese who carried out the reprisals against Northern infiltration were in league with the American military. The covert activities, however, only minimally irritated the North. The Americans wanted to step them up to deter the North but also worried that the escalation would expose the United States' role in the war.

In August 1964, in the Tonkin Gulf, the North Vietnamese navy attacked American destroyers sailing in what the United States claimed were international waters in a program that supported the harassment but was a component of a different U.S. operation. Two days later the American ships, in a troubled sea, mistakenly believed that they were again under attack, and assaulted an imaginary enemy. Washington officials also believed in the second attack, although over the next several months they suppressed growing doubts about its reality. At the time Johnson put skepticism behind him, and a one-time retaliatory bombing raid upped the ante.

The president decided on this raid in part as domestic strategy in an election year. He wanted to show himself a prudent but strong defender of American interests in his campaign against Republican Barry Goldwater, who was reputedly a reckless advocate of nuclear war. Not reckless, neither was Johnson weak. In part the fantasy skirmish conveniently allowed Johnson to secure congressional backing for policies he might later want to carry out. In the Gulf of Tonkin Resolution, the legislature recorded its support and, Johnson recognized at the time, a commitment to any necessary future actions. The president felt he had to have such an imprimatur and had, he said, been carrying around a version of it in his pocket for weeks. That is, the administration had been looking for an incident that would bring the United States openly into the conflict, a scenario in which it would respond to provocation, and that would enable the executive to get something like a declaration of war, which it might want down the road. In part Johnson acted to shore up the morale of

Figure 6. Thomas Schelling (Courtesy of the Harvard University Archives)

the South Vietnamese. A show of American power would help their war effort, for they needed to know that the United States would stand with them.

American action also embraced a strategic idea. The United States was warning the North that it would protect its client in Southeast Asia. But this idea was murky, since for the record the Americans were not at war in Vietnam. The "reprisal" cautioned the northerners that they had better not attack the United States anymore. But if the threat worked, the North Vietnamese would merely take more care in their attacks, and the aim of the United States to disguise its own involvement would assist them. Of course, to the extent that the strategic idea was coherent it might be that Johnson intended to tell the northerners that the United States was invested in Vietnam, or that the North would pay for any successes of the guerrillas in the South.

Finally, one must say that speculation on Johnson's motives is a bit nonsensical in light of the knowledge that the second North Vietnamese naval clash never occurred. The United States had been provoking the northerners, and they had responded with a first attack. They themselves knew, however, that they had been falsely accused of a second and then bombed. Must they not have thought that the United States had concocted the incident in order to escalate the war?[27] The now routine if oversimplified analysis of Johnson's behavior is of a case of presidential deception.

In 1964 Schelling was consulting with the Defense Department officials whom his ideas of deterrence had shaped. His *Arms and Influence* (1966) made Johnson's Tonkin Gulf reprisal a centerpiece example of rational signaling.[28] The account was instant analysis but based on some insider knowledge, and showed how the strategists applied theory to the cluttered reality of war.

According to Schelling the bombing was an "unusually fitting" military action. It displayed America's reputation for "civilized restraint and for resolve and initiative." One's positive judgment about the actions, Schelling noted, was bound to be "aesthetic," but as an appreciative observer, he saw "an expressive bit of repartee," a "riposte," an "articulate" deed in "the idiom of reprisal." It was neat and just in its "symbolic relation of response to a provocation" and in "the psychology of communication." Schelling reverted to his analogy of the punishment of children. He quoted the famous French psychologist Jean Piaget on the nature of childhood aggression, and saluted the decision as a brilliant way of showing how America penalized an opponent's misconduct.

The Harvard theorist quoted with approval Congress's view of the president's decision as "soundly conceived and skillfully executed." Under the circumstances the United States "could not have done less and should not have done more." The president had devised "a communication that would be received by the North Vietnamese and the Chinese with high fidelity." But Schelling warned that the air strike was "an extreme case of articulate action" and that in ordinary cases diplomacy "by maneuver" was "typically a good deal clumsier, with actions less subject to careful control for the message they embody, subject to background noise from uncontrollable events, and subject to misinterpretation." Schelling even admitted, in conclusion, that the signal might have not been as audible to the North Vietnamese as it was to the Congress.[29]

There was a fragment of truth in Schelling's overall ideas. People can communicate. If I say, "I will meet you at Twenty-third and Pine at 4:00 o'clock," in the usual case, we can meet up at four. And although words and actions

---

[27] My interpretation of Tonkin is indebted to Edwin E. Moïse's careful study, *Tonkin Gulf and the Escalation of the Vietnam War* (Chapel Hill: University of North Carolina Press, 1996), esp. pp. xi–xiii, 1–30.

[28] Kaplan, *The Wizards of Armageddon*, pp. 332–36.

[29] Schelling, *Arms and Influence*, pp. 141–51, 170–72.

often mean to others something different than what is intended, people convey their intentions, sometimes in a complicated manner. From these propositions, Schelling spun out notions that heightened the rational aspect of this process, which war, especially, decreases. As Kennedy's only trusted military advisor, General Maxwell Taylor, commented on an earlier essay of Schelling's, "Too metaphysical for me."[30] Schelling postulated a purity about war that it does not have. He tended to regard personal rivalries, conflicting priorities, bureaucratic conflicts, dispersed efforts, and various snafus as unnecessary and extraneous conditions. But they do not *intrude* on war. They are *intrinsic* to war, just as they are intrinsic to human life in general.[31] In addition to the limitations of the theory, Schelling misconceived the factual substance of the affair in the Tonkin Gulf.

The Civilian Strategists on Vietnam

Schelling's view became unfairly summarized as graduated escalation, but the latter did capture a variety of conceptions academics and scholarly policymakers had propounded.[32] The outcome of the missile crisis had energized the men around Kennedy. The experience was particularly important for the RAND theorists who were in the Department of Defense. Maxwell Taylor said that Cuba convinced the civilians that they might optimistically face the insurgency in Vietnam. Alexis Johnson, deputy undersecretary of state, a minor figure in the Cuban Ex Comm deliberations, and Douglas Dillon, secretary of the treasury, made the same point, albeit in retrospect, as did high-ranking Defense Department official Paul Warnke. Neustadt wrote that particularly after Cuba, McNamara believed that if "a problem were brought to his shop, he would cut [solve] it."[33] Clark Clifford, who was to become secretary of defense in 1968, warned Lyndon Johnson in 1965 that the misapplication of the Cuban experience could be disastrous.[34] Scholars and policymakers apprehensive about how to understand their responsibility for Vietnam have subsequently noted the role of Cuba. McNamara, for example, later said that, because Cuba was successful,

---

[30] Quoted from Tactical Nuclear Weapons, T-229–69, June 1, 1962, Box 33, Maxwell Taylor Papers, courtesy of David Rosenberg and Marc Trachtenberg.

[31] For the inspiration for this passage see Sherry, *American Air Power*, p. 165.

[32] See the Schelling-inspired essay by William E. Simons, "The Vietnam Intervention, 1964–65" (originally a 1969 RAND study) in *The Limits of Coercive Diplomacy*, ed. Alexander George and William E. Simons, 2nd ed. (Boulder, Colo.: Westview Press, 1994), pp. 144–210, wherein the author attempts to show the relevance of "signaling theory" about the "opponent's compliance behavior."

[33] Taylor and Ball cited from Neustadt and May, *Thinking in Time*, pp. 78–88, 305 n. 6; Warnke, Oral History, tape 2 (January 1969), pp. 5–8, LBJ Library.

[34] See Mann's discussion in *A Grand Delusion*, pp. 453–54; and Clark Clifford, *Counsel to the President: A Memoir* (New York: Random House, 1991), pp. 410–11, 418–21.

he may have applied its learning to Vietnam, but then, he concluded, in so doing he also avoided a resort to nuclear weapons in Southeast Asia, which otherwise might have been an option.[35] The shorthand for this learning, false or true, was baptized as graduated escalation.

One did not have to be a strategic genius to come up with graduated escalation. It is encapsulated in advice such as, Don't use a tank to kill a flea. You started with the minimal respectable response that indicated the end you wanted to achieve. Operating from a strong position, you implicitly cautioned the adversary that unless you got your way, further and more severe responses were indefinitely available. In October 1962, according to the received wisdom, the Soviets had collapsed in the first round, when they withdrew their missiles in the face of a wobbly blockade. They were the second most powerful nation on earth, and nuclear weapons were at issue. How much easier would it be with a fourth-rate power, when the United States had an array of conventional assets, in addition to those at the nuclear level!

In the real world, matters were more complex, and policymakers pointed out to one another the uncertainties of a slippery slope, of bit by bit becoming committed to inevitable increases in blood and treasure for a minor objective. Yet slow but sure involvement was also exactly what was demanded. Running for election and then worried about his Great Society, LBJ did not make the war a priority when he made the basic decisions. Apprehensive about polarization between Democrats and Republicans in foreign policy, as had occurred in the early 1950s, he eschewed a public debate. Johnson feared, moreover, Russian or Chinese intervention should he be too belligerent. The complex equation of how bombing of the North would influence its role in a weak South also perplexed the Americans. Then, the fragility of the southern government meant that the United States had to move slowly, and military logistics on the American side additionally precluded the rapid, mass deployment of troops. Graduated escalation promised at its start no great expenditures, only power held majestically in reserve. Cuba showed that the United States need not move up "the ladder of escalation." The policy was finally, at its low end, continuous with what had gone before—temporizing.

As the Johnson administration slid into Vietnam, what is noteworthy is not a strategic concept that scholars might formulate in graduate study in a center of higher learning, but the absence of such a concept. The leadership moved hesitantly ahead. The fundamental commitment, born of a determination not to lose Vietnam but also of the uncertainly of Johnson and his advisors about what they should do, was compatible with *any* of the strategic theories advanced in the 1960s. In the real world, William Kaufmann, Schelling, and even the military counterinsurgency theorists had ideas that amounted to much the

---

[35] Blight and Welch, *On the Brink*, pp. 106, 155–56, 170, 194; McNamara, *In Retrospect* (New York: Random House, 1995), pp. 323, 332, 338–39.

same thing—going slow. As one commentator has written, they all supported a middle way between withdrawal and militarization.[36] In academic circles the niceties of each notion made careers in major universities. In Washington one or all of them might serve as a rationale for what would have been done on other grounds. For the president, Bundy repeatedly dressed up the decisions as graduated escalation—or flexible response, sustained reprisal or pressure, measured or proportionate response, controlled escalation, war-fighting, counterforce, and even covert operations or quasi-guerrilla action. Johnson got a respectable label for what he was doing.[37]

INTELLECTUAL GENERALS

When McNamara arrived in Washington, statesmen placed a premium on military figures who could pass muster as defense intellectuals, but the services only slowly learned the grammar of the new conversations. While the army and navy and air force subsequently picked out young officers for advanced study at civilian institutions, those who already had it gained a new eminence. Henry Kissinger noted that the military proudly put forward its academic generals but possibly overestimated their ability, while the civilians were carried away by the fact that any soldier might achieve a doctoral degree.[38] Andrew Goodpaster, who had a Princeton Ph.D., already had some repute in the 1950s and later served Nixon in the 1970s, and Alexander Haig, who did graduate work at Georgetown, also rose in the Nixon administration. But earlier George "Abe" Lincoln, who spent much of his career teaching social science at West Point, had participated in political-military planning in the Pentagon.

Most important were Maxwell Taylor and Roger Hilsman. Hilsman, a former army officer in the State Department, attracted Kennedy and others to counterinsurgency in the early sixties. But after Kennedy's assassination he rapidly lost influence and left the administration. More prominent was Taylor, chief of staff under Eisenhower, who became a hero for Democrats when he criticized the Republican doctrines of massive retaliation in a popular book,

---

[36] David Stigerwald, "The Paradoxes of Kennedy Liberalism," *Reviews in American History* 28 (2000): 640.

[37] These phrases and similar ones recur over and over again in the documents in FRUS 1964–68, vol. 1, *Vietnam, 1964*; vol. 2, *Vietnam, January–June, 1965*; vol. 3, *Vietnam, July–December, 1965*. See also the other examples from one of the many excellent discussions of Lawrence Freedman in his "On the Tiger's Back: The Development of the Concept of Escalation," in Kolkowicz, *Logic of Nuclear Terror*, pp. 136, 138. Based largely on *"The Pentagon Papers"* (which I discuss in chapter 9), Stephen Peter Rosen, "Vietnam and the American Theory of Limited War," *International Security* 7 (1982): 83–113, is also useful in documenting the role of theory in the escalation in Vietnam.

[38] Henry Kissinger, *White House Years* (Boston: Little, Brown, 1979), p. 41.

The Uncertain Trumpet (1960), after he left the service. A few years later, disagreement with Eisenhower and the ability to write a book gave Taylor an edge with Kennedy. He came out of retirement to become an advisor in the Democratic White House, then chair of the Chiefs, and ambassador in Vietnam. He continued to be a significant figure in the Johnson administration. He was the one influential military man whom Kennedy respected, and Johnson's national security advisors felt that they could talk to him. Passable as an intellect, he advocated a version of graduated escalation.

The essential problem for the military was that when these men rose in prominence among the ranks of political decision makers, they lost contact with the service viewpoints, and were often regarded as traitors to their caste. They maintained leverage only because their perspective was that of the civilians and not that of the military. Taylor was an excellent example. Moreover, the intellectual generals were so few that they evolved no distinctive approach to defense policy. Rather, the generals who counted were those excluded from high policy circles but relied upon to conduct the war.

McNamara

Graduated escalation obfuscated the war for McNamara. In the aftermath of the Gulf of Tonkin, the secretary orchestrated Rolling Thunder, the policy of bombing the North that began in early 1965, after Johnson's election. But while McNamara wanted to confront the Communists with the threat and actuality of force until the United States got its way, he did not like the war as war. He detested the generals and admirals with their taste for blood, their mental thickness, and their persistent squabbling over resources with little regard for what a unified defense posture should be. If the civilians in the Department of Defense managed the conflict, McNamara believed, he could steer clear of many of the concerns he had about the military. Moreover, taking a page from Schelling, McNamara, in his head, would not be running a war. Vietnam was rather a laboratory to understand how the United States might tackle insurgencies, and the conflict there continued the play of "communication" between the United States and the Soviet Union that the missile crisis had prompted. According to the civilians in the Department of Defense, Rolling Thunder was a complicated game of signals with the North, as much psychological as military.

The Joint Chiefs of Staff never accepted the strategy of signaling, but their lack of influence with McNamara combined with their inability to agree on alternatives allowed the civilians to triumph. The generals thought RAND ideas undefined and confused, and advocated a military campaign to destroy the North.[39] Nonetheless, by the end of 1965 the services had transformed

---

[39] See for example JCS to McNamara, June 2, 1964; and November 23, 1964, FRUS 1964–68, vol. 1, *Vietnam, 1964*, pp. 437–39, and 932–35, respectively.

McNamara's bombing more straightforwardly into the tactic of violence it was. In spite of the micromanagement of targets and the restrictive rules of engagement McNamara imposed on the brass, *growing and continuing* graduated escalation gave the generals more of what they wanted: a major commitment to defeat the enemy. The secretary of defense saw the fight through the lens of strategic theory, and when he comprehended that he was not carrying out an applied social science experiment, he turned against the bombers. By then, however—at the end of 1965 and early 1966—the United States was immersed in a genuine war. The civilian strategists may have influenced McNamara. At least they shrouded his mind from what was occurring.[40] When the shroud was lifted in 1966 and 1967, the United States engaged upwards of four hundred thousand troops and conducted a full bombing campaign over Vietnam.

WALT WHITMAN ROSTOW

Rostow was an MIT economist who held high offices in the Kennedy and Johnson administrations. He matriculated at Yale in the early 1930s at the age of sixteen and received his B.A. in three years. After attending Oxford as a Rhodes scholar, he returned to Yale and earned a doctorate in economics in 1940. During the war he worked for the OSS, and then the air force, where, like many others we have met, he studied the effectiveness of the air warfare against Germany. Indeed, Rostow at that time became an advocate of certain kinds of bombing as the key to the defeat of an enemy. By 1950 he was a professor of economics at MIT and helped to build its Center for International Studies. His importance as a policy intellectual in the 1950s and 1960s derived from his espousal of "modernization," about which he wrote a run of books.

In the early part of his career in the 1930s and 1940s, Rostow considered himself a man of the left. From the time he entered Yale, he wanted to construct a theory of political and economic change that would rescue Marxist insights from the totalitarianism of the Communists. If he could detect the laws of historical development, science could guide American policy. But these laws were different from what Marx had thought, and need not be put to work for the sort of meretricious cause Lenin and Stalin advanced. Rostow's own research supplemented that of scholars of political development who were looking at the way traditional societies adapted to the economic leadership of the West and made the transition to industrialized life. Many studies now exist of this social science literature, which argues that the modernization theorists were presumptively ethnocentric. They believed that Western capitalism represented the one good path and that a liberal political

---

[40] These themes are evident in McMaster, *Dereliction of Duty.*

and economic telos existed in history. Historians have also urged that in the Cold War these theories rationalized American economic and political intervention in the underdeveloped world. It is easy with hindsight to see these aspects of this social-science project, but it must be recalled that these scholars responded to a real problem. Industrial society starkly differed from that which was not industrial, and Rostow wanted to alleviate the misery of the latter, bereft of technology and education.[41]

In 1960 he published *The Stages of Economic Growth*, the most famous book on modernization, and one that legitimated the approach to foreign aid in the early 1960s. The volume was subtitled *A Non-Communist Manifesto*, which called to mind Marx's nineteenth-century tract and Rostow's own ambitions. He aimed to uncover the forces that drove change. Rostow was no economic determinist but did believe that all societies would develop their own industrial civilization. How they would do so depended on the peculiar mix of social and political values in the "modernizing élite." The determinism at work mixed technology and culture. He worried, however, that "scavengers of modernization" would warp these forces and produce social orders less worthwhile than those that had flowered in the West. The Soviet Union exemplified modernization gone awry. The Russians had an effective state, but Communism was "a disease of the transition" from traditional society.[42] Neurotic social and political commitments had given birth to the USSR. Its formidable bureaucracy took what could have been the means to a democratic welfare state and created a nation devoted to military expansion.

To counter this system, Rostow looked at the emergence of modernity in the West. He analyzed the "takeoff" period and the engine of industrial maturity that led to eras of high mass consumption in countries such as Britain, France, and the United States. Modernization was inevitable, but it could happen benignly in only one way. Rostow worried that the Communists would threaten the developing nations—the southern world. *The Stages of Economic Growth* told how the United States might assist these nations and how they could take the good route and prevent Communists from distorting the transition. Rostow focused on the takeoff era and noted how the West could shape modernizing elites in countries at risk, and with technology, expertise, and financial aid increase the prospects of democratic government when these countries reached their modern period. One wanted to prevent a small group of revolutionaries from the imposition of a totalitarian regime.[43]

---

[41] See Michael E. Latham, *Modernization as Ideology: American Social Science and "Nation Building" in the Kennedy Era* (Chapel Hill: University of North Carolina Press, 2000), and David Engerman et al., eds., *Staging Growth: Modernization, Development, and the Global Cold War* (Amherst: University of Massachusetts Press, 2003).

[42] W. W. Rostow, *The Dynamics of Soviet Society* (New York: Norton, 1953), p. 81; and *The Diffusion of Power: An Essay in Recent History* (New York: Macmillan, 1972), pp. 87–88.

[43] Rostow, *Stages of Economic Growth* (New York: Cambridge University Press, 1960), pp. esp. 25–29, 50–51, 131–33, 141–43, 162–64.

Figure 7. Walt Rostow at a meeting in the Cabinet Room (LBJ Library photo by Yoichi R. Okamoto)

Rostow was a presence in Cambridge, Massachusetts, when Kennedy was on the lookout for advisors, and in the late 1950s attracted JFK's interest.[44] In 1961 he became a member of McGeorge Bundy's National Security Council staff, positioned to exploit postwar social science to influence policy.

In the 1950s critics had pointed to another side to Rostow. Some people had deprecated the torrent of publications on which he placed such a high value, and his view that policymakers needed a theory of history as a guide.[45] He wrote an early speech for Eisenhower that was rejected for its empty, pompous language.[46] In 1961 Rostow remarked to a congressional committee that the NSC "would be vastly improved if it had an independent staff of first-rate men freed of ties to particular bureaucracies, paid to think in terms of the totality of our policy problems, empowered to lay proposals on the table." Outgoing defense secretary Thomas Gates, asked to comment on Rostow's proposal,

[44] See Rostow Memos, Pre Presidency, POF Box 64A, JFK Library.

[45] Rostow, *The Diffusion of Power*, pp. 87–88; and, for examples of Rostow's self-promoting fluency, see Box 10, Millikan Papers, MIT.

[46] Bowie and Immerman, *Waging Peace*, pp. 110–11, 115.

complained that such "an ivory tower staff" would be free "of all experience and association with the problems."[47] In the White House, Rostow urged that policymakers should not "waste time" on theoretical papers[48] but recalled that Washington knew him as "a long-winded idea man."[49] Kennedy grew tired of his ebullient lectures.[50] He moved Rostow from Bundy's aegis at the end of 1961, out of the White House, to head the Policy Planning Staff in the State Department, where, as we have already seen, men of greater power or intellect were contemptuous of him. Henry Kissinger apparently also thought of him as "a fool."[51]

In 1964 and 1965, when Johnson set policy in Vietnam, Rostow had little influence. At the same time, from 1961 on, he had supported sustained intervention in Vietnam and had written memos advocating bombing and graduated military action.[52] In the immediate aftermath of the Bay of Pigs he sponsored "a maximum effort—military, economic, political, and diplomatic" in Vietnam. Bombing the North would stop the flow of revolutionaries to the South. Not only could the United States be victorious there, but success would take people's minds from Cuba.[53]

Modernization theory in the style of *The Stages of Economic Growth* rationalized Kennedy's program of foreign aid. Rostow commented that leaders from developing countries always referred to "the concept of take-off" to JFK but barely disguised their interest in American funds.[54] Modernization was the way to talk about money. Nonetheless, many of the policy intellectuals with ideas like Rostow's were convinced that the challenges to the United States would come in the underdeveloped world, and their ideas complemented the rhetorical stress on conventional weaponry for struggles "on the periphery." Rostow modified his theories to apply to modernizing societies that were actually under Communist military attack. Not only did he advocate the techniques of counterinsurgency and guerilla warfare popular at the time. He also put them into his own peculiar context. The military might do partial service in Southeast Asia as a modernizing elite, and armed assistance could provide a shield behind which development might lift South Vietnam into the takeoff phase. Behind the shield, economic aid could provide the capital necessary to promote

---

[47] Rostow and Gates quoted in Roherty, *Decisions of McNamara*, p. 41.

[48] FRUS, 1961–63, vol. 8, *National Security Policy*, p. 55.

[49] Rostow, Oral History no. 1, p. 13, LBJ Library.

[50] Freedman, *Kennedy's Wars,* pp. 317, 338.

[51] According to Daniel Ellsberg, *Secrets: A Memoir of Vietnam and the Pentagon Papers* (New York: Viking, 2002), p. 348.

[52] See Rostow, Oral History, no. 1, pp. 9–10; Box 13, Rostow Papers, LBJ Library; Parrot to JFK, March 22, 1962, FRUS, 1961–63, vol. 8, *National Security Policy*, pp. 254–55.

[53] Rostow Memorandum, April 24, 1961, in *The Cuban Missile Crisis, 1962: A National Security Archive Documents Reader*, ed. Laurence Chang and Peter Kornbluh (New York: New Press, 1998), p. 19.

[54] Rostow, Oral History, p. 14, JFK Library.

growth. With any luck, the insurgency in the South would slowly go away, and the country would emerge as a fledging industrial democracy, perhaps on the model of South Korea.[55]

Such ideas made it easy for Rostow to support the Johnson administration in Vietnam in 1964 and 1965—and to press for more action—although his impact was limited. Then, in 1966, LBJ brought Rostow back to the White House to replace Bundy as national security advisor, a strikingly important job. The appointment signified Rostow's willingness to prosecute the war. Johnson also desired to spite Bundy, who detested Rostow, and to have nearby a learned mind that fervently backed the president. But even though Rostow had the last laugh, he was too late to have a distinctive conceptual inspiration on Vietnam. He was faced with a policy in place, whose implementation he had early and vigorously confirmed, but he did not contribute in a way that would move applied scholarship forward. William Bundy said that he made no mark. Instead, said George Ball, Rostow "cast a malign spell over Johnson, encouraging all of the President's worst instincts by rationalizing them with factitious historical parallels."[56]

In Vietnam the *ideas* of intellectuals were notable neither for their perspicuity nor for their causal efficacy. Theories were often wrongheaded, but theorists qua theorists were not usually relevant to running policy. To the extent that the intellectuals themselves were influential, it is hard to make the case that the conceptions they took from the world of thought were crucial. Rusk and Bundy had the greatest power, but their interest in academic debate minimal. The most striking effect that thinkers had on officials—RAND strategists with McNamara, or Bundy or Rostow with Johnson—was to characterize policy in such a way that its nature was disguised and matters positively explained if there was a perception that they had gone awry.

NET ASSESSMENT

By the late 1960s Vietnam and McNamara, together, had given RAND's systems analysis and its relatives in war planning a bad name in Washington, and a distinctive RAND intellectual style went into decline. But, bureaucratically entrenched, the essentials of the inclination did not die, and the fundamentals of systems analysis were preserved in a nominally different enterprise. Net assessment came into its own only after the period I have investigated. Promoted by the

---

[55] Rostow, interview, February 22, 2002.

[56] Bundy to Ball, July 6, 1976; Ball to Bundy, August 23, 1976, Box 2, Additional Bundy Papers, Mudd Library, Princeton University. For examples of Rostow's historical reasoning see Rostow to LBJ, April 14, 1966, and September 19, 1966, FRUS, 1964–68, vol. 4, *Vietnam, 1966*, pp. 348, 647.

group around Albert Wohlstetter, net assessment was associated with Andrew Marshall, a longtime employee at RAND who left there in 1972 to direct a new office of net assessment in the Department of Defense. The net assessor comprehensively studied the likely dynamics involved in future competition with a (Soviet) adversary or in the evolution of war. The endeavor promised to bring together operational military analyses and intelligence data, which were supposed previously to have been separate. Net assessment also admitted to more subjectivity and appraisal than systems analysis. Net assessment calculated the interactions of various military confrontations that might occur. It put them in the context of the total society's mobilization for battle, and based the results on an examination of the traditions of such conflicts, cultural patterns of strategy, and the changing geopolitical aims of the combatants.[57]

[57] One view of net assessment is given in Pickett, Roche, and Watts, "Net Assessment," pp. 158–85.

CHAPTER 8

The Kennedy School of Government, 1964–1971

IN THE 1950s and early 1960s the Harvard Department of Government was out of step with other leading universities, which had institutes devoted to the scientific study of policy.[1] Even its name suggested commitment to something slightly different from political science. While Harvard's prestige insured that its employees were well represented in policymaking circles, two older scholars, William Y. Elliott and Carl J. Friedrich, who had credentials as political theorists, still dominated the department. More freestanding scholarly entities on the campus offered younger faculty fashionable niches, although officials regularly thought of closing the most significant of these, the Harvard School of Public Administration—the Lucius Littauer Center. The drowsy center had existed since 1935 but was a stepchild in Cambridge, an administrative unit that faculty in the departments of economics and government jointly ran. While the connection to Harvard had made Littauer more than respectable, training in public administration lacked the excellence associated with Harvard's schools of law and medicine. As one evaluating committee put it, the master's degree that the center awarded had "never been entirely satisfactory," and the students "not fully up to the standards of the Arts and Sciences departments."[2] The center contributed little to the field of security studies that scholars in places like Princeton and Hopkins had established some fifteen years before, and often MIT's Center for International Studies welcomed Harvard faculty interested in geopolitical strategy.

The situation changed at the end of 1963 when the family of John Kennedy initiated plans for the presidential library that would house material from the administration of the assassinated leader, immediately elevated to martyrdom. First Arthur Schlesinger Jr. and then McGeorge Bundy promoted a library and an accompanying "Institute in Memory of President Kennedy" or "Kennedy Center for the Politics of Democracy" or (finally) "Institute of Politics" that were physically and intellectually grand.[3] At one point in the complicated negotiations, it looked like Kennedy's alma mater would erect a Kennedy School of Government that would replace Littauer, and attach this school to a presidential library. Harvard would not just upgrade its training of graduate students

---

[1] A contemporary survey is in Gene M. Lyons and Louis Morton, *Schools for Strategy: Education and Research in National Security Affairs* (New York: Praeger, 1965), pp. 146–54.

[2] Visiting Committee Report, 1966–71, HUE 44.171.14, Harvard University Archives.

[3] Kennedy School Folders, Box 1, McGeorge Bundy Papers, JFK Library.

Figure 8. Richard Neustadt at a Kennedy School meeting. To Jacqueline Kennedy's left are Averell Harriman, Michael Forrestal, and Neustadt (Courtesy of the Harvard University Archives.)

and redesign a graduate program. The Kennedys and the new center would boost Harvard into the forefront of policy science and create a new public conversation about politics oriented to the majesty of JFK's Camelot.

At the same time that civilian strategists were prominent in the Defense Department, Harvard developed in this new setting its own style of strategic thought that complemented RAND's ideas.

THE INSTITUTE OF POLITICS

By early 1964 Robert Kennedy, John Kennedy's brother and spokesman for the family, had urged Harvard to recruit Richard Neustadt from Columbia to play a prominent role in the endeavor that would initially receive $10 million from the family's Kennedy Library Company, as well as other donations linked to the family's fortunes. The Department of Government was not entirely gracious in accepting this benefaction, but only the recently tenured Henry Kissinger argued, on grounds he claimed of principle, that the department ought to turn Neustadt down[4] (and the Kennedys and their money). As soon as Neustadt arrived in 1965, he organized a new graduate program formed around an Institute of Politics in the planned Kennedy School. This institute would offer a central program of public policy, when the Kennedy School of Government

---

[4] Kissinger to Maas, October 13, 1964, KSG Papers: UA V.434.11 General Correspondence, N-Z, Neustadt, Harvard University Archives.

took over for Littauer in 1966. The goals for the early 1970s were a building, a broadened curriculum, and a world-class faculty.

Neustadt and the people around him eloquently stated that the new institution would bring science to bear on politics. The modest ends that Neustadt had pursued at Columbia received a sharper focus, and an ambitious group of policy scientists would work them out at Harvard. "The university['s] response to a national crisis" should be to create "a new profession." The United States must "devote a share of its highest intellectual talent, and the most modern scientific methods, to the public service." Harvard would train intellectual generalists who would combine wisdom with their own individual expertise to govern public affairs. Reformed areas of inquiry "calculated to serve as the basis for practical decisions" and "to help the scholar and practitioner to bridge the growing gap that separates them" would secure social scientific study. Echoing RAND ideas, Harvard proposed to promote the careers of those who could go back and forth between the government, on the one side, and law, business, and the university, on the other. The Kennedy School would influence "the administration of government at all levels." The institution would deal in "organized learning" and make "systematic Efforts to capture lessons learned."[5]

NEUSTADT'S THOUGHT

Neustadt was now more suspicious of the benign nature of democratic polity. In his examination of negotiations in the executive, he wanted to see not just how leaders might get more power, but to explore how the decisions themselves might be made better—how the president, by administrative jujitsu, might use bureaucracies to achieve his goals; how outcomes might more closely resemble the executive's objectives that were the best guide to desirable policy.

Neustadt emphasized three concerns. First, he perfected the case-study method that "Skybolt and Nassau" had advanced. He would draw his conclusions from a look at the common features in a series of past decisions—most crucially some were successes and some failures. Second, because he dealt with recent history, Neustadt investigated these case studies using structured interviews with participants in the decision making. In fact, he became known for his belief that such interviews overshadowed the importance of the written record.[6] Analytical but friendly probing of policymakers—"critical oral his-

[5] "Toward A New Profession," HUE 44.2.2; Dean's Report, 1966–67, HUE 44.166.75; and see *The John F. Kennedy School of Government: The First Fifty Years* (Cambridge, Mass.: Ballinger, 1986), HUE 44.186.42A, Harvard University Archives.

[6] Richard E. Neustadt, *Alliance Politics* (New York: Columbia University Press, 1970), p. 7.

tory"—was more likely to get at the truth than documents, often written "for the record" and concealing both motive and goal. Neustadt consulted in a treacherous Washington environment that, for him, tainted the paper trail. He did not have the historian's sense that he might interrogate the documents themselves, which at least had the advantage of being contemporary with the events under study. Nor did he sense that memory might be frail, or the intentions of policymakers protective, or less than honorable. As an insider, he also believed that they would reveal the truth to him, despite his awareness that the same people could write documents that obfuscated. He had none of the suspicion of the historian of those in power. His preference for interviews in any event highlighted his distance from historians, who were usually dealing with the dead.

Over the years, the sort of scholarship Neustadt promulgated built a special relationship between scholars like him who had a connection to the upper reaches of the federal bureaucracy. His strategy fit in with the view that specialist historians with exceptional clearances might work for the government. In early 1963 he advocated an instant history of the Kennedy administration, provided that the White House staff oversaw the work of the historian chosen to do the job.[7] The scholarship of Neustadt and his colleagues distinguished between academics like themselves and those less favored in Washington, who might be denied interviews and confidential documents.[8] Neustadt recognized that perspectives more hostile to Washington existed but innocently assumed that intimacy with the powerful presented minimal problems of professional compromise.

As Neustadt elaborated a mental picture of how Harvard would study public policy, he refined his view of the most problematic aspect of the presidency. The professor assumed that democratic politics—or American politics—defined acceptable aims, and wondered why things so often went awry. What caused the various crises that were the staple of politics?

The answer to this question defined the third concern: competing bureaucracies hindered the desired expression of purpose. Neustadt formulated in an understated but straightforward way the crucial element of his view. The scholar had to take in policies not as the outcome of plans rationally decided upon, but as the product of bargains among the various people involved in making decisions. Their personal histories and those of their agencies limited—or empowered—the functionaries who ran them. A web of ongoing commitments caught up administrators, and engaged them in a variety of struggles and alliances that might or might not be pertinent to the decisions at hand.

[7] Neustadt to Schlesinger, January 7, 1963, Box 18, Neustadt Papers, JFK Library.
[8] For an example see Coulam, *Illusions of Choice*, pp. xi–xii, 391–93.

This context had previously led Neustadt to ignore ends and to argue that the president merely had the power to persuade officialdom.[9]

Neustadt now focused on how bureaucratic jousts, which often produced misapprehensions or bungling, might explain policy outcomes. Political science of the sort Neustadt practiced could assist people like the president to untangle these snarls, and enable policy, whatever it was, to be carried out more efficaciously. As one critic has noted, this "second wave" of theorizing was more contentious—it gave greater prominence to the obstructive role of institutions.[10]

ANALYSIS OF THE MODEL

One way to see the distinctiveness of this interpretation of political life is to look by contrast at historical knowledge. As a form of understanding, histories of politics and diplomacy are narratives about how purposes, intentions, or goals are revealed over time. Persons in communities can display these purposes, but so too can communities themselves: historical individuals such as groups, organizations, institutions, cultures, nations. The activities defining purpose may be frustrated or aborted. The relevant individuals may not like what the fruition of their wills amounts to in the world. Nor can persons at the time be fully aware themselves of the culmination or abandonment of their aims or those of the institutions, cultures, or nations of which they are members. Most important, historians presuppose that their sort of understanding can only emerge in time, with "historical perspective," as they say. One cannot write a history of a conflict until it is *over*. A reason "Skybolt and Nassau" was off the mark *as history* was that, despite access to the documents, the author did not write from a temporal distance and thus could not take hold of historical truth.

Historians are also hard pressed to judge that alternative courses of action would have had better effects, or that persons had much latitude in their choices. Ambiguity of effort is conventional in historical appraisal. Yet the enterprise presumes that we learn in the unraveling of events over time how purposes evolve and come to fruition. Historians regularly confront the distractions that constitute impediments to their central story. In diplomatic history, for example, public statements, conscious lack of clarity, and outright lies often conceal purpose. Accident, weakness, inconstancy of effort, personal grievance, or subsidiary bureaucracies often subvert, temporarily or permanently, the ends of a country's foreign policy. The frustration of aims or the fault of

---

[9] These ideas were worked out in Neustadt, *Alliance Politics*.

[10] Robert Abt, "Bureaucratic Politics and American Foreign Policy: A Critique," *Policy Sciences* 4 (1973): 467–90.

organizations in such frustration is a staple of investigations by reflective students of the past.

The philosopher G. F. Hegel got at the problem when he spoke of "the cunning of reason." Hegel noted that political struggles abounded with contesting and only semiunderstood selfish interests, many of which seemed to cancel one another out. Yet, he claimed, the result was the advance of a greater purpose, never fully understood by the politicians involved, and never fully the conscious purpose of persons. Ordinary historians conventionally point to irony—things often turn out with a twisted connection to original aims. There is "a law of unintended consequences." Garden-variety factors account for much historical irony. Sometimes, say, diplomacy is topsy-turvy because a stronger power has overridden the purposes of officials. Sometimes policymakers are replaced, and the ends of older decision-makers are misconceived or deliberately altered. Anyone who has worked on a historical problem using original sources and has traced the development of policies can testify to the accidents that drive policy off course, the conscious "tacking" that frequently occurs, and the insistent background noise of dealing with incompletely committed subordinates, administrative stubbornness, and missed communications.

As important as any of these empirical variables is the additional fact that many political beliefs consist in a vision of far-off goals, a moral ethos about the worth of these goals, and expectation for apocalyptic success. Politics is very much a means to action that gives an aspect of complete reality to mere anticipation. In these circumstances, historical irony is commonplace, and materializes because what politicians say may have little to do with what they do, or with what happens.

In addition to ignoring the peculiar way goals come to completion for historians and to placing obstacles at center stage, scholars like Neustadt often assumed that their approach yielded a historical account of what occurred. Yet as a form of knowledge, history must differ from what is available to policymakers. As I have noted, historical knowledge depends on a temporal perspective. Events take on their historical meaning with the passage of time, and it is logically impossible that an actor could examine himself as a historian would. Woodrow Wilson could not see himself as initiating an American foreign policy impulse that would later have the doubtful connotation *Wilsonian.* Nor could Lyndon Johnson know in 1964 that subsequent sympathetic historians might describe his efforts as those of *a failed Wilsonian.* Wilson could not know he was starting a tradition, and in 1964 LBJ had not yet failed.

Neustadt argued that actors might use potted but nonetheless sophisticated packages of narratives of past events to negotiate the present. But the intent could never have been for the actors to have historical knowledge of themselves. Historical knowledge is never autobiographical—it requires that the actors be seen not as they see themselves but as others see them. They could not, a priori, have an idea of what they were doing as historical figures—let us say of what their aims were in all their complexity, how these aims appeared to others, how others might rightly oppose them, and how things turned out. People could not learn these things until they became the objects of history, and until historians exposed them to the pitiless inspection with which they scrutinized the past. Instead, for Neustadt, policymakers learned to circumvent obstacles in their immediate path. He designed his work not to understand the past but to manipulate the present and to bring about a desired policy outcome. As one theorist-policymaker, Morton Halperin, observed, the ideas about bureaucracy, once absorbed, allowed the politician to behave more rationally *in government.*[11]

The knowledge available to policymakers must be more akin to the partial and limited knowledge we have of ourselves than to historical knowledge and the knowledge that others have of us, which are both crueler. Anyone who has gone to a dinner party and spoken of absent acquaintances must understand the difference between the way people appear to themselves and the way others regularly describe them. We judge the calculations, motives, moral decision-making, and even minor foibles of individuals far more ruthlessly than do the individuals concerned. This is not just an observation about dinner parties and history. One aspect of civility is the delicate dialectic that militates against our telling others what we think of them, in return for which they do the same in order to make social life possible. Civility is never mere civility. People could not function were they to understand themselves the way others do. Policymakers, like others, construct for themselves a sense of what they are doing that will differ from what others think, as well as from the perhaps even more unforgiving but similar accounts that historians will give of their activities. Indeed, such construction presents a special problem for public officials, many of whose actions are subject to far more open and less circumspect discussion than the actions of most of us. Diplomats must deal with excessive obsequiousness (sometimes from commentators and scholars) as well as excessive lack of civility (sometimes from commentators and scholars).[12]

Policymakers understand this phenomenon when they deny access to their papers until after their deaths, and sometimes longer. While they recognize that the importance of such papers necessitates their use, statesmen also recognize that what is found will not only differ from their sense of things but may also undermine their self-worth. In promotion of the importance of oral history over documents, Neustadt displayed a lack of interest for the written record that policymakers did not share. They are far more comfortable talking about their views of what has happened in the recent past than they are with the release of documents.

---

[11] Interview with Halperin, March 4, 2003.

[12] My use of civility is barely covered in the comprehensive set of studies edited by Leroy S. Rouner, *Civility* (Notre Dame, Ind.: University of Notre Dame Press, 2000).

Historical knowledge of politics and foreign affairs is essentially based on documentary resources. Its heartlessness is that it is no respecter of persons, and in this way different from the kinder interviews that defined Neustadt's approach.

Neustadt rightly never claimed that policymakers might themselves act as if they had at the time historical knowledge of their own activities. But in addition to the use of his approach as a tool for decision makers, it also became a way to understand the meaning of events that was supposed to be comparable to, even a substitute for, history.[13] But history cannot in the first instance be concerned with navigating the ship of state. It rather analyzes, after the fact, what happened and why, without a primary focus on whether outcomes were desired or desirable. Disciplinary point of view was also critical. When Neustadt issued a new edition of "Skybolt and Nassau," over a quarter of a century later, his "later reflections" did not mention the historical meaning of the events.[14]

The countertradition among my intellectuals—Kennan, Morgenthau, and as I shall note Kissinger—dismissed social science and relied on history. The positivist instrumentalists returned the complement: RAND wanted to replace history with "synthetic history," the results of simulation and gaming. Neustadt's followers hoped to use the past to circumvent its pitfalls.

There is a deep tension here. Historical knowledge, which gives insight into the meaning of policy, can conflict with what I shall call the actor-knowledge generated at RAND and Harvard. On the one hand, in its inability to obtain historical perspective—the meaning of events studied historically—actor-knowledge will have wrongly understood what is going on. On the other, as Friedrich Nietzsche pointed out a long time ago in his work on history, historical knowledge may make the bearer of that knowledge sick, unable to do work in the world. Such knowledge tends to undermine a sense of the efficacious and desirable nature of outcomes persons can will.[15] The point of view of the actor is necessary to agency. Historical knowledge is more spectatorial.[16]

THE MAY GROUP

Neustadt brought his ideas to bear on contemporary politics. He also organized the Kennedy School and simultaneously implemented its first research program. Following on the heels of colloquia at Harvard's Center for International

---

[13] These confusions are exemplified in Graham T. Allison and Morton H. Halperin, "Bureaucratic Politics: A Paradigm and some Policy Implications," *World Politics* 24, Supplement (1972): 40–79.

[14] *Report to JFK: The Skybolt Crisis in Perspective* (Ithaca: Cornell University Press, 1999).

[15] This is the point of his essay, usually translated into English as "The Use and Abuse of History," which I have used in the pamphlet of that name (Indianapolis: Bobbs-Merrill, 1957), 2nd ed.

[16] See Richard Moran, *Authority and Estrangement: An Essay on Self-Knowledge* (Princeton: Princeton University Press, 2001), pp. 64–65, 100–101.

Affairs in the late 1950s, a seminar took shape in early 1966. The Faculty Study Group on Bureaucracy, Politics, and Policy in the Institute of Politics— or more informally over a longer time "the May Group"—was named after its convener, Ernest May. A diplomatic historian who had consulted in Washington, May too wanted to forge links with policymakers to make decisions better[17] and had proposed special treatment for governmental historians who might assist officials.[18] He befriended Neustadt and influenced his views on how history might contribute to scientific administration. In addition to Neustadt and May, in the late 1960s, the group included many who had worked in the Kennedy and Johnson administrations and had RAND affiliations—William Kaufmann, Thomas Schelling, Adam Yarmolinsky, and Carl Kaysen. The interests of the May Group eventuated in a famous course, On the Uses of History. As team-teachers Neustadt and May introduced an imaginative case-study method to train students about policymaking. The teachers "invented" cases—say a North Korean attack on the South in 1966—and supplied documents from various perspectives, while asking students to respond to such events as responsible policymakers. Neustadt and May published a book about the course, *Thinking in Time*.[19]

Emphasizing foreign policy, the May Group began its deliberations at a distracting moment. The war in Vietnam had become hotly contested. Universities were in turmoil, a fact underscored for the May Group in November 1966 when Defense secretary McNamara traveled to Harvard as an honorary member of the Kennedy School to inaugurate the Institute of Politics. McNamara made a presentation after a quarrel with students that embarrassed the policy academics. Scholars in the May Group believed McNamara to be "a profoundly sensitive, subtle, and humane personality," and the protests stunned them. In a letter of apology to the secretary, Neustadt implied that the demonstration indicated fascism's appearance in America. McNamara's reception was all the more troubling, Neustadt wrote, because "I'm grateful to you above all else for being almost the only man in creation, Mac Bundy aside, who fully and completely grasps the whole of my ambition for this Institute and School."[20]

In a connected issue, the scholars in Cambridge also worried about maintaining their professional authority against a popular group of radical historians and social scientists, embittered by their opposition to current policy in Southeast Asia. The "revisionists" attacked American diplomacy in the whole post–

[17] Neustadt and May, *Thinking in Time*, pp. xviii–xx; Neustadt, *Alliance Politics*, p. 160. See the files in May Group, Study Group (Cont)-Z, KSG Records, UAV 708.6; and "Research Proposal," May Group, Lovett, Robert —N, UAV 708.8, Harvard University Archives.

[18] See the discussion in chapter 4 of May's *"Lessons" of the Past*.

[19] Neustadt and May, *Thinking in Time*, quote at p. xi.

[20] See the documents in the McNamara file, Honorary Associates, KSG Files General Office Correspondence, UAV 708.50, Harvard University Archives.

World War II period as imperialist and aggressive, and thus easily construed the war in Vietnam as the expected outcome of older policies. The Kennedy School took issue with these interpretations but felt pressed to develop a credible alternative orientation to the recent past.[21]

Finally, a financial crisis loomed. From 1963 and early 1964, the Kennedys were interested in the public character of the Institute of Politics. They had a vague vision of scholarly enterprise that would yet have the glamour of Hollywood. They did not want "just another Harvard building" with "another Harvard program,"[22] and by the late 1960s the family was in revolt about the academic thrust of Neustadt's ideas. After Robert Kennedy's murder in 1968, his brother, Massachusetts senator Edward Kennedy, commented that Neustadt was creating "a modernized Littauer" and complained that the family had always wanted a more popular and high-profile tribute to the president. This dispute occurred simultaneously with controversies over other funding and over where the Kennedy Library Corporation and Harvard would construct both the library and the Kennedy School. Neustadt and his colleagues feared that his plans, which required money for academic programs and professorships, might come to naught if the Kennedys backed out.

By 1969 circumventing the fiscal issues was critical, and the Harvard scholars called on their political contacts to protect their image of the school, to assist in raising money for it, and to keep the Kennedys on board. Operationally important to these efforts were Michael Forrestal and Averell Harriman, two men close to the Kennedy family whom we have previously met advising John Kennedy to overthrow the government of South Vietnam in 1963. Symbolically important was McGeorge Bundy, who had resigned as LBJ's national security advisor in 1966 to head the Ford Foundation, bruised by his association with the war. Asking Bundy to recall his Harvard connections, Neustadt said that the school was a tribute to JFK but particularly to the president's "extraordinary efforts to bring trained intelligence to bear on public problems." Of greatest significance was Robert McNamara, who too had Harvard connections. When McNamara left the Johnson administration in 1967–68, injured by Vietnam, Neustadt wanted to appoint him at the institute for as long as he wished, and enlisted the Kennedys to land McNamara in Cambridge. Although his appointment did not come to fruition, McNamara became one of Neustadt's "key advisors." As head of the World Bank in 1969, McNamara was instrumental in convincing the Kennedys of the importance of Neustadt's plan and in salvaging the finances of the Kennedy School with Kennedy money.[23]

---

[21] On revisionism, Harriman Project, Faculty Studies Programs, 1969–74, UAV 708.65, Harvard University Archives.

[22] See Kennedy School, January 1964–April 1965; and September 1964–October 1964, esp. Edward Kennedy Memo, December 30, 1963, Box 1, McGeorge Bundy Papers, JFK Library.

[23] Kennedy to Neustadt, April 16, 1969; Neustadt to Bundy, March 24, 1970; Neustadt to McNamara, March 3, 1969, and McNamara to Harriman, April 10, 1969; and Neustadt to Price,

THE SALIENCE OF BUREAUCRATIC POLITICS

As scholars, the members of the May Group made their first project a most difficult one. While they shared a consensual distaste for the war, they focused on policy in Vietnam and asked: Why was the United States there? What had gone awry? Reflecting on the aspirations of the political leadership they served, the May Group tried to figure out why "some of the best minds of the age" in "positions of great influence" had been unsuccessful in Southeast Asia. These "talented political leaders" had operated "from the best principles of American democracy." How could it be that the United States was so problematically committed? In a tangential way, the May Group reproached the American military for the war. In addition, the May Group called upon history to explain why Washington had failed. False analogies—Munich and Vietnam, Korea and Vietnam—rather than appropriate ones—such as the relevance of the French experience to the American one—had misled policymakers. Moreover, had the president's men been more historically adept at understanding where they and their peers had come from, in terms of their lived experience of the recent past, such a self-conscious historical perspective might have changed the mathematical odds of making better decisions.[24]

Primarily, however, Harvard's policy scientists thought Vietnam exemplified the truth of Neustadt's evolving model that now received a name—bureaucratic politics. The ongoing trouble in Southeast Asia was antithetical to what they had wanted themselves as a policy outcome, and what they would have predicted from the work of their sober, sensible, and decent former Harvard colleagues and friends, who had held office, or were still in office. Matters had not come out as planned. The May Group premised that the intentions of political leadership went unrealized, and specifically presumed that bureaucracy had transformed purpose in foreign policy. The central problem was not that of Bundy and McNamara. Bureaucratic politics allowed scholars to appreciate the gap between what Harvard conceived as the aims of policymakers in Washington and the results of their actions. The civilians in high places were victims of poor administration, bad communication, competitive organizational interests, and inadequate deliberation that resulted from the pace of everyday business. The problem was "the machinery of government." Large enterprises were "a major barrier between human aspiration and human achievement."[25]

July 5, 1968, on McNamara, Neustadt Directors Files, Box 2, Correspondence with Kennedy, UAV 434.5172.5, Harvard University Archives; Neustadt to Perkins, January 29, 1965, IOP 1964–65, Box 17; to McNamara, November 30, 1967, Box 8, N 1967–68, Robert Kennedy Papers, JFK Library.

[24] *Thinking in Time*, pp. 75–90, 161–71.

[25] "Retrospect," December 1969, May Group, Lovett–N, UAV 708.8, Harvard University Archives.

One cannot help asking what could be more wide of the mark, as if Lyndon Johnson and the men around him, rightly or wrongly, could have subdued Asian Communism on their own. If we look at the achievement of any collective aim, bureaucracy is the means of achievement. Suppose LBJ had been defeated for the presidency in 1964 and had retired to his ranch in Johnson City, Texas. Further suppose that from there he decided as a private citizen to maintain an anti-Communist South Vietnam and enlisted "the Harvards" to aid him. What would have been his chances without the globe-spanning institutions of the American government? Bureaucracies are imperfect bearers of large purpose, but they are the only instrumentalities we have to will it.

The rise of bureaucratic politics as an explanatory scheme demands clarification, and its social origins make it partly comprehensible. The defenders of bureaucratic politics frequently asserted that where you stood depended on where you sat, and they exemplified this aphorism.[26] The men in the May Group depended financially on the goodwill of the policymaking elite they were investigating, and never made deep criticisms of this elite despite their dislike for American involvement in Southeast Asia. The policy scientists faced a dilemma that appeared insoluble. They wanted to explore what they perceived as the disaster of the war without blaming those who were, for good or ill, plainly responsible for it. Bureaucratic politics resolved this problem. The politicians who took the United States into the war and who had been celebrated as "can-do" decision makers suddenly became victims of institutional mismanagement.

Indeed, McGeorge Bundy explicitly worried that some would make the accusation that through the Kennedy School "the Kennedys are taking over history too," to secure a base for less than unbiased views abut Camelot. But Neustadt argued that just the opposite case could be made. The affiliation with Cambridge diluted Kennedy interests because of Harvard's reputation for dispassionate scholarship.[27] A few years later, as head of the Ford Foundation, Bundy financed a new Program for Science and International Affairs at the Kennedy School. The idea was "a major initiative to promote university-based research" in security studies because of Bundy's concern that they were not "deeply rooted in the academic world."[28]

Although the Kennedy School came into existence much later than SAIS or the Princeton Center for International Studies, it arose as the premier institution for the study of decision making. It ultimately overshadowed RAND itself. Like the other academic institutes of policy, Harvard too exhibited the irony

---

[26] See for example, Allison and Halperin, "Bureaucratic Politics," p. 73.

[27] Neustadt to Lovett, January 3, 1967, History Project, A–Ar, Institute, May, UAV 708.6, Harvard University Archives.

[28] I have taken this description from Stephen Miller's review "*International Security* at Twenty-Five," *International Security* 26 (2001–2): 5–6. Miller was then editor of the journal that had been founded with this infusion of Ford Foundation money in 1976.

of postwar social science. The assertion of scientific impartiality and objectivity in investigation went hand in hand with a greater commitment not to scholarship but to involvement in politics and punditry. And the greater involvement with real politics simultaneously contracted the range of political views espoused within the intellectual community. When scholars augmented their advisory roles to politicians, they became less able to articulate controversial ideas. But Harvard's case was also unique. Nowhere else was scholarship so clearly subservient to the outlook of a specific group of policymakers.

THE ESSENCE OF DECISION

The May Group pondered more questions than Vietnam. This forum produced the most extraordinary work about one of the favorite topics of the Kennedy School, the Cuban Missile Crisis. While institutions might frustrate human effort, on other occasions they might provide the site for the enhancement of purpose. Again and again, Harvard scholars returned to October 1962 and Kennedy's executive branch for lessons to guide the American policymaker in what they regarded as the greatest example of quality decision-making—a counterpoint to what had gone on, or was going on, in Vietnam. Graham Allison, a student of Neustadt's who served as the secretary of the Study Group on Bureaucracy, Politics, and Policy, received his doctoral degree in the late 1960s. In 1971 he published *Essence of Decision: Explaining the Cuban Missile Crisis,* based on his dissertation and his ideas about the group's discussion topics.[29] For over thirty years the volume influenced the discipline of international relations and exemplified the historical and social scientific analysis associated with the May Group and the Kennedy School. Scholars credited *Essence of Decision* with a demonstration of the worth of this sort of analysis, just as they credited Albert Wohlstetter's report of 1954, "The Selection and Use of Strategic Air Bases," with validation of RAND social science. On the strength of the book Allison went on to become dean of the Kennedy School.[30]

Essence of Decision was heralded for two reasons. First, it offered a compelling substantive elucidation of the missile crisis. Second, it provided a unique methodology for the investigation of foreign affairs. Allison laid out three alternative accounts to inspect public policy: the rational actor; organizational behavior; and governmental politics constructs. But the discussions of these constructs did not successively follow each other. An exploration of

---

[29] Allison, *The Essence of Decision.*

[30] A new edition—rewritten, longer, and coauthored with Philip Zelikow, a younger scholar for a time connected to Harvard policy studies—brought the original up to date in 1999 and presents the opportunity to make a historical interpretation of the role of the original in the history of the study of international politics, Allison and Zelikow, *The Essence of Decision: Explaining the Cuban Missile Crisis,* 2nd ed. (New York: Longman, 1999).

the missile crisis as each construct understood it separated each theoretical discussion from its siblings. Allison enriched each successive description by reference to the constructs that had gone before. He said that he adhered to the logical positivist model of scientific explanation, promoted by philosopher Carl Hempel.[31] There was an overarching model of explanation, and then three different points of view to which Allison attended but which he could not rank. Finally, the book explicitly used history to explore how we could make better decisions in the future. History and social science could jointly improve policy. Allison praised the decisions of October 1962 and hoped that we could codify their principles if we had a more adequate grasp of what had occurred in the Ex Comm.

The rational-actor construct assumed that the achievement or nonachievement of thoughtfully considered and agreed upon ends was necessary and sufficient to appraise decisions. This impulse was found, for example, in RAND social scientists and Thomas Schelling.[32]

So the book first investigated the missile crisis in its terms. Here we got the most celebratory depiction of President Kennedy and his executive committee. But Allison considered that depiction insufficient. He complicated his "first cut" by a look at decision making in the two further constructs of organizational behavior and governmental politics.

Scholars have been troubled to differentiate these last two constructs—one that stressed decisions as the standard outputs of organizations; the other that produced decisions through bureaucratic infighting. Both elevated the nonrational aspects of policy, and the last was bureaucratic politics à la Neustadt. Together they suggested why events often did not follow the ends of planners, why surprises filled the history of the implementation of a policy. Some aspects of the missile crisis became more transparent once the focus was off the conscious ideas of high officials, what they hoped to accomplish, and what they thought their adversaries were up to.

When Allison figured matters out in 1971, what did he say happened in Cuba? The question of a nuclear Germany is at the center of scholarly comprehension of the missiles in Cuba. Allison missed this entirely. He did not get it wrong, so much as he did not see the relevance of Germany to Cuba at all. A revised edition published some thirty years later highlighted the early failure. The new edition underscored the German problem and had an extended ten-page discussion of Berlin and several other references to the question of a nuclear Germany.[33]

The methodology also had problems. Allison in fact did not use the logical positivist model of explanation. There were no "statements of generalizations"

---

[31] Allison, *The Essence of Decision*, pp. 278–79, 327–28.
[32] For example, Schelling, *The Strategy of Conflict*.
[33] Allison and Zelikow, *The Essence of Decision*, pp. 99–108.

that were candidates for laws, no depiction of "boundary conditions," no attempts to draw deductive inferences in the manner that Hempel said should take place. Omitting even an "explanation sketch" that Hempel said might be employed in history, Allison proceeded in a manner more familiar to historians, mixing narrative with interpretation. He weighed proposed truths against the data that were assumed to support them and tested evidence in various ways.

This strategy was more complex than positivism allowed, and Allison's three vying constructs emphasized even greater complexity. Much of *Essence of Decision* was antithetic to logical positivism, for these constructs were incompatible. At the same time, in the crunch, Allison said that we needed a grand model that would incorporate all that was good in the constructs, or that we must combine constructs to get a more comprehensive scientific explanation.[34]

Allison had three different stories, each of which examined the missile crisis. The bottom line was hateful to positivism—that scholars at this time could not do better than "multiple, overlapping, competing conceptual models."[35] In fact, the author often attributed the expressed views not to himself but to anonymous "analysts" of the missile crisis, who believed in different constructs.

Allison thus did not produce an integrated account, although he discussed social-science methodology and logical philosophy. Yet the message was simple. To study this material was like watching *Rashomon*, Akira Kurosawa's famous movie of 1951 about a sexual encounter, where the filmmaker treated viewers to different versions of the same event given by various participants.

It is easy to speculate about why this book appeared in 1971. Like the May Group's explanation of what had gone wrong in Vietnam, *Essence* partly resulted from the confusions of the 1960s as scholars of public policy connected to Harvard interpreted these confusions. Vietnam hovered in the background. Allison wrote about Cuba, but he and his peers worried about why RAND ideas, which Allison took to be influential, had gone haywire in Southeast Asia. The consequence of these qualms was a stylish relativism, and the discussions of the May Group that preceded the publication of *Essence of Decision* had noted the reasoning of Thomas Kuhn's *Structure of Scientific Revolutions* of 1962.[36] Kuhn, a Harvard product in physics and philosophy, had argued that the hard sciences themselves did not progress. They were subject, as academic discourse had it, to altering and incommensurable "paradigms."[37] Allison put these ideas to work in Cuba, when he nodded not only to the greatness of Kennedy's effort but also to the inscrutability of effort. Harvard's response to the 1960s was like that of a lot of people. Things were not certain, the world

---

[34] See, for example Allison, *The Essence of Decision*, pp. ix, 251, quote at p. 275.

[35] Allison and Zelikow, *The Essence of Decision*, p. 401.

[36] See the material in Bureaucratic Politics Group, Black Caucus–Campaign; and May Group, Lovett–N, Institute of Politics Papers, UAV 708.8, Harvard University Archives.

[37] For a discussion see Bruce Kuklick, *A History of Philosophy in America* (New York: Oxford University Press, 2001), pp. 269–72.

won't conform to our wishes, we can't control what is going on, we are left with our own perspectives. Allison elevated these anxieties to respectability.

Bureaucratic politics was a tool to get policymakers off the hook of Vietnam. The scholar had to see that policies could go awry because of unproductive contacts, organizational sclerosis, and contests among agencies. But in the evolution of the bureaucratic-politics model, a darker message had emerged. Vietnam intimated that these problems were not solved as easily as Neustadt had hoped—they were so great as to have distorted the purposes of able and intelligent statesmen-experts. With *Essence of Decision*, however, Harvard found a further way to exonerate its people who were making policy in Washington. Actors could never be sure of what was happening. The interpretation of history and current events was always in doubt, subject to the distortions of "conceptual lenses," "conceptual models," "conceptual frameworks," "vantage points," and so on. As Allison put it, the notion of comprehensive truth was "really a metaphor."[38] About the only certainty in Cambridge was that at least in October 1962 Harvard's Jack Kennedy and his Harvard advisors had done a good job.

Where are we left with this seminal text? With respect to alternative conceptual schemes, scholars are about where they were some time ago—blindly staggering around. We have, however, made some progress substantively. Allison was off the mark in 1971 in neglecting the problem of a nuclear Germany and its relation to the missile crisis. In making amends for this oversight, the new edition best refuted the old. Historical research had helped. History might have helped more if Allison were not committed at the outset to the view that there could not be an overall explanation.

These are sober conclusions to come to. *Essence of Decision* was for a long time a standard text used to teach public policy, to train men and women how to make better decisions. But the book did not have much of a grip on the basic issue of the missile crisis. Allison said that tangential aspects of the crisis were crucial, and did not tell students about crucial aspects. If Cuba were an example, students could not learn from an advanced degree in public policy how to figure out the fundamental issues necessary to make a decision. We also need to mull over what Allison was doing when he sketched his perspectivalism. Although the issue was not discussed, perspectivalism does not make much practical assistance available if one is looking today for a way to make the best decision. Perspectivalism says that when people in the future explain what you have done, the chances are that they will not be able to tell whether you could have done better or worse. This is not a comfortable conclusion to come to if one is engaged in the preparation of individuals for careers in public service.

---

[38] Allison, *The Essence of Decision*, pp. ix, 251, 275; Allison and Zelikow, *The Essence of Decision*, p. 401.

CHAPTER 9

The Pentagon Papers

VIETNAM DISTRESSED the intellectuals, especially those in positions of power, who felt, even if wrongly, "the blame, guilt, and all the rest of it"—as one of them put it[1]—for a war gone awry. While Dean Rusk remained tight-lipped about his contribution to the foreign policies of the 1960s, Walt Rostow was a fascinating exception among my groups of strategists and actively defended his commitments. Most of the others, believing themselves in part answerable for bad things, used their facility with ideas to envision the war in a way that would diminish their accountability. We have seen this attitude at work in the Kennedy School of Government, but it took different forms. Townsend Hoopes, a long-serving Democratic official, became the first, but not the last, to blame the Republicans. Puzzling over the problem in a work of 1968, *The Limits of Intervention*, and then five years later in *The Devil and John Foster Dulles*, Hoopes argued that Dulles "must bear a large measure of responsibility." He had made such "a deep imprint on the national psyche" and was such "a subliminal influence" that presidents after Eisenhower could not escape the secretary of state's anti-Communism.[2] Kennedy White House aide Arthur Schlesinger Jr. had celebrated the control of the Ex Comm in its deliberations over Cuba. When the same men were accused of making the decisions over Vietnam, Schlesinger proposed early on a different but soon to be conventional explanation of motives. His book of 1967, *The Bitter Heritage,* endorsed "the quagmire thesis." As if by accident the United States had embroiled itself in Southeast Asia, and one commitment had produced another until, without any wayward intent, a brutal and unwinnable war bogged down America. It was not only idle but unfair "to seek out guilty men," wrote Schlesinger. Vietnam was "a tragedy without villains."[3] Paul Warnke, an associate of some of the intellectuals treated in this book, added that Vietnam was a "conceptual" and "tactical" "miscalculation," but the "vice" of critics was to impugn "laudable" intentions.[4]

Suddenly the experts who had previously claimed that foreign policy under their guidance would epitomize rational control changed their minds and ar-

---

[1] Adam Yarolinsky, Oral History (1970), p. 27, LBJ Library.

[2] Hoopes, *The Devil and John Foster Dulles* (Boston: Little, Brown, 1973), pp. 257, 405.

[3] *The Bitter Heritage: Vietnam and the American Democracy, 1941–1966* (Boston: Houghton Mifflin, 1967), pp. 31–32.

[4] Warnke Oral History (1969), Tape 2, pp. 5–8, LBJ Library.

gued that decision makers were impotent in Vietnam. As Richard Smoke asserted, critics of Vietnam and the national security state looked for "obtuseness
or maleficence" as the causes of the war. Since the civilian strategists had for
twenty years promoted these variables (in the guise of military stupidity and
Soviet evil) as fundamental to understanding conflict, critics might unsurpris-
ingly have fallen back on them. But Smoke assured his readers that the true
villains were "historical inevitability and tragedy"[5]—two variables new to policy scholars of the postwar period.

    The most substantial exercise in exculpation was a forty-seven-volume book
known as *The Pentagon Papers*, which itself spawned further similar sorts of
efforts.

ORIGINS OF *THE PENTAGON PAPERS*

In November 1966, convinced that his strategy for winning the war was not
working and distressed about his own role in the conflict, Secretary of Defense
Robert McNamara traveled to Cambridge, Massachusetts, as I have noted, as
part of a program to celebrate the opening of the Kennedy School. He spent
some time at his alma mater, the Harvard Business School, and then spoke to
some undergraduates whom Richard Neustadt had assembled. On his way to
another appointment, a meeting of Henry Kissinger's graduate seminar in international relations, McNamara confronted students who trapped his car and
questioned him. To prove that he could not be intimidated, McNamara clam-
bered onto the hood of the vehicle and told the angry gathering that, at Berkeley
in the 1930s, he had done just what it was doing. This was not true, since
McNamara had been a well-dressed, unadventurous student leader at a less
politicized institution. In any event, his Harvard challengers would have none
of it. They jeered this attempt to overcome the generation gap as they jeered
innumerable such attempts. He said, "I was tougher than you then and I'm
tougher today. I was more courteous then and . . . today." A few minutes later,
the secretary jumped off his car and made his way, unnerved, through an under-
ground tunnel to Kissinger's class.

    McNamara spent the evening with Neustadt and some faculty of the new
school. He had a more restrained and intellectual version of the argument that
had taken place with the students, and gave the disarming performance noted
in the last chapter. The academics asked why the United States had gotten
involved in Vietnam and what mistakes it had made. McNamara took the opportunity to reveal that he had urged Neustadt to do a study of Vietnam for
over a year. The secretary praised Neustadt's "Skybolt and Nassau" and said
that a comparable examination ought to be made of the war. Scholars should

---

[5] Smoke, "National Security Affairs," p. 327.

determine why Vietnam was not going as hoped in order to steer clear of such "errors" in the future.[6]

Neustadt had submitted his report on Skybolt to the president in mid-November 1963. He had suggested to Kennedy that some conclusions were too sensitive to be put on paper, and asked for a meeting. Kennedy had agreed to see him after he returned from his trip to Dallas, Texas, where he was assassinated. Now, in 1966, Neustadt related that he had given some thought to what he was going to say to the president. He acknowledged that he had considered asking whether the United States could expect to do better with its South Vietnamese allies than it had done with its British ones in 1962. The question, Neustadt said, "haunt[ed]" him.[7] As I have argued, by 1966, Neustadt was also implying that scholars might explain unsuccessful policy not by looking at American goals or individual purpose but at bureaucratic failure.

In early 1967 McNamara assigned a six-person staff to answer some "dirty questions" about the war, some of which were historical but all of which were oriented to getting information relevant to decision making in Vietnam.[8] At about the same time, in the spring, Neustadt was again asked to undertake a report. After he indicated his willingness, however, he was told there would be no such study.

McNamara vacillated. The most astute commentator on his motives believed that the secretary was sorrowful about the war. A historical project would help him and the country see where they had fallen short and assuage the guilt. McNamara wrote in his memoirs that, by 1967, the administration's ideas were not working and the costs of the war were greater than he could have imagined. How could the United States have prevented the disaster? Where had he gone wrong? "The thought that scholars would surely wish to explore these questions once the war had ended was increasingly on my mind."[9] He worried, rightly I believe, that posterity in the guise of "the judgment of History" would tear him to pieces.

By mid-1967 the secretary finally decided to move ahead with a report. Nonetheless, he tried to keep the work a secret from Lyndon Johnson and his national security advisor, Walt Rostow, and McNamara dissembled about the study's scope to Secretary of State Dean Rusk.[10] McNamara believed that he

---

[6] For this incident see Deborah Shapley, *Promise and Power: The Life and Times of Robert McNamara* (Boston: Little, Brown, 1993), pp. 376–77. The material on the meeting is in McNamara, Honorary Associates, K SG Papers: General Office UAV708.50, Harvard University Archives; and McNamara, *In Retrospect: The Tragedy and Lessons of Vietnam*, expanded ed. (New York: Vintage, 1996), pp. 254–56. For an example of the Neustadt-May academic connection, see their jointly authored book *Thinking in Time*.

[7] Neustadt, *Alliance Politics* (New York: Columbia University Press, 1970), pp. 150–51.

[8] Leslie Gelb, "Misreading the Pentagon Papers," op-ed, *New York Times*, June 29, 2001.

[9] *In Retrospect*, p. 280.

[10] Interview with Morton Halperin, March 4, 2003.

was being disloyal to the administration, but his determination to do the right thing (and to absolve himself) led him to act.

McNamara assigned organization of the report to the office of International Security Affairs, the political-military branch of the Pentagon under the department's assistant secretary John McNaughton (and after his death, his successor Paul Warnke). McNamara instructed one of his staff, Morton Halperin, to oversee the writing of this "encyclopedic history of the Vietnam War." Apparently the secretary still also had the example of Skybolt in mind and suggested that Neustadt's Harvard colleague Ernest May be given day-to-day responsibility for the project. When May turned him down, one of Halperin's assistants, Leslie Gelb, got the job. In his technocratic way, however, McNamara then had nothing to with it. He wanted the project "exhaustive and objective" and did not want to be seen as influencing its substance. Soon after the work was finished, Gelb reported that his aim was to preserve documents and to show how bureaucracies functioned.[11] But because the desire for secrecy had ruled out interviews, the ideal of "Skybolt and Nassau," with its oral histories, went unfulfilled.

SOCIAL SCIENTISTS BECOME HISTORIANS

The study was not completed until early 1969, many months after McNamara had left office. Thirty-six midlevel officials, drawn from various agencies, had worked off-and-on on the project. Only very few had claims to be historians. Many had RAND connections, and some military men who worked with civilians in the Pentagon and shared McNamara's concern for the war participated.[12] With allowances for how one counted, the end product was bound in forty-seven volumes, some four thousand pages of documents and three thousand pages of historical writing. The documents were included in thirty-seven studies on topics pertinent to American involvement in the war, mainly organized around events that defined a time period presumed to be critical, for example, the Geneva Conference of 1954, the Kennedy commitments of 1961, and the Gulf of Tonkin decisions of 1964. The "book" ended with volumes that contained "negotiating positions" of the American government through early 1968. Not only had different hands crafted the projects, but more than one official had also worked on most. The authors were granted anonymity to promote candor, but the results were uneven and often repetitive. The docu-

---

[11] See *New York Times*, December 30, 1971, p. 10. A more detailed account, along the same lines, appears in John Prados and Margaret Pratt Porter, eds., *Inside the Pentagon Papers* (Lawrence: University Press of Kansas, 2004), pp. 12–17.

[12] Prados and Porter, *Inside the Pentagon Papers*, pp. 15–23, discuss what is known about individual authors.

mentary-history aspect of the project often meant that the analysts interpreted their charge to be to abbreviate the many cables and aide-mémoires that came under their inquiry. Often the studies looked like what they were: committee summaries of documents by hurried and overworked officials. The best volumes were problem-oriented and answered questions crucial for thoughtful Americans in the late 1960s. For example, if the United States had supported Ho Chi Minh in the early period, would American policy have averted disaster? Gelb believed that the failure to prod high-level officials in conversation frustrated the overall end.

More important than not conducting interviews, the authors generally did not immerse themselves in the historical literature on American foreign affairs, or on the economic and social history of Asia. They had little distance from the standard views of American diplomats, and the commentary in the volumes usually relied on secondary sources that conventionally supported the policies of the United States. Even in the "interpretative" texts, long excerpts from undigested documents appeared, the writing was regularly unclear, and the historical narrative was amateurish. The tone of the studies was what one would expect. One author commented that the project's leaders shaded formulations to the "responsible center." The writers were officials in the Department of Defense who upheld its priorities but who shared McNamara's dislike of the war and his view of the ineffectiveness of the bombing and concern for its morality.[13]

The authors had access to material generated in the Pentagon and much else besides, but despite the comprehensive nature of the research, the writers did not see many documents written at high levels in the State Department and, more significantly, records of some decisions in the White House.[14] Because of their origin, the volumes focused almost exclusively on American debates and were particularly deficient in understanding the positions of adversaries. The studies apportioned more responsibility to generals and gave more weight to the opinion of working-level Defense Department officials than was warranted. The documentary bias probably also increased the need of these officials to explain the responsibility of civilian officials in the Pentagon in an acceptable way and also fed a tendency to blame the high military of the Joint Chiefs of Staff. The authors did not reproach people like them-

[13] Jardini, "Out of the Blue Yonder," pp. 281–82, 419–20, 512. Quote by Mel Gurtov from Prados and Porter, *Inside the Pentagon Papers*, p. 25.

[14] The four "negotiating" volumes did rely on State Department materials. See the outstanding edition edited by George C. Herring, *The Secret Diplomacy of the Vietnam War: The Negotiating Volumes of the Pentagon Papers* (Austin: University of Texas Press, 1983). There is a complete edition in microfiche: John Prados, ed., National Security Archive, *U.S. Policy in the Vietnam War*, vol. 2, 1969–75 (Alexandria, Va.: Chadwyck-Healey, 2003).

selves or their bosses and had no detachment from McNamara (or his successor, Clark Clifford).[15]

The most arresting deficiency was that the authors collectively ignored how the United States consciously molded political forces and power balances within South Vietnam itself to make the rump-nation a vehicle suitable for American intervention. Instead the authors assumed the rectitude of the containment of China; of damming the spread of Communism; of maintaining United States military power; and of the preservation of American prestige abroad. And they certainly accepted without notice the justice of armed intervention in any state whose fall might have a ripple effect on United States' interests.[16]

In their compilation of the study, the officials worried that other agencies less tormented than the Department of Defense might end the project or suppress it when released.[17] Halperin thought that Walt Rostow wanted all copies of the book destroyed.[18] Dean Rusk intimated that disgruntled and disloyal bureaucrats had prepared the studies in part as "campaign documents for Bobby Kennedy," who, before his murder in 1968, had been running for the presidency against Johnson's policy.[19] But there was also a straightforward pro-American bias at work in Gelb's contributions. Organizing the material and presenting an overall sense of the issues, Gelb digested each case, but often went beyond what was available to the reader in the study itself. In one instance Gelb's précis argued with anti-American interpretations of the war made in the middle and late 1960s and allowed the inference that the point of his exercise was to defuse radical criticism.[20] Overall, the volumes described the origins of the war and its course that put the best face possible on the activity of McNamara and his assistants.

None of this discussion is meant to detract from the value of the enterprise, and far more significant from my perspective than research deficiencies and

---

[15] An excellent early review of the volumes is *"The Pentagon Papers*: An Assessment," by Ernest R. May, Samuel R. Williamson, and Alexander Woodside, initially a presentation at the American Historical Association in 1971. I have used the copy annotated with William Bundy's notes, in Pentagon Papers Review, Box 1, Additional Bundy Papers, Mudd Library, Princeton University.

[16] George McT. Kahin, *"The Pentagon Papers*: A Critical Evaluation," *American Political Science Review* 69 (1975): 676, 680, 684. This review, and a companion piece by H. Bradford Westerfield, "What Use Are Three Versions of the Pentagon Papers?" (pp. 685–96) are outstanding.

[17] Tom Wells, *Wild Man: The Life and Times of Daniel Ellsberg* (New York: Palgrave, 2001), pp. 313–14.

[18] Ellsberg, *Secrets*, p. 243.

[19] Rusk, *As I Saw It*, pp. 575–77.

[20] On this interesting issue see Noam Chomsky, "The Pentagon Papers as Propaganda and as History," in *Senator Mike Gravel Edition, The Pentagon Papers: Critical Essays*, vol. 5. , eds. Chomsky and Howard Zinn (Boston: Beacon Press, 1972), pp. 179–101, citing Gelb in Gravel, vol. 1, pp. 260, 264–65, 333.

interpretative political biases is the overall sense the researchers gave of the unfolding of the war. Many of the case studies called attention to bureaucratic politics, but emphasized that the troubles in the way of rationality ran so deep that officials could not have made better policy. Americans had not executed an unjust strategy. Rather, departments at odds, failures of intelligence, and lapses of communication had altered policy for the worse. No one wanted what had happened, but no one could find remedies. Bureaucratic politics enabled the authors to distance themselves—and their political superiors—from liability for Vietnam. As Morton Halperin later observed, Vietnam made bureaucratic politics "fashionable."[21] The volumes reduced the action-oriented decision makers who had come to Washington confident about impressing their wills on the world to impotent witnesses to forces that they could not control.

Part of this change in view was a function of the authors' engagement with historical research in primary sources. Different from that of the policymaker, the perspective of the historian imposed itself on the authors as they worked, and they welcomed this perspective as one that mitigated not just their own burden but the burden of their predecessors in Washington. Thus, the studies noted that although diplomats made mistakes, alternative decisions would not necessarily have eventuated in better consequences. Moreover, the novice historians believed that constraints operated on the choices open to decision makers. The statesman had a tiny ability to influence what happened. Gelb wrote that the forty-seven volumes had in them qualities of Herman Melville's great novel of doomed human destiny, *Moby-Dick*. Vietnam was a tale of how chance, determinism, and free will commingled, said Gelb, and we learned to our sorrow how fated were our decisions, how narrow the realm of freedom.[22]

All of the skeptical remarks that I have made in this book about the policy-oriented certainties of the civilian strategists turn up in this material, sometimes prefacing or concluding analyses, sometimes an aspect of the argument. The requirements of historical understanding in part inflicted this skepticism on the fledgling historians. They embraced it to distance themselves from blame. Bureaucratic politics helped in the process. The reversal in mental outlook was remarkable.

ENTER ELLSBERG

These studies were officially titled "United States–Vietnam Relations, 1945–1967." They were the source of *The Pentagon Papers*, the documents leaked to the press, which began to publish them in June 1971, in a celebrated series

[21] Morton Halperin interview, March 4, 2003.
[22] Gelb Memo, in *United States–Vietnam Relations, 1945–1967*, 12 vols. (Washington, D.C.: U.S. Govt. Print. Office, 1971), vol. 1, pp. ix–x.

of events. Daniel Ellsberg had given the material to the newspapers, and his story is the first and perhaps most important narrative of how the policymaking community used *The Pentagon Papers* to pardon itself over Vietnam. Ellsberg had graduated from Harvard in 1952. After a year of graduate study at Cambridge, England, he had joined the marines but returned to Harvard as a junior member of its Society of Fellows, earning a Ph.D. in economics in 1963. His specialty was bargaining, the field of his mentor Thomas Schelling. Harvard recognized Ellsberg as one of the youngest members of the elite group of students of strategy. His work was abstract, and he was a philosophical positivist. But Ellsberg also wrote elegantly and urged that RAND's notion of rationality was narrow and had to be made more complex. He opened what seemed like a stunning governmental career as a consultant, gaining experience through the 1960s in various agencies, putting his intelligence to work, and deprecating the tradition of "literary" discussion of strategy.[23]

In Henry Kissinger's classes at Harvard Ellsberg had lectured on "The Political Uses of Madness," elaborating the more complex ideas of rationality at issue in bargaining. When Nixon told his advisors to warn the Communists in Asia that he was "a madman" who might do anything to end the Vietnam War on terms acceptable to him, he might have actualized Ellsberg's observations.[24] At RAND Wohlstetter appreciated Ellsberg's ability. Consulting for the Defense and State departments in the early 1960s, Ellsberg participated informally in Neustadt's work on Skybolt, and Neustadt encouraged him to pursue case studies of international security affairs.[25] After he left RAND in 1964, Ellsberg joined the Defense Department full time, where Vietnam became his area of concern, but he went to Vietnam as a civilian working for State. By 1967 he was back at RAND, although his friends in the Pentagon obtained his services for McNamara's historical enterprise. In Ellsberg's version of the story, which is almost certainly exaggerated, he had told a friend that the Department of Defense ought to undertake a study of the war, along the lines that Neustadt had used in his report on Skybolt.[26]

By 1967 Ellsberg was, like McNamara, confused about the morality of the war and the prudence of the American commitment, but he was still at RAND

---

[23] Ellsberg, "Theories of Rational Choice Under Uncertainty" (B.A. thesis, 1953), esp. 35–36, 164; and "Risk, Ambiguity and Decision' (Ph.D. thesis, 1962), esp. p. viii, both in Harvard University Archives; and "The Crude Analysis of Strategic Choices," *American Economic Review* 51 (1961): 478.

[24] See Ellsberg, "The Theory and Practice of Blackmail," RAND P-3883 (1968), which was the first publication of the lecture series that Ellsberg had done in Boston in 1959. It was eventually published in *Bargaining*, ed. Oran R. Young (Urbana: University of Illinois Press, 1975), pp. 342–63.

[25] Neustadt to Rowen, May 14, 1964, Box 16, R; Neustadt to Ellsberg, February 20, 1965, Box 15, Correspondence 61–65, 2 of 2, Neustadt Papers, JFK Library.

[26] See Peter Schrag, *Test of Loyalty: Daniel Ellsberg and the Rituals of Secret Government* (New York: Simon and Schuster, 1974), p. 35.

in 1969, and even prepared a paper on options in Vietnam for Henry Kissinger, who had by that time advanced to power as Nixon's national security advisor. Ellsberg did not cut his ties to RAND till early 1970, by which time he had xeroxed the text of "United States–Vietnam Relations, 1945–1967," top-secret copies of which had been stored at RAND.[27]

Ellsberg read the Pentagon history assiduously not just to understand the war but also to distance it as far as possible from himself. Ellsberg had been unreflective about American foreign policy, his patriotism best displayed in his "gung ho" interest in combat when he was in Vietnam in the mid-1960s. He later said that it was embarrassing to him that everything he wrote during the 1950s and 1960s was predicated on the American "right" to win in Vietnam in ways the Americans defined.[28] The lack of reflection carried over into his later ruminations on American foreign policy, which were also naive, especially since his scholarship was about political bargaining. *The Pentagon Papers*, which like all historical material displayed a variety of motives, and incidentally predictable political dissembling, shocked Ellsberg. By the late 1960s, what he called the lying and deceit of politicians and policymakers had permanently altered his perspective. He had no sense that political morality might be of a different sort than that which was appropriate for a private person. He could not separate an idealized notion of truth-telling (which he thought he exemplified) from the (base) aspects of a public information policy in a real polity. In this respect, Ellsberg's thinking exemplified the formalism of many RAND-influenced scholars. His training served as a poor substitute for a grasp of how the world worked.

Ellsberg's change of heart traumatized him, frequently bringing the man to tears and visible distress. One historian has noted that in this respect he was like his sometime boss and acquaintance, McNamara,[29] although the 1960s did more to influence Ellsberg. In the middle and late sixties his marriage came apart, he experimented sexually, used drugs, and engaged in many sophomoric bull sessions, all the while lamenting the war and his role in it. These activities euphemistically describe a lost soul. Moreover, his Harvard and RAND supporters had been wrong about his potential. Despite his ability, he was unable to complete work yet was convinced of his own genius. By the late 1960s and the early 1970s his career had come to a dead-end. The

---

[27] My narrative of the preparation of the volumes and of Ellsberg's role is indebted to Schrag, *Test of Loyalty*, pp. 9–54, whose outstanding text is unfortunately undocumented; and David Rudenstine, *The Day the Presses Stopped: A History of the Pentagon Papers Case* (Berkeley and Los Angeles: University of California Press, 1996), pp. 18–29, 33–47, which leans heavily on Schrag.

[28] Ellsberg, "Introduction," in *Papers on the War* (New York: Simon and Schuster, 1972), p. 24.

[29] Rudenstine, *Pentagon Papers*, p. 33.

professional problems exacerbated the erosion of his moral ballast and complicated his self-absorption.[30]

At the same time, Ellsberg had numerous advocates. He had had to search his conscience to find his way, and his articulate commitment stirred the admiration of many. As he put it, his decision to release the documents lay in finding in himself "loyalties long unconsulted."[31] He gave *The Pentagon Papers* to the *New York Times* in the spring of 1971.

Shortly before the newspapers printed them, Ellsberg delivered a talk in Boston, "The Responsibility of Officials in a Criminal War." As in many of his lectures at the time expressing his mea culpa, Ellsberg recounted to his audience that in the past months he had read Albert Speer's *Inside the Third Reich,* published in English in 1970. He read to his auditors segments of the book and portrayed Speer to them as a humane liberal who would not have been out of place at a meeting of the National Security Council of the United States in the 1960s. Ellsberg also said that many of the members of the NSC would have been comfortable writing Nazi memoranda. He concluded that all the officials he knew who contributed to the Vietnam War must live with their "willful, irresponsible ignorance and neglect of human consequences" and "active association with the whole course of events."[32]

Ellsberg conceived of the Department of Defense volumes as a series of case studies such as Neustadt's Skybolt report, which Ellsberg continued to think of as a paradigm. Extrapolating from the individual narratives, Ellsberg himself theorized about the war. He induced generalizations that would enable researchers to predict and give good advice in the future. His interest was "analysis" and not the "telling [of] the story"—or stories—on which the analysis relied. From examination of the case studies Ellsberg constructed a "decision model."[33] Neustadt's report influenced Ellsberg in more than structure. The paper on Skybolt had concluded that bureaucratic politics produced the "irrational" decisions that had been made, and this formulation cropped up frequently in Ellsberg's own explanation of Vietnam.[34]

He had first approached the war with the conviction that presidents wanted victory over Asian Communism and hired experts who would tell them how to reach that goal. Thus Ellsberg expected to find faulty information and bad advice. But, he argued, in several of the case histories the experts had accurately and pessimistically urged that available resources could not win the war. The experts such as Ellsberg, then, were not to blame!

[30] Wells, *Wild Man*, supports my view of Ellsberg.

[31] Quoted in Shrag, *Test of Loyalty*, p. 41.

[32] Ellsberg, "The Responsibility of Officials in a Criminal War," in *Papers on the War*, pp. 308–9; and Schrag, *Test*, p. 27.

[33] Ellsberg, "Introduction," pp. 18–19, and "The Quagmire Myth and the Stalemate Machine," pp. 43, 49, 100, in *Papers on the War*.

[34] Ellsberg, "Quagmire," e.g., pp. 70, 86, 88–89, 92.

What then were the presidents doing if they were not following the advice? How did Ellsberg explain that policymakers forsook a model of rational accomplishment? He answered that they were trying not to lose. They strung matters out in Vietnam, without going to all-out war. And why did they do this? In addition to *The Pentagon Papers*, Ellsberg read the just-published "revisionist" monographs on the origins of the Cold War from 1945 to 1950. Based on newly released documents, this scholarly literature in some respects responded to the climate of the 1960s and, as we have already noted, also troubled the May Group at Harvard. Cold War revisionists saw in American imperialism after 1945 the origins of the later imperialism in Vietnam.

Moreover, these historians found the sources of McCarthyism in the anti-Communist rhetoric of the Truman administration. According to revisionists, Truman's rhetoric justified a foreign policy that Congress and the public had found unattractive when it was defended on its (true) economic and social grounds. Truman had wanted foreign aid to rebuild a prosperous and capitalist Europe. When he was met with skepticism, he sold the policy instead in terms of a global fight against Communism. Later, when the Democrats allowed China to go Communist and responded only halfheartedly in Korea, the Republican Right used the anti-Communist public information policy of the Democrats to bludgeon the Democrats themselves. The GOP had forced Truman and Acheson from office, considering them criminally negligent in respect to Communism. But according to the revisionist historians, the Democrats had crafted the tools of the hyperbolic public information program that Republicans used.

As he perused *The Pentagon Papers* in the late 1960s and early 1970s, Ellsberg came to believe that policymakers under Eisenhower, Kennedy, and Johnson, but especially Democrats, took from the experience of 1947–52 a crucial lesson: one could not remain in office if perceived as weak on Asian Communism. Thus, in Vietnam when each president tried to avoid defeat, the aim was not to win, but to stay in power. Domestic politics explained the irrationality of Vietnam.[35]

Ellsberg could find in the record much evidence to back up his conclusion, and political liberals in the 1960s have acknowledged that they supported the war to prevent a right-wing backlash. But Ellsberg barely noted that liberal interests might be served if reproach for the war could be laid at the door of the conservative extreme.[36] The left-liberal scholars on whom Ellsberg relied for his historical knowledge of the late 1940s may have fallaciously found in the Truman administration the fear of anti-Communism that they believed had

---

[35] Ellsberg, "Quagmire," pp. 29, 35, 43, 84–86; and for his attempt to think through his views, see particularly "Introduction," pp. 9–12, both in *Papers on the War.*

[36] In "Introduction," *Papers on the War*, p. 12n, Ellsberg is remarkably prescient in deconstructing this historical explanation, but he does not carry forward his investigation.

flowered in the 1960s after an earlier germination. That is, perhaps the revisionists would benefit from faulting people in the past as the real sources of the problems of the late 1960s. In that way these scholars could distance themselves from the traumas of Vietnam. Most reflective Americans needed to find someone else culpable for Southeast Asia.

In any event Ellsberg—and in part the revisionist historians on whom he relied—had generated a space between themselves and accountability for the war. According to Ellsberg, the advisors who had not been optimistic about American prospects in Vietnam had told statesmen the truth. The (liberal and moderate) statesmen themselves had not tried to conquer that country. Instead, the leaders—and the experts they employed—were keeping the United States out of the hands of Republican reactionaries. Fascism tinged the real (right-wing) enemy.

PLACING BLAME

The Pentagon Papers initiated an attempt both to understand the war and to find out who else but the authors should pay for it. The published study continued to function in this way, as Ellsberg's use of it to build a "decision model" illustrated.[37] Other books that relied on the documentary history carried on this project. A conspicuous instance was the volume that Leslie Gelb, who had overseen the compilation of the reports, coauthored with Richard Betts. They published *The Irony of Vietnam: The System Worked* in 1979. The two wrote about an American political system designed to operate consensually and to produce commitments that carried over into the long term with wide public support. Thus in Vietnam the system did what it was supposed to do, the authors explained, because of the overarching agreement on anti-Communist containment. Various bureaucracies reinforced this reiterated national aim. Realistic policymakers always passed up extremes for continued moderate sustenance of the cause but acknowledged to themselves the dubious nature of the enterprise. Vietnam, Gelb and Betts concluded, taught that leadership ought to encourage the pragmatism of domestic politics, rather than the ideological commitment of foreign affairs. A good system had produced a bad result. The authors wrote that American statesmen believed that they had no choices, even that the system "took *choice* away." Policymakers were prisoners "of the larger political system that fed on itself, trapping all its participants."

In the exoneration of people like himself, Gelb (and his coauthor) propounded the mystification that history had taught him. Gone was the notion that individuals could control events, or secure the conditions of better deci-

---

[37] See Gelb's op-ed essay, "Misreading the Pentagon Papers," which was printed just as Ellsberg's biography, *Wild Man*, was published.

sions. Quoting Franz Kafka's *The Trial*, the authors stated that answers to critical questions such as whether the war was good or bad "will forever remain elusive." Writing history was "a treacherous exercise," and provoked debates that would go on "as long as people are interested in truth."[38] Certainties for making effective decisions had been easily available from the late 1940s to the early 1960s for the civilian strategist. Suddenly they vanished.

NIXON

One of the motives pushing Ellsberg to release the documents was that the war had gone on after Richard Nixon defeated Hubert Humphrey, Johnson's vice president. Nixon appeared to Ellsberg as great a war criminal as the men around Lyndon Johnson. When the documents first began to appear in the newspapers in 1971, the uncontrolled leak of secrets appalled Nixon's national security advisor, Henry Kissinger. He urged Nixon in 1971 to act against his former student and employee, telling the president that Ellsberg was a "genius" but "unbalanced."[39] One result of Kissinger's "cranking up" of the president was a series of legal maneuvers in which the Republican administration attempted to stop the publication of the documents and then to jail Ellsberg. In landmark decisions, the newspapers continued to print excerpts from the study, and the Supreme Court threw out the administration's cases. These events weakened Nixon and convinced people like Ellsberg of his bankrupt policies. But a far more significant result of Kissinger's harangue of Nixon was the confirmation for the president of the nature of the liberal conspiracy against his administration.

In a chain of events whose sequence is still clouded, the president and his assistants created "the plumbers." They were primarily to stop the leaks that, in the case of Ellsberg, might imperil Nixon's foreign policy, although Ellsberg's particular offense was to reveal secrets of Democratic administrations. The plumbers broke into the office of Ellsberg's psychiatrist to get information. Not unreasonably, Nixon believed that men like Ellsberg had gotten the United States into Vietnam, and that they were in the late 1960s and early 1970s, out of guilt, undermining Republican efforts to extract America from the conflict. Beset by enemies like Ellsberg, the executive branch gave bigger jobs to a reconstituted group of plumbers, such as a burglary in the Watergate Hotel of the offices of the Democratic National Committee, to learn about its activities.

---

[38] Gelb and Betts, *The Irony of Vietnam: The System Worked* (Washington, D.C.: Brookings, 1979), pp. 2, 24, 241, 245, on the way the good system worked; 25, 352, on lack of choice; 9, 352, on mystery of history; 299, 352, on Kafka.

[39] Rudenstine, *Pentagon Papers*, p. 121.

Nixon could not have responded more appropriately for Ellsberg and many foreign-policy strategists predisposed to allocate blame for Vietnam to someone else. In the 1960s the heavy was the system and not the people in it. At the very end of the decade commentators like Ellsberg shifted fault to the militant GOP anti-Communists of the late 1940s and early 1950s. Then Nixon, who had come of age in the McCarthy period and made his career in it, took over the presidency. He soon pursued the same sort of foreign policy that policy scientists had come to repudiate. Nixon's fingerprints were all over the creation of the conditions in the McCarthy period that led to Vietnam and the continued disaster of the war. Almost on cue the new president reentered national politics to assist many intellectuals in the hunt for culprits. The dénouement of the Nixon administration finally gave liberals a scapegoat who would be accountable for all the troubles of the United States in the late 1960s and early 1970s, which is not to say that the blame was wrongly placed.

CHAPTER 10

Henry Kissinger

Before his tenure as national security advisor and secretary of state in the 1970s, Henry Kissinger had made a substantial academic reputation. His rise to power was the high point for intellectuals in politics in the period we are surveying. But Kissinger conflicted with the RAND strategists who were implicated in Vietnam and the Harvard policy scientists who invented bureaucratic politics. Although Kissinger thought of these men as his peers, and certainly absorbed their ideas, he brought to bear on diplomacy a distinctive sensibility distant from the emphases of social science, yet illustrating some of its concerns.

EARLY LIFE AND CAREER

Kissinger was a German Jew whose family fled its home in Fürth, Germany, in 1938, after persecution by the Nazis. As a teenager in New York City, he worked in a shaving-brush factory while he attended high-school classes and, then, at night, City College. In 1943 Kissinger was drafted and went to Germany at the end of 1944 and 1945. Already recognized for his brainpower, he served in Division Counterintelligence and, as the war ended, was part of a denazification unit.

In 1947 Kissinger left Germany and the army and enrolled at Harvard on the GI Bill, where he first obtained a B.A. in 1950 after three years, added on to the two years of credits from City College. His senior honors thesis, "The Meaning of History: Reflections on Spengler, Toynbee, and Kant," was famous in the Harvard Department of Government. Kissinger had secured the patronage of William Y. Elliott, who encouraged the young man to go on for a doctoral degree at Harvard. His dissertation of 1954, which appeared as a book in 1957 as *A World Restored: Metternich, Castlereagh and the Restoration of Peace: 1812–1822* continued Kissinger's observations on the course of history.

His peers in Cambridge regarded him as a gifted but unsocial grind who studied in his room and bit his nails till his fingers bled. His mental prowess was undeniable but, according to standard reports, he was pretentiously solemn, obsequious to professors, awkward and calculating with his contemporaries. A gloomy young man in the style of central European scholars, he worried about order in civilization, expatiated on the role of statesmen in promoting the stability of states, and prognosticated about the disintegration of cultures. His cumbersome prose mirrored his lugubrious thoughts.

Still befriended by Elliott, Kissinger began an academic career at Harvard but shifted his attention to the defense intellectuals of the 1950s, nuclear strategy, and America's global alliances. He influenced elite opinion-makers close to the Council on Foreign Relations in New York and developed a relationship with a powerful Republican politician, Governor Nelson Rockefeller of New York. Nonetheless, his progress at Harvard was tortured. In a period when McGeorge Bundy quickly rose to a tenured position in the Department of Government and then the deanship without a doctoral degree or significant publications, Kissinger—a far more accomplished scholar—merely hung on in Cambridge. In the mid-1950s, Elliott even tried unsuccessfully to get MIT to employ him because Kissinger's prospects were so bleak.[1]

As even one of his close friends wrote, Cambridge regarded Kissinger as "ambitious and power hungry," "a schemer who chose his patrons with a deliberation worthy of a greater objective."[2] Another old Harvard acquaintance said he was "a wanderer with no moral center . . . only an operational imperative."[3] The distaste that his academic colleagues felt now fills pages of the literature on Kissinger. They knew him as Henry "Ass" Kissinger. They gossiped that he lifted his scholarship on current American policies from more original thought and that he changed with the fashions. One of these academics famously joked, "I wonder who's Kissinger now?" Richard Neustadt, a gentle man who was around Harvard much of this time, remarked that Kissinger was a bad person, who left every institution with which he was associated worse than when he entered it. "Weak and sycophantic, acting like a courtier, but not truly evil," wrote another colleague.[4] McGeorge Bundy later regretted the modest assistance he gave Kissinger. According to Bundy's biographer, Bundy thought Kissinger "an unpleasant opportunist."[5]

Kissinger's memoirs of 1979 noted that Bundy had responded to him with the "subconscious condescension" reserved for people, by New England standards, of "exotic backgrounds and excessively intense personal style."[6] It is hard not to conclude that part of Kissinger's problem was Cambridge's attitude

[1] Box 3, Correspondence, March 1955, Folder 113, Dean of Humanities Papers, AC 20, MIT Archives.

[2] Stephen R. Graubard, *Kissinger: Portrait of a Mind* (New York: Norton, 1973), p. 119.

[3] Ralph Blumenfeld et al., *Henry Kissinger: The Public and Private Story* (New York: New American Library, 1974), p. 86.

[4] William Bundy, Notes for Book Appearances (ca. 1998), Box 9, Additional Bundy Papers, Mudd Library, Princeton University.

[5] For "Ass" Kissinger, see Kai Bird, *The Color of Truth: McGeorge Bundy and William Bundy: Brothers in Arms: A Biography* (New York: Simon and Schuster, 1998), p. 142; "Kissinger now," quoted in Herken, *Counsels of War*, p. 99; Bundy on Kissinger, Bird, pp. 143–44; Neustadt conversations, 1978–79. For more see Isaacson, *Kissinger*, pp. 79, 100, 114.

[6] Kissinger, *White House Years*, pp. 13–14.

toward "outsiders" that had only slowly given way to appointments based on merit and not lineage, as well as Harvard's entrenched anti-Semitism.

At the end of the 1961–62 school year, after almost ten years, Kissinger got a permanent position in Government at Harvard. But at the same time that many of his colleagues were invited to assist Kennedy, Kissinger was left out. He was a consultant of minor import through the 1960s.

PHILOSOPHER OF HISTORY

Three hundred and eighty-eight pages long, Kissinger's B.A. thesis, "The Meaning of History," was the most intellectually creative and sustained piece of work that he wrote, and a key exposition of his concerns.[7] He picked up the views of the *Existenz* philosophy that rose to prominence in the 1930s and 1940s. Suspicious of a religious orientation to the universe, European thinkers tried to understand the ghastly events that had almost destroyed Western civilization between 1914 and 1945. With the revelations of the Nazi death camps after World War II, existentialists like Jean-Paul Sartre became popular figures with the educated public in both Europe and the United States. These philosophers rejected the progress and rationality predicated on an orderly cosmos. Instead, human persons were "thrown" into a particular cultural world, their being defined by their relentless passage through time. The individual's ordinary focus on "everydayness" only half suppressed the terror of dying. Because of death, care and anxiety filled the living. Thoughtful people needed to lead an existence that accepted these hard truths and to eschew social conformity— *mauvaise foi* or bad faith. Human beings had a radical freedom that they could not slough off, and supernatural truths that theology might uphold could not guarantee significance. In this meaningless universe, Sartre concluded, individuals must make themselves, and he called for the necessity of commitment— acts of will—even though such commitment might have no further warrant and even if it amounted to nothing. At the same time the philosophers of *Existenz* more than hinted that significance was to be found in the collective dedication to politics.

By 1950 Kissinger was no longer a practicing Jew, and not even religious. "The Meaning of History" effectively located humankind in a Godless and mechanistic world, and on its first page noted how the individual faced the

[7] "The Meaning of History" is available on microfilm in the Harvard University Archives. The one book seriously to evaluate Kissinger's thesis is Peter W. Dickson, *Kissinger and the Meaning of History* (New York: Cambridge University Press, 1978), which is excellent but has major shortcomings. Indeed, no one has refined Dickson's discussion, and subsequent writers on Kissinger have dumbed-down Dickson or ignored the thesis altogether. See, for example, Jussi Hanhimäki, *The Flawed Architect: Henry Kissinger and American Foreign Policy* (New York: Oxford University Press, 2004), pp. 5–8.

"directedness" of a certain kind of life.[8] But while Kissinger accepted human existence in the natural and not the supernatural world, he defended a nondeterministic account of human action.

For him the central issue was the justifiability of historical knowledge. If physics and biology essentially described the world, history might be a comforting narrative but could never really explain why things were the way they were. Physical and natural science would provide a causal account. The human story could then have no point, and history could not be a genuine form of knowing. On the other hand, if history disclosed something beyond what the sciences taught, it had meaning. For the individual this issue was that of free will. If the natural world produced people, their choices were determined. They could not display the will that made for freedom and that (jointly) gave history value. In exploring whether historical knowledge—as opposed to a tale told by an idiot—existed, Kissinger argued that he was taking up the most important metaphysical problems of (personal) freedom and (collective, historical) meaning. To solve these problems he elaborated a complex vision.

The philosopher Hegel was known for his dialectical reasoning in which, from a competing thesis and antithesis, a synthesis emerged that ensuing debate itself modified. Commentators often studied the history of philosophy in a way that acknowledged Hegel. The rationalism of Descartes, Spinoza, and Leibniz contrasted with the succeeding empiricism of Locke, Berkeley, and Hume. Kant synthesized the two traditions, but Hegel went beyond Kant. To explain how history might be a form of knowledge, Kissinger constructed a similar sort of dialectic, and this apparatus is critical to seeing his point of view. The historical theorists Oswald Spengler and Arnold Toynbee represented the thesis and antithesis.

Spengler's *Decline of the West* postulated that all cultures had the same inevitable cyclic pattern of birth, growth, decay, and death, but Spengler also believed that the cosmos was inherently "organic," governed by mental forms, and thus the question of the significance of history did not arise, for in some way it was an emanation of thought and, ipso facto, meaningful. Kissinger called Spengler a "transcendentalist."[9] But since the ideas at work in history were deterministic, resulting in the fated rise and fall of cultures, Spengler ruled out human freedom from the start. In contrast to this position, for Kissinger, stood the "empiricist" Toynbee. His then not yet completed *A Study of History* (1934–61) interpreted the rise of cultures on the basis of factual evidence. Toynbee allowed for failure and success based on human choice, which took place within the context of the "challenge and response" of peoples to the environment. But, for Kissinger, Toynbee's theory did not allow human beings to escape the clutch of the natural world. When cultures failed, the

---

[8] "Meaning of History," p. 1.
[9] "Meaning of History," p. 132.

environment did not befriend them. When they succeeded, the environment supported their endeavor. Human purpose was ineffectual, and historians might just as well study climate and geography.[10]

Spengler conceived meaning without freedom. Toynbee, said Kissinger, allowed freedom without meaning. According to Kissinger, his interpretation of Kant fused these two inadequate ideas of transcendentalism and empiricism. Kant had urged that our knowledge of the natural world depended on both the organizing framework supplied by the mind and presented data. Unlike Descartes, Spinoza, and Leibniz, Kant believed that sense contents were essential to knowledge, but unlike Locke, Berkeley, and Hume, Kant believed that mind was active in knowing. Kissinger waded into the difficulties of Kantian scholarship to defend his outlook on history. He argued that, for Kant, nature depended not on the actuality of a prior mental world (that is, an infinite mind for which Hegel later argued and that Spengler later accepted), but on the less speculative premise that no one could rule out such a world. In philosophical jargon Kissinger was adopting the perspective of late-nineteenth-century neo-Kantians that "the transcendental unity of apperception" was a valid ideal. One could not exclude the idea that a coherent structure of intelligibility conditioned nature. We could not refute the view that natural science was inadequate in its depiction of human beings. We could not prove that the biological and physical world was ultimate, for the proof would require that we adopt a stance by which we could measure how nonscientific understanding added nothing to, or reduced itself to, science. But taking such a stance meant that we transcended the biological and physical! The proof exemplified the state of affairs that the proof itself was supposed to rule out.

Because of this supposition, Kissinger asserted that no one could disprove belief in free choice or in historical knowledge. But this argument did not guarantee that we actually made free choices or that history was a success story. The argument only guaranteed that we could reject claims about the uselessness of our efforts or the meaninglessness of history. As Kissinger repeatedly stated (with many others), Kant denied knowledge to make room for faith. The position revealed the influence of one of Kissinger's mentors at Harvard, the Kantian Carl J. Friedrich. Friedrich took an uncomplicated view of the outcome of Kant's practical philosophy. The goal of moral action for Kant was universal peace. More circumspect, Kissinger echoed this sentiment only in a chastened form. History did not guarantee meaning, but the hidden purpose of conjoint human willing might be lasting peace.[11] Thus, Kant's syn-

---

[10] "Meaning of History," pp. 198n, 245.

[11] For Friedrich's position, which Kissinger cited, see Carl J. Friedrich, ed., *The Philosophy of Kant: Immanuel Kant's Moral and Political Writings* (New York: Modern Library, 1949), especially, pp. xl–xlv of the introduction. Less important is Friedrich's *Inevitable Peace* (Cambridge: Harvard University Press, 1948). Dickson has an outstanding and more complex account of the

thesis permitted Kissinger to assert, against Spengler and Toynbee, both free will and historical meaning—at least we could not prove them wrong.

Kant was not, however, the last word. Kissinger elaborated how his own Kantian-inspired position could meet mid-twentieth-century concerns. Thinkers like Sartre, Kissinger suggested, chose one of two options. They believed in the need to choose even though choice was meaningless—witness the decisionism that arose in Hans Morgenthau's teachers. Or existentialists inconsistently believed in absolute goals—Sartre's claim that people made themselves obscured his certainty about left politics. Kissinger proposed a middle path. He placed the realm of meaning in the problematic growth of civilizations. Kissinger dismissed Spengler's argument that the collapse of cultures was unavoidable, and may have felt a greater affinity with Toynbee's quasi-Christian belief in an uncertain form of cultural ascent. But Kissinger, like Kant, had a more individualistic belief in the significance of the human person than did Spengler or Toynbee. At the same time the individual's contribution to history came through politics, the collective endeavor that shaped civilizations. Kissinger concluded that because meaning was only possible, momentous choices would recognize limits, tolerance, and the dignity of others. Yet he insinuated that there were no universal values, and that life frequently frustrated intention. Our larger purposes might issue in "totally incommensurate consequences."[12]

In asserting the possibility of meaning in the political conflicts called history, Kissinger rejected a role for experts who could make politics rational. Although very much part of the world of RAND and those scholars who would later attach themselves to the Kennedy School, he was outside their orbits. There were no "merely technical" solutions to political problems, "the dilemmas of the soul." "Political scientists," wrote Kissinger, "should cease condemning their profession for not living up to their misnomer."[13]

At some point in his work on the thesis Kissinger learned about logical positivism, the scientific philosophy that was becoming prominent in the United States and that, as I have argued, many of the RAND theorists espoused. A central doctrine of the positivists was that all moral and metaphysical positions were, literally, cognitively meaningless. This doctrine flourished on the notion that meaning adhered to individual propositions whose truth or falsity was empirically verified. If propositions could not pass the verifiability test, they had to be thrown out. Kissinger recognized that the conception of meaning in his senior thesis would never pass muster by the positivist criterion, and in an addendum he sketched a view of meaning adumbrating that of the chief opponents of positivism—like W. V. O. Quine—who were promoting a holistic

---

intricacies of Kant's political ideas and their relation to his moral philosophy, although I believe that Dickson misses Kissinger's minimalist views about what Kant had really warranted.

[12] "Meaning of History," pp. 4, 234, 285–86, 342, 345.

[13] "Meaning of History," pp. 6–9, 341.

theory of significance involving a system of propositions, rather than a theory that emphasized propositions taken one by one.[14]

The thesis is arguably a work of genius, despite its portentous reasoning, heavy language, and lapses into incomprehensibility. As an adoring biographer rightfully pointed out, Kissinger had worked out a coherent point of view; one can find in his writings a "portrait of a mind."[15] "The Meaning of History" displayed Kissinger's intellectual ambition and a position that was not unlike that of conservative European existentialists like Martin Heidegger. Human existence was a mystic relation to the universe, and while choice never expressed righteousness in a straightforward way, nature need not frustrate man.[16] Nothing could relieve a person from giving his own meaning to life and elevating himself above necessity, and resolute action for its own sake might be obligatory. Our handiwork was in doubt, but authentic human beings were called upon to make choices that did not just reflect convention. Ethics resided in an inward personal state where an individual uniquely recognized responsibility. Kissinger made explicit the premises of the countertradition of Kennan and Morgenthau and brought their views to fruition in American foreign policy circles.

Kissinger's doctoral dissertation of 1954, four years later, was less prepossessing. He took some of his philosophical ideas and learned how concrete historical circumstances might corroborate them. In *A World Restored* these circumstances were the struggles between French militarism and its adversaries in Britain and Austria-Hungary in the early nineteenth century, and the combination of negotiations, threats, and war that the great powers employed. Kissinger told how the diplomats had ended conflict in Europe after the period of the Napoleonic wars and created a state system that eventuated in a century of peace. Kissinger wanted to understand empirically how meaning was lodged in history, and how men imposed their values on the world. The senior

---

[14] The addendum is perhaps the most interesting part of Kissinger's lengthy essay. The critique of positivism was indebted to his teacher and Harvard logician Henry Scheffer, whom I suspect introduced Kissinger to positivism. Scheffer had written a pathbreaking article on logic at the beginning of the century, for which he ultimately received a permanent position at Harvard, but he had never done anything else, and throughout his career he was "stuck" in the thought of early-twentieth-century American logicians such as Charles Peirce and Josiah Royce. Scheffer did, however, embody the "holist," antipositivist conception of meaning that was promulgated in the Harvard Department of Philosophy throughout the twentieth century. W.V.O. Quine, among others, was a proponent of such a conception in the second half of the century. Through Scheffer, Kissinger sketched a version based on the philosophy of the first half of the century and argued that various systems of meaning might exist with different first principles or "axioms." The philosophical adversaries of the positivists ultimately achieved great success, but Kissinger's position, though clear, was underdeveloped, and he did not understand some of the logical issues with which he was dealing.

[15] See Stephen R. Graubard, *Kissinger*, with its subtitle; but see esp. pp. 1–12.

[16] "Meaning of History," p. 327.

thesis was about theory, the dissertation about practice, although the conclusions of the doctorate were less grandiose than what was implicit in the earlier writing. *A World Restored* claimed that the order of nation-states embodied meaning. Flawed and constantly at risk, this order was still the most that we could ask for in human life. Equilibrium was ever subject to the imperfections of the cultures for which the statesmen spoke, and to their own personal failings, exacerbated by the intrinsic but contingent problems of the era in which they lived.

In part the book elaborated a version of the popular realism of international relations theory. At the heart of diplomacy was force. Security and not justice were paramount, although somehow the search for stability elevated national life beyond the self-interest of individual states. Kissinger demonstrated that realism was true not by conjecture, but by showing how the history of Europe displayed its truth. Individuals most contributed to the uncertain positive agglutination of meaning in history in the world of power-political statecraft. When diplomats promoted order, they supremely carried value in the world.

A final aspect of this book has intrigued commentators. Many commentators have claimed—and Kissinger implied—that while *A World Restored* was about nineteenth-century diplomacy, it was also about the Cold War. With various phrases Kissinger distinguished between states committed to legitimacy—whatever constellation of powers and their interconnections dominant at the time—and revolutionary states, which challenged whatever the constellation was. Conventional states aimed at an authoritative establishment through accepted standards of negotiation. No such accommodations could be made with revolutionary states. They did not accept the rules and instead placed the parameters of the system itself at issue in every confrontation. Aside from the easy equation of the USSR with the prototypical revolutionary state, Kissinger suspected attempts to reach a utopia. Perfection and permanence were denied to humanity, and to think that one could get them was overweening, an attempt to escape history. Kissinger always looked to the antirevolutionary states for whatever wisdom existed. Yet he also recognized that a lack of commitment to the revolutionary ideals needed to galvanize nation-states would blemish the work of conservatives and insure its impermanence.

Kissinger expressed his views in his persistent accolades to one of his heroes, Metternich, who triumphed over the revolutionary Napoleon. Kissinger praised Metternich's "diplomacy par excellence, pure manipulation," his "masterful manipulation," "brilliant manipulation." Yet at the same time Kissinger allowed that although Metternich "was not a cynic where his deepest values were concerned," "construction" and not just manipulation would have enriched his statesmanship.[17] Realpolitik in diplomacy was always wed to a con-

---

[17] Kissinger, *A World Restored: The Politics of Conservatism in a Revolutionary Age* (New York: Houghton Mifflin, 1957, 1964, 1969), pp. 213, 312–13, 83, 11.

ception of moral order, but such an order was always subordinate to interests because the realist was a legitimist and not a revolutionary. The ideal statesman had to bring together two inevitably incompatible claims.[18] Realism was required of any sane statesman, but without ideology it could never sustain a nation. Yet ideology inevitably undermined realism.

Commentators concluded from the book that in the mid–twentieth century the United States must methodically thwart the Soviet Union. Americans would be foolish to expect some quasi-permanent agreement between the United States and Russians. And Kissinger embodied this interpretation in his views of the then contemporary scene. Moreover, although he accepted the moral outlook of realism, he was inconsistent—as was Hans Morgenthau—about the historical laws associated with the balance of power. This conflict is evident from the time of his doctoral dissertation through later works such as *Diplomacy* (1994). For him, power politics "could not be denied." Nations were "bound" to follow its dictates. Yet Kissinger criticized American diplomats in the twentieth century for ignoring the lessons of realpolitik—as if they had a choice. When he recounted how Communist leaders calculated their advances and retreats against the West, Kissinger often condemned their wickedness and cynicism—as if they too had a choice.[19]

THEORIST OF NUCLEAR WAR

Kissinger's foray into nineteenth-century diplomatic history showed courage or naïveté in a period in which policy intellectuals were studying the transformation in international politics that, they believed, the atomic bomb had caused. Yet even *A World Restored* indicated Kissinger's desire to contribute to this debate. The pre- and post-1945 worlds were continuous. For him Revolutionary France, Nazi Germany, and Communist Russia presented to the rest of the state system identical sorts of problems, and atomic weaponry, although a critical element in the equations of postwar politics, was subsidiary to the issue of conventional versus revolutionary states. This position put Kissinger outside the consensus of policy scientists at RAND and elsewhere. At the same time, highlighting the hostility of the Soviet Union was common currency among defense intellectuals. Finally, Kissinger walked a tightrope between RAND intellectuals and those of his colleagues at Harvard who would accentuate bureaucratic politics. Like Neustadt, Kissinger scorned bureaucracy in poli-

---

[18] The same impulses are found in his briefer study of Bismarck, often alleged to be his real hero: Kissinger, "The White Revolutionary: Reflections on Bismarck," *Daedalus*, summer 1968, pp. 888–924.

[19] For examples see *Diplomacy* (New York: Simon and Schuster, 1994), pp. 294–95, 314, 350, 686; quotes at 370 and 421. There is also a tension in Kissinger's belief that the revolutionary Soviet state was also realistic in its diplomacy.

cymaking, but his remedy was never its rationalization. Instead, he displayed contempt for the mediocrity of bureaucrats. The statesman had to overcome them through force of will, guile, and vision. In this respect, he resembled the RAND theorists who focused on the creative intelligence of intellectuals in politics. In addition to his distaste for bureaucracy, however, Kissinger dismissed the idea that a technocracy could carry out foreign policy. Diplomacy was misconceived as a game, and was rather an activity adjudicating forces that, for Kissinger in his more metaphysical moments, represented the tragic immersion of human beings in time and history. His sensibility was antithetical to American instrumentalism.[20]

Two books that Kissinger wrote as a Harvard faculty member, *Nuclear Weapons and Foreign Policy* (1957) and *The Necessity for Choice* (1961), carved out his own position in the field of nuclear policy. Like his Harvard (and RAND) associates with whom he had such a troubled relation, Kissinger rejected a stereotyped version of Republican diplomacy. No intellectual could earn his spurs in the 1950s and early 1960s defending Eisenhower and reliance on atomic weaponry. But Kissinger also wished to transcend the ambience and Democratic commitment of the civilian strategists. His link to Nelson Rockefeller made sense. Rockefeller wanted foreign policy advice that would distance him from liberal Democrats, from Eisenhower, and from Eisenhower's vice president and Rockefeller's chief opponent for leadership in the GOP, Richard Nixon. As scholars correctly saw, rather than establishing an independent voice, Kissinger's writings adapted the ideas of RAND theorists to whom Kissinger gave insufficient credit.[21] At the same time, he differed little from Thomas Schelling and Herman Kahn, who had also elaborated on the work of others. The damning accusation that Kissinger popularized and traded on other people's efforts neglected to note that he had pulled off what was beyond the ability of most of the strategists. He conveyed to the foreign-policy public the concerns over nuclear weaponry prominent among thinkers from the late 1940s to the early 1960s.

On the other side, the tactical nature of his writings about atomic policy compromised Kissinger's accomplishment. *Nuclear Weapons and Foreign Policy* promoted the graded use of the nuclear arsenal in a way that made it continuous with conventional weaponry in a version of the war-fighting briefly in fashion at RAND. Kissinger embraced the latest style, although his book conveyed some of the complexities of nuclear strategy to the sorts of people who read *Foreign Affairs*. Then, four years later, *The Necessity for Choice* discarded this doctrine as other theorists had and replaced it with the standard strategy of second-strike deterrence. Kissinger's intellectual work appeared to be the outcome not of scholarly inquiry but of self-interest. In fact, later in his

---

[20] The best statement is found in Kissinger, *World Restored*, pp. 312–32.
[21] See for example Brodie to Kissinger, May 2 1958, Box 1, Brodie Papers, UCLA.

career he could never clarify the tension in his own mind between war-fighting and more conventional beliefs about mutual deterrence.

KISSINGER IN POWER

Kissinger spent the 1960s much more as a spectator rather than even a minor player in the world of politics. But when Nixon beat Rockefeller for the Republican presidential nomination in 1968, Kissinger emerged as a natural for an important national security position in a Nixon White House. Nixon would conciliate the defeated Rockefeller with Kissinger's appointment. At the same time, the president-elect wanted his own intellectual, at least one, to show that he was equal to Kennedy. Nixon hated Harvard academics, felt inferior to them, yet craved their approval. He recognized in Kissinger a kindred spirit, even though Kissinger was himself a Harvard man. Both were poor outsiders who had fought their way up. Their enemies accused them of opportunism and duplicity. Symbols of resentment played a part in their bonding. Together Nixon and Kissinger developed a curious and sometimes uneasy rapprochement built on a cruel but cunning appraisal of international politics and a ruthless suppression of foreign policy bureaucrats. When Nixon would denigrate the Ivy League State Department and Harvard Jews to "Dr. Kissinger," the professor knew that the president, in his weird argot, was talking about the same Cambridge types who had also stood in Kissinger's way. As Kissinger put it, it was not necessary to turn philosophers into kings, or kings into philosophers, but to have the thinker and the politician work imaginatively together.[22] Nixon gave him that opportunity.

The Truman administration had created the National Security Council in 1947 as part of the reforms that had established the office of the secretary of defense. But the position of advisor for national security did not really exist for Truman and was unimportant for Eisenhower. Kennedy and Johnson made the special assistant, in the persons of McGeorge Bundy and Walt Rostow, a figure of substance, although the NSC remained a somnolent institution. Accentuating developments that began under Kennedy, Nixon concentrated foreign policy decision-making in an NSC staff that Kissinger led.[23]

As national security advisor and then later as both advisor and secretary of state, Kissinger implemented a thoughtful strategy, but it was not a theory he had learned in graduate school or as a professor at Harvard. Rather, it was the working out of what he repeatedly called a vision of diplomatic behavior, the

---

[22] "The Policymaker and the Intellectual," *The Reporter*, March 5, 1959, p. 35.

[23] See the summary in Andrew Preston, "The Little State Department: McGeorge Bundy and the National Security Council Staff, 1961–65," *Presidential Studies Quarterly* 31 (2001): 636–41.

elaboration of a "conceptual structure" for international politics that he had been meditating on for almost twenty years. The most effective statesmen, Kissinger believed, were those who had systematized "a conceptual basis for political action." The test of his stewardship would be the development of a pattern of response, a behavioral routine, for the most likely challenges the United States would face.[24] Much of this was academic verbiage, but Kissinger did promote a strategic concept.

Vietnam and World Order

Standing outside of the decision making of the 1960s, Kissinger comfortably believed that Democrats had misconceived the Vietnam War, from which the United States had to extricate itself expeditiously. But although a paramount issue of the 1968 campaign, the war was never for Kissinger himself a core problem. Like Kennedy, Kissinger had changed his mind about the USSR in the 1960s. He thought not only that good Soviet-American relations were essential for global political life but also that nuclear weapons and the technological advances in their development were the chief threat to these relations. The strategic superiority that had forced the Soviet Union to back down in 1962 had vanished. The Test Ban Treaty that Kennedy had negotiated in 1963 implied this fact, and by the early 1970s parity was a reality for Kissinger. The United States could not bestride the world as it had in the 1940s and 1950s. The European settlement that Kennedy arrived at with the Soviets in the early 1960s initiated an era in which the United States would operate in a world with competing nation-states, or at least with two such states. Managing this operation became critical because of nuclear weapons, as it had for Kennedy. The issues were too grave to construe as an ideological war that the fall of Communism would resolve. Such a collapse would not occur now that the USSR was the military equal of the United States. From Kissinger's perspective Vietnam was tangential and had prevented the Johnson administration and his Harvard peers from perceiving the alteration in world politics as the Russians gained atomic equality.

The battle between democracy and totalitarianism should no longer dominate foreign policy. It was too hazardous to the planet to regard the USSR as an implacable foe, for such a scenario could only lead to the end of the world. While issues of human liberty were important, the "first objective" was "to reduce the danger of international war."[25] Although he sometimes disliked the

---

[24] I have taken these, most elegant, formulations of his ideas from Kissinger, *Nuclear Weapons*, pp. 410, 434.

[25] Henry A. Kissinger, *American Foreign Policy*, expanded ed. (New York: Norton, 1969, 1974), p. 206.

word, Kissinger sought a condominium of power, a system in which America and Russia would share the burdens of order. The two would put relations "on a new foundation of restraint, cooperation, and steadily evolving confidence . . . [and] a spectrum of agreements on joint efforts with regard to the environment, space, health, and promising negotiations on economic relations."[26] For realpolitik to achieve an equilibrium, rather than to degenerate into crises and war, Kissinger wanted some consensus on the rules of engagement for a U.S.-USSR system.[27]

To actualize this idea was to solve a problem. The USSR had not made itself over from a revolutionary state to a legitimate state in the twenty-five years after World War II. Yet by adroit diplomacy Kissinger could assist the Soviet Union, or pressure it, to transform itself. Kissinger held out to the Soviets reciprocal engagements and activities, joint ventures and programs that would incrementally construct conciliatory if always revocable areas of restraint and cooperation. The United States would help the USSR increase its standard of living and create the infrastructure for a bourgeois, legitimate state. Kissinger was "forcing the Soviet Union into a cooperative relationship with the rest of the world . . . that [would] . . . over a period of time mitigate their system."[28]

Kissinger and Nixon opened relations with China to intimate to the Russians that they needed the United States in a world not defined by ideology. Communism no longer joined China and the USSR, nor separated China from the United States. If the Soviet Union accepted the Americans' offer to erect a new world order, the United States would help it maintain its sphere of influence against China. But if the Russians did not take the bait, they would face the prospect of a China allied to the United States.

Vietnam tested Kissinger's version of the détente that Kennedy had begun. If a war of ideals was no longer central, then Vietnam should no longer matter so much to the United States, and it did not to Kissinger. Indochina, he said, *had been viewed* "from our perspective of a monolithic Communist world." There *had been* "an assumption that this was a test case of a global confrontation." But now the United States could put Vietnam in "a more regional perspective" and had "no national interest in a predominant American position in this area and we will not seek to achieve it."[29] Nonetheless, the credit and honor of the Americans, who must bow out without humiliation, did matter. In the metamorphosis of the war in Vietnam into a local struggle for independence, Kissinger hoped to call on the Soviet Union, which like the United States had an interest in the moderation of emergent nationalism. On its side, the USSR could demonstrate its evolution from revolutionary state by helping

---

[26] Kissinger, *American Foreign Policy*, p. 156.
[27] See *Diplomacy*, pp. 421, 733–61.
[28] Kissinger, *American Foreign Policy*, p. 214.
[29] Kissinger, *American Foreign Policy*, pp. 225–26.

the United States to extricate itself from the war—or, as perhaps the Soviets saw it, by giving the Americans one last victory.

The other critical test of Kissinger's concept was SALT, the Strategic Arms Limitations Talks, which continued the impulses that had led to Kennedy's Test Ban Treaty. Identified by many with détente, SALT attempted to control the nuclear weapons that, in the first place, had made it necessary for Kissinger to leverage the Soviet Union into legitimacy. Premised on "geopolitical equilibrium," the SALT negotiations flowed from "an underlying philosophy and a specific perception of international reality."[30] The two great powers could not dominate one another and had to cooperate to manage the weapons of mass destruction.[31]

Like the nineteenth-century diplomats he wrote about, Kissinger fell short of his goals. Although the USSR may have supported him in muscling enough concessions from North Vietnam to allow the United States to leave South Vietnam in early 1973, the Soviet ability and desire to coerce the northerners were minimal. In 1954 the Geneva Conference had taken France from the field in Indochina, and China and Russia had pushed Ho Chi Minh to give up a military victory in his grasp for a political victory a few years later. The latter took over two bloody decades and, in 1971 and 1972, the North Vietnamese were unwilling to trust their allies about what they might get in the future. North Vietnam suspected promises about long-term political solutions available if it would abate the fighting. De-escalation would only allow the United States to consolidate its position. At least by 1969–72, if not much earlier, saving America's face did not attract the northerners, or they distrusted face-saving as an explanation of American diplomacy. Some evidence indicates that they wanted to embarrass the United States, even if they had to suffer in the process. This test of détente proved imperfect to some; to others a Russian failure to honor the new relation with America; and to still others foolishness on Kissinger's part to think that anything had changed.

SALT agreements were reached, but were always clouded, and never expressed to their critics the alteration of direction Kissinger presumed to have forced on the USSR, or inveigled it to take. SALT became merely one more arena in which the adversaries carried on their ideological shouting match. In part this lack of success stemmed from the fact that Kissinger's domestic opponents like Democratic senator Henry Jackson of Washington and many conservative Republicans would not accept his view of the USSR's legitimacy. For them, Kissinger foolishly envisaged compromises. SALT should only function as a tool to defeat the Russians. The hostile critique later persuaded Kissinger to reinterpret what he had been doing in his time in power. Soon

[30] Kissinger, *American Foreign Policy,* p. 139.

[31] Kissinger, "Statement Before the Committee on Foreign Relations . . . 1979" in *For the Record: Selected Statements 1977–1980* (Boston: Little, Brown, 1981), p. 192.

after he went out of office in 1977, he claimed that the USSR had "assault[ed]" the "international equilibrium."[32] He recalled that détente was only "a method for conducting the Cold War."[33]

Kissinger had the same flaws as he imputed to Metternich, and they in part accounted for the criticism. The Austrian was a brilliant tactician but lacked a moral imperative that could have guided his diplomacy. Kissinger gave even the educated elite in the United States a poor substitute for the global war for freedom that they had found in the Truman Doctrine and Kennan's containment. In his emphasis on realpolitik, Kissinger downgraded the principle of an American-led moral order and ideological conflict against a brutal enemy. The secretary's critics at home did not believe that the USSR was a strong state with which America would permanently have to do business, and clung to the view that the Russians represented an evil that the United States must vanquish.[34]

Kissinger presented a revised account of his point of view in the three-volume memoir on his years in power, almost four thousand pages long. This project—the first two volumes completed in 1979 and 1981, the third in 1999—co-opted for literature the global politics of the 1970s. Richard Neustadt early on argued that the memoirs were designed as a stumbling block to all future attempts to understand the period.[35]

From the perspective of these memoirs I have erred in concentrating on a vision that only ambiguously guided Kissinger's time in office. In the volumes Kissinger intimated that the agreements with the Russians did not break new ground, as one might have thought. To protect himself against the critics of the late 1970s who chastised him and Nixon for being soft on the USSR, Kissinger protested that his policies had anti-Russian aspects, as they undoubtedly did. In the last volume, written after the collapse of the Soviet Union, he went further. Conventional commentators attributed its demise to unrelenting pressure on the Russians by conservative Republicans after Kissinger. The breakup proved that détente was the wrong policy, for it was premised on a permanent USSR. Kissinger thus argued in the 1990s that his diplomacy fit with the harder, ideological line that was thought to have brought the Soviets down. That is, in the memoirs a gifted participant attempted a history that justified his activities by making them comport with later views that he saw as triumphant.

[32] Kissinger, "Statement," *For the Record,* p. 217.

[33] Kissinger, *Years of Renewal* (New York: Simon and Schuster, 1999), p. 248. See the more ambiguous remarks, already backtracking, in "Footsteps of History" (1980) in *For the Record,* p. 262.

[34] An excellent succinct analysis is given in Seyom Brown, *The Crises of Power: An Interpretation of United States Foreign Policy during the Kissinger Years* (New York: Columbia University Press, 1979), pp. 141–53.

[35] Neustadt conversations, 1978–79.

KISSINGER ON SOUTHEAST ASIA

After Lyndon Johnson had refused to run for reelection, Richard Nixon had defeated the Democratic vice president, Hubert Humphrey. But when Nixon took over in 1969, American power in Vietnam had crested. Graduated escalation had stalemated the battle in bloody and seeming unending conflict that left well over five hundred thousand American troops in Vietnam. Bundy and McNamara were gone from LBJ's government, and in the spring of 1968, under pressure, Johnson had capped the level of American forces, halted the bombing of the North, and was negotiating the United States out of the war. Although some commentators have argued that the antiwar movement prolonged the fighting,[36] by this time politicians were responding to a deep and widespread public demand that the United States get out of Vietnam as quickly as practicable. Legislators determined to reduce executive prerogatives, to secure an American retreat, and to terminate support for the Southeast Asian allies dominated the Congresses that took office in 1969 and the next several years.

Nixon could not resist these domestic imperatives in 1969 and soon recalled some American troops, a move consistent with what the Democrats had been doing in 1968. This unilateral de-escalation evolved into a series of scheduled reductions. Kissinger recognized how this would complicate diplomacy with the North Vietnamese, with whom he bargained for a phased withdrawal that would salvage American pride and, he hoped, the non-Communist governments in Indochina. To offset the diminution of American power the Republican administration announced a policy of "Vietnamization," or "the Nixon Doctrine," that would replace American troops with Asian ones generously assisted by American supplies and materiel. But no one thought that the South Vietnamese alone would bear the increased burden of fighting both insurgents in the south and the army of North Vietnam. Regular decreases took both the carrot and stick from Kissinger's hands. To influence the North Vietnamese from his weakened position, Nixon slowly decided to resume the air war on the enemy.

Because Johnson at the end of his term had stopped the bombing in the north, to start it again lacked appeal. Instead Nixon—as had Johnson at the end of his term—focused on the south and on the eastern boundaries of Laos and Cambodia that for so long had harbored the North Vietnamese infiltrators to the south, comrades in arms of the Laotian and Cambodian Communists. Only later did use of air power against the north itself again become prominent. Nixon and Kissinger hoped to trade the end of such bombing for concessions

[36] See Adam Garfinkle, *Telltale Hearts: The Origins and Impact of the Vietnam Antiwar Movement* (New York: St. Martin's, 1995).

that would allow the Americans a dignified exit that might indefinitely preserve the south. Kissinger, however, was more eager to get out and Nixon more committed to staying, more trustful that continued violence would save his ally.

As I have suggested, the administration hoped that détente would persuade the Soviet Union to make the North Vietnamese more tractable. "Playing the China card," however, only complicated the deal with the Russians, for as the United States warmed up to China, North Vietnam became the USSR's strongest ally along the China border. Moreover, Nixon and Kissinger were in a feeble position at home. Bombs were one of the few means the administration had at its disposal to force the North Vietnamese to allow the Americans to leave with "honor," as Kissinger and Nixon repeatedly put it. But in creating a bargaining position through bombing, they infuriated their congressional adversaries who seemed determined, from the perspective of the administration, to achieve the humiliation of the United States, and who at least gave little thought to the problems that would accompany an immediate collapse of American power.

The president and his national security advisor wanted more than the traffic would bear, although the continued fighting put not insignificant pressure on the North Vietnamese. According to Kissinger, they attached value "to qualities like cleverness and cunning as opposed to attributes like probity . . . esteemed in the Western world."[37] More important, however, than the moral differences Kissinger perceived between Asian integrity and his own was the balance of forces. Air power aimed to give the United States a strategic departure from Indochina and a non-Communist government there. But bombs were not enough. Indeed, although more potent than many observers allowed, bombs were inadequate when contrasted to the diminished number of American troops, the public and congressional cry to disengage, and the legislative drive to end the military and economic aid to the United States' sinking clients.

In early 1973, after greater bombing had destabilized the Laotian and Cambodian governments and B-52s had unleashed extraordinary tonnage on North Vietnam, Kissinger signed a cease-fire agreement with the northerners that allowed the ground forces of the United States to depart. Soon after, north and south were again embattled. The south was finally defeated in May 1975 after some attempts by American statesmen to prop up the government and much hand-wringing about diplomatic commitments. Later the disaster that befell Cambodia under the rule of the Khmer Rouge was often seen as having its origins in American policies of the late 1960s and early 1970s. Carrying the war to Cambodia, critics plausibly argued, had energized a malign Communist

---

[37] Harriman, Memorandum of Conversation, August 2, 1966, FRUS, 1964–68, vol. 4, *Vietnam 1966*, p. 543.

group that came to power because the United States had generated chaos in that country.

Numerous commentators vilified the policies of the administration, especially excoriating its efforts in Cambodia.[38] All of them adopted a variant of the views expressed in an early and powerful work by William Shawcross, *Sideshow: Kissinger, Nixon, and the Destruction of Cambodia*.[39] Published in 1979, *Sideshow* argued that Kissinger (and Nixon) bombed Cambodia to gain time for the Vietnamization of the war in the south. The administration understood that the North Vietnamese could not resist the early prospect of taking all of Indochina, but such a wider war would compel the north to slow down in the south. On this view, the war in Cambodia bought a couple of years for South Vietnam, and permitted "a decent interval" to occur between the disengagement of the United States and the victory of the North Vietnamese. The sacrifice of Cambodia preserved the status of America as a guarantor nation. There was a further turn on this interpretative stance, although not entirely compatible with it. Nixon believed, some scholars argued, that the enemy would disregard any cease-fire agreement worked out between the United States and North Vietnam. Nonetheless, Nixon went through a diplomatic charade. If the North Vietnamese broke such an agreement, he felt the executive could circumvent congressional disapproval. Only such a "legal" document would allow him to reenter the war and reinstitute bombing the north for its abrogation of a cease-fire.[40] Shawcross's interpretation gained credibility immediately, because in response to *Sideshow*, Kissinger rewrote portions of the first volume of his memoirs, just due for publication when *Sideshow* appeared. Unfortunately for Kissinger, his publishers had released galleys of his book to the press, and comparison of them to the published volume showed that Kissinger had changed the emphases of his treatment of Cambodia. The alterations indicated that the final version disguised his beliefs at the time about some of the consequences of the air war.[41]

Shawcross and the many who have followed him in the last quarter-century have joined their negative appraisal of Nixon's and Kissinger's policies to a similar appraisal of the men's lack of virtue. The air war on the north and the

---

[38] Among them: William Bundy, *A Tangled Web: The Making of Foreign Policy in the Nixon Presidency* (New York: Hill and Wang, 1998); Jeffrey Kimball, *Nixon's Vietnam War* (Lawrence: University Press of Kansas, 1998); Christopher Hitchens, *The Trial of Henry Kissinger* (New York: Verso, 2001); and Larry Berman, *No Peace, No Honor: Nixon, Kissinger, and Betrayal in Vietnam* (New York: Free Press, 2001). An outstanding comprehensive look at the literature is Jussi Hanhimäki's "Selling the Decent Interval: Kissinger, Triangular Diplomacy, and the End of the Vietnam War, 1971–73," *Diplomacy and Statecraft* 14 (2003): 159–94.

[39] I have used the Touchstone edition of 1987, which has a new introduction and a very useful appendix on the controversy the book originally generated when published in 1979.

[40] Berman, *No Peace, No Honor*, pp. 186–88.

[41] The best, careful, analysis appears in the *New York Times* for October 31, 1979, p. A10.

disaster of Cambodian policy demonstrated the viciousness of their impresarios, and it is difficult to disentangle the two. Yet the diplomacy deserves more scrutiny.

Nixon and Kissinger took power in impossible circumstances. The troop withdrawals forced on Nixon as a predictable leader of a mass democracy also handed him an insoluble dilemma. The expanded bombing, as a last-ditch effort, sought to protect American soldiers while fortifying the frail U.S. allies whose existence was at stake. The harshest commentators could say only that this policy had little conceptual underpinning and was at most "a managed retreat." Disgusted by the policy, however, analysts attributed it to the basic lack of moral feeling at the heart of Nixon's and Kissinger's characters. If history were only ethical critique, this might be satisfactory.[42]

Kissinger's and Nixon's literary enemies conflated Kissinger's intentions with the results of the policies—the communization not only of South Vietnam but also of Laos and Cambodia, and the dreadful loss of life there. Shawcross wrote that whatever the administration meant for Cambodia, history must judge statesmen by the consequences of their actions. Among many others, he asserted that Nixon and Kissinger "created catastrophe." At the same time, Shawcross asserted that "no one could have foreseen the consequences at home and abroad." Other authors noted that Kissinger and Nixon were forced into some of their maneuvers and that matters turned out the opposite of what they had wanted.[43] Even the argument that Kissinger "knew" that all he could achieve was a decent interval between the withdrawal of the United States and the collapse of South Vietnam rests, first, on ambiguous evidence. It rests on a belief in Kissinger's ability to see the future that neither he nor anyone else had.[44] Most important, it undervalues Nixon's intense focus on the extrication of the United States in a way that preserved what, to him, was its self-respect as a great power. Nixon may have had little reason to support his ally and fight Communism to the last, but the president actualized sentiments that were on the lips of all Americans in the twenty-five years after World War II.[45]

The end was still ugly. The north did not secure a victory in 1975 at a minor cost, using small arms that the victors had collected from the departing French in 1954. Instead, the intrusion of the United States into Indochina had increased

---

[42] Jeffrey Kimball's *The Vietnam War Files: Uncovering the Secret History of Nixon-Era Strategy* (Lawrence: University Press of Kansas, 2004) has a synthetic account of the policies that is joined to moral condemnation. Quote from Bundy, *Web*, p. 302.

[43] Shawcross, *Sideshow*, p. 396, and repeated on pp. 443–44. Also Bundy, *Web*, pp. 368–71; and Kimball, *Nixon's Vietnam*, pp. 331, 333.

[44] The best assemblage of the evidence is in Isaacson, *Kissinger*, pp. 161, 313, 484–86. See also Hanhimäki, *Flawed Architect*, pp. 230ff., 284.

[45] Readers will find a good survey of the thinking in Pierre Asselin, *A Bitter Peace: Washington, Hanoi, and the Making of the Paris Agreement* (Chapel Hill: University of North Carolina Press, 2002).

the stakes, the destructiveness, and the hostility among all the sides in Vietnam. In Cambodia the victory of the Khmer Rouge empowered murderous reformers, who gave Communism a bad name even with the Left in the 1980s. Nixon and Kissinger added to the violence Lyndon Johnson unleashed on Southeast Asia, and very few commentators believed that the benefits outweighed the costs. Walt Rostow was a striking exception.

As the topics of this book have made apparent, it is a nice question how the results of action are connected to human purposes. When effects contravene the intentions of the actors, are they merely unintended consequences, or something more? Shawcross and those who have followed him have condemned Kissinger for the consequences not because he intended them but because they believed that Kissinger was repellent. And there is some evidence that Kissinger was dimly aware by 1971, and then more increasingly, that the world was transmuting his diplomatic goals.[46] But there is a more appropriate way to examine these goals.

Shawcross stated that Cambodia's interests were "consciously sacrificed" to the vision of an American "strategic design," and other bitter critics have talked about a "strategy," a "strategic plan," and a "grand design" that the Nixon administration possessed.[47] But a strategic concept was just what Kissinger claimed to add to American diplomacy. He even acknowledged the accompanying compromises and political adjustments that his later critics noted.[48] Moreover, Kissinger recognized historical irony, if they did not. History transmogrified human designs, but we could still not dismiss the possibility of progress, certainly when statesmen acted with self-conscious decisiveness.

In April 1970, in a notorious act of will, Nixon presided over an "incursion" into Cambodia that attempted, mainly through bombing, to create the conditions for a decorous retreat by the United States and the indefinite maintenance in power of the South Vietnamese government. Nixon ignored the State and Defense departments, whom he rightly believed would scuttle the move, and worked only with Kissinger and his White House staff. Shortly afterwards, a group of Kissinger's former Harvard colleagues met with him to protest American policy. The group included devotees of both the bureaucratic-politics (Richard Neustadt) and the rational-actor (Thomas Schelling) models.[49] Kis-

---

[46] An excellent example, cited by his foes, comes from H. R. Haldeman's diary of the end of 1970, which has Kissinger worrying that an early settlement in Vietnam might be something to be avoided because the south might collapse before the presidential election of 1972, thus creating a problem for Nixon's reelection bid. See Kimball, *Nixon's Vietnam*, p. 239; and Hitchens, *Trial*, passim.

[47] Shawcross, *Sideshow*, p. 396; Bundy, *Web*, p. 302; and Kimball, *Nixon's Vietnam*, pp. 370–71.

[48] See, for example, Kimball, *Nixon's Vietnam*, pp. 370–71.

[49] A full report of the meeting is given in the Harvard *Crimson*, May 19, 1970, and is recounted in Shawcross, *Sideshow*, p. 156; and see the discussion of Simon and Arrow in chapter 2.

singer apparently told them that the administration wanted a three-year "fire break" for South Vietnam. They urged Kissinger to resign and told him that they had lost confidence in the diplomacy of the United States and would no longer consult for their country.[50] Yet Nixon, with Kissinger, was the best embodiment of the rational-actor model that RAND strategists were likely to see. According to RAND, ultimate ends were not, could not, be open to cognitive discussion. The values displayed in such ends had no further justification than the adherence to them by the leadership. Additionally, a dictatorial society, as Kenneth Arrow had called it, made the most rational and integrated decisions. One will exercised authority over the multitude of competing wills that ordinarily diffused the consistent expression of purpose. Moreover, in their disregard of the foreign policy bureaucracies, Nixon and Kissinger reflected the views of men like Neustadt who saw the pitfalls of the bureaucracies and who wanted, certainly in a more well-mannered way, to overcome their problems for the executive. At any rate Kissinger's former Harvard colleagues did not invoke the model of bureaucratic politics to argue that he was not to blame for what had happened.

Despite Kissinger's contempt for Harvard, and its for him, he and Nixon embodied the theories of RAND. The two men also recognized the power of bureaucracies to upset policy by circumventing them. But these facts underscored a truth about historical irony that Kissinger himself often noted. People often do not like it when they get what they wish for.

Kissinger as a Model

Kissinger was the defense intellectual of the postwar era supremely gifted in translating ideas into politics. Yet his success in applying knowledge to the polis would not have been possible without his alliance with Nixon, an American leader known for his dismissal of the role of intellect in public life. According to all the commentators, reckoning political advantage guided Nixon more than principle. Moreover, Kissinger's wisdom in power must be compared to the views of his fellow realist thinkers George Kennan and Hans Morgenthau, both of whom hostilely opposed the Johnson and Nixon administrations' decisions. It is hard to make the case that even similar theoretical views cash out with like actions, although no one can show that Kennan and Morgenthau would not have acted like Kissinger had they been given the chance. Finally, in implementing a strategic concept, Kissinger ranks, among

---

[50] Neustadt, esp. letter not sent, July 15, 1970, Box 24, Neustadt Papers, JFK Library.

the people I have studied, with Dwight Eisenhower. Eisenhower made effective a point of view but was uninterested in learning from the scholarly community, disdained its theories, and dealt with it uncomfortably. To call attention to these facts suggests the peculiar way ideas were potent in diplomacy from 1945 to 1975.

CHAPTER 11

Diplomats on Foreign Policy, 1976–2000

THE IMPACT of the events of 1962–75 on defense intellectuals was evident for a much longer time than the immediate period after the publication of *The Pentagon Papers* in 1971 and the conclusion of the war in 1975. Through the end of the twentieth century, the strategists provided those involved in Vietnam with techniques of exoneration. This chapter considers several pieces of writing, indicating how the civilians involved in foreign policy shaped the interpretation of the 1960s for the next thirty years. In laying out their elucidation of the era, I emphasize the repeated efforts of Secretary of Defense Robert McNamara.

McGeorge Bundy

In 1988 McGeorge Bundy published *Danger and Survival*, a long, densely written book about nuclear issues from World War II to the 1980s. It was the closest Bundy would come to a published memoir. Although he wrote in part as a historian, he acknowledged that he also designed his narrative to explicate the big events that he knew much about personally, such as the dropping of the atomic bomb (the rationale for which he had worked on as a young man with Secretary of War Henry Stimson) and the missile crisis of 1962. The context in which Bundy wrote this book in the 1980s also needs to be considered. Bundy (and many Democrats like him) responded to the triumph of Ronald Reagan's Republicanism, to its forceful critique of a weak or misguided Democratic foreign policy, and to what looked to Bundy like an excessive buildup of military hardware. Centered in Cambridge, Massachusetts, opponents of Reagan pointed to a new arms race, the horrors of nuclear war, and Republican-generated strategic instability as the real dangers. They looked to the recent past to shore up their arguments for arms control and a more modest emphasis on defense spending than the Republicans offered.

These scholarly ideas were of a piece with the lack of interest in history of many students of strategy. If the problem was an abstracted arms race, there was no need to examine the ups and downs central to the political disputes between and United States and the Soviet Union, and how these concerns might moderate or increase the perceived need for military options. Another reason that people like Bundy seized on these ideas was that they made the

Vietnam War a minor current in the history of American foreign policy, and stressed instead atomic diplomacy in which men like Bundy felt their record was better. Henry Kissinger wrote that "anyone who knew Bundy is aware of how much he suffered from what he believed—perhaps excessively—to be his share of the responsibility for what began in idealism and ended in disaster."[1] For Bundy in the 1980s, the nuclear race was the politics. One could underscore responsible arms control as the central thread of international affairs, downplaying Southeast Asia. Finally, concentration on nuclear issues included one of the signal successes of American policy, the missile crisis.

A serious man, Bundy walked a narrow line to explore an ambiguous past in which he had an important part. When he embraced the arms control agenda of the 1980s, Bundy showed a more refined sense of the dangers of nuclear weapons than he had in the 1960s. In a multiauthored *Foreign Affairs* essay of 1982 he became one of a renowned "Gang of Four" advocating "no first use" of atomic weapons,[2] and he projected this sensitivity into the earlier period. When *Danger and Survival* revisited the missile crisis, it focused on an arms race that it was typical for all great powers to engage in and ignored the specific Cold War battles, which had gotten the United States into Vietnam. The result was that Bundy did not have to gaze at his role in the war in Southeast Asia, although he also found himself exaggerating America's responsibility for the Cuban missiles.

In studying Cuba in 1988, Bundy was most intrigued with questions of deterrence, and a then standard view that something like assured destruction—rough parity between two opponents—was the best way to avoid an armed contest. Bundy barely glanced at the issue of Germany and Khrushchev's bellicosity over West Berlin. This Soviet hostility made the missile crisis a complex affair whose explanation must transcend the simple accusation of an American grab for power. The missile crisis came about, in part, because the Russians were convinced that the Americans might give Germany nuclear weapons. The USSR did not appreciate that the United States was also leery about German assertiveness (just as the Americans did not appreciate the divisions in the Communist world).

Bundy minimized the political struggle between Communism and democracy that defined the Cold War (and landed the United States in Vietnam) for a more technical grasp of issues of nuclear arms. But then he found less in the Cuban record to defend American behavior than he might. Instead, he debated how Soviet feelings of "decisive nuclear inferiority" might have destabilized great power relations in the early 1960s. Examining Roswell Gilpatric's speech

---

[1] Kissinger to Sulzberger, September 24, 1996, Chron 1996, Box 10, Additional William Bundy Papers, Mudd Library, Princeton University.

[2] Bundy et al., "Nuclear Weapons and the Atlantic Alliance," *Foreign Affairs* 61 (1982): 53–68.

a year before the crisis, Bundy worried that the Soviets might have been led to feel overwhelmed. In earlier published writings, he had argued that nuclear "superiority" had not been an issue in 1962 and that the two sides were stalemated.[3] Now in *Danger and Survival* Bundy led himself up to the belief that an amplified American nuclear buildup and an overestimation of Russian strength had been the crux of the crisis. The Russians might have acted in Cuba because of the legitimate fear that American rocket rattling had produced. This was not entirely false, but Bundy made the United States more aggressive than may have been warranted. He then saved himself by noting that the Americans could never actually have taken advantage of this superiority because they felt themselves at risk and vulnerable. But this appraisal of their psyche spoke only to Bundy's ability at the last minute to get himself off the hook and not to the logic of his argument.

The price of mental peace over Vietnam was mental anguish over nuclear war. On the one hand, Bundy did not want to revisit Vietnam and, thus, ideological battle between the United States and the USSR. On the other hand, to explain the concepts of deterrence and arms control pointed to American fomenting of the missile crisis.[4]

McNamara

Much has been written about Robert McNamara, a most influential secretary of defense and, because of the conduct of the Vietnam War, one of the most hated Americans of the second half of the twentieth century. McNamara was a decent man who wanted honorably to serve his country in a difficult hour. He also took seriously questions of defense and tried to think them through more systematically than any other public official. Yet it is not easy to find in the record positive acknowledgment of his personal strengths in office. A sympathetic biography of McNamara is needed, since it is hard to imagine that someone could be as unappealing as critics have made the secretary out to be.[5]

McNamara was impressively intelligent and hardworking, and these characteristics and a dominant persona had carried him from humble beginnings to

[3] Bundy, "To Cap the Volcano," *Foreign Affairs* 48 (1969): 11.

[4] A large section of *Danger and Survival: Choices about the Bomb in the First Fifty Years* (New York: Random House, 1988) bears careful reading: see pp. 339–457.

[5] Studying McNamara has become a small industry. I have relied on Paul Hendrickson, *The Living and the Dead: Robert McNamara and Five Lives of a Lost War* (New York: Knopf, 1996); McMaster, *Dereliction of Duty*; Shapley, *Promise and Power*; Trewhitt, *McNamara*; and Stephen Twing, *Myths, Models and U.S. Foreign Policy: The Cultural Shaping of Three Cold Warriors* (Boulder, Colo.: Lynne Rienner, 1998). The 1996 paperback edition of his memoir, *In Retrospect: The Tragedy and Lessons of Vietnam* (New York: Vintage) contains a rich collection of responses to the book.

Figure 9. Secretary Robert McNamara (LBJ Library photo by Yoichi R. Okamoto)

a position of prominence. He equated virtue with brainpower and made a basic assumption that IQ guaranteed morality. He placed the most value on intelligence as measured by cultural stereotypes, academic prestige, and test scores. One of his few childhood memories was of getting the highest grades in his one-room school and thereby successfully competing for the front-row seat against "invariably Chinese, Japanese, and Jews." In old age he was proud of the fact that he was one of three sophomore Phi Beta Kappas at the University of California, Berkeley.[6] His memoir recounted that his group of "Whiz Kids" whom Ford had hired after the war had achieved the best marks ever in the battery of standardized tests that Ford administered, and in picking his staff in the Department of Defense, McNamara also presumed that a certain sort of mental prowess would be the key to success. As he put it, people had to meet his "standards of intelligence, education, and experience." One of his great achievements, he wrote, was to bring into the Department of Defense "Rhodes scholars and editors of the Harvard and Yale Law Reviews." As he came to doubt Vietnam, he was swayed by the fact that demonstrations against the war occurred at superior universities, as he evaluated prestige. As he computed GPAs, the best students were the most opposed.[7]

---

[6] McNamara tells his interviewer this in Errol Morris's film *The Fog of War* (2004).

[7] This portrait of McNamara is drawn from the early pages of *In Retrospect,* esp. pp. 4, 11, 12, 17, 252–54; McNamara Oral History, no. 1 (1975), p. 6, LBJ Library; Shapley, *Promise and Power*, pp. vii–xvi, 614–15. *The Fog of War* also supports my picture.

McNamara also had an interest in the life of the mind. As an automobile executive, he had lived in Ann Arbor and consorted with University of Michigan faculty and not the automobile executives who lived in the exclusive suburbs of Detroit. He wanted "to raise our children in a university environment." In Washington, he was known for his bookish pursuits, and attended the "Hickory Hill seminars" over which the president's brother, Attorney General Robert Kennedy, presided. McNamara read Albert Camus and Arnold Toynbee, as well as such popular favorites as Barbara Tuchman's *Guns of August* and John Kenneth Galbraith's *Affluent Society*. He quoted Aeschylus, Montaigne's *Essays*, and the poetry of Whitman and Kipling. Heavy academic volumes were always on his reading desk. David Halberstam wrote long ago that McNamara "liked to be philosophical."[8]

Yet McNamara did not have much of a contemplative bent. He repeatedly cited T. S. Eliot's lines from "Four Quartets"—We shall not cease from exploration / And the end of all our exploring / Will be to arrive where we started / And know the place for the first time." He talked about how Robert Frost had written about the fork in the woods and that it had "made all the difference" that the poet had taken "the one less traveled by." But the secretary had spent his career making technocratic decisions. Nothing in his life suggested that he thought about ends. He thrived on calculation of means and refused to explore his inner self—indeed he could not. From the sixties on he was alienated from his three children.[9] Unlike Frost, he had unerringly chosen the well-worn worldly path, and not that of the lonely seeker or the conventional family man or the zealous scholar.

His intimates have described McNamara as an isolated character—cold and unattractive. Even friends and allies who saw him when he was relaxed and sometimes even wryly humorous noted his emotional distance and his lack of feeling for people. Some of his enemies early on believed that an overweening high-mindedness and unwillingness to listen to others held the potential for disaster. He had taken over the Department of Defense with an explicit desire to "do good" in public life and was filled with an awareness of this own honesty and integrity—he had been an Eagle Scout in his youth. Even back when his stewardship of the Pentagon was full of promise, hostile commentators lamented that his commitment to a moral politics was abstract. James Reston, an influential journalist, said that "some element of personal doubt, some respect for human weakness, some knowledge of history" was missing in the secretary. One critic (Ward Just) complained that one of America's great tragedies was not being spared McNamara's "unspeakable arrogance." Intolerant and without humility, he was, to the military, someone who cared "about mankind, but not very much about men." Someone else wrote that he had gotten

[8] Halberstam, *The Best and the Brightest* (New York: Random House, 1972), p. 237.
[9] *In Retrospect* gives some sense of this on pp. xxii, 216–17, 258, 313.

A's in college but flunked life. At the end of his time in office, when he believed that his policies were catastrophic, he would sit in his office and cry, or burst into tears before embarrassed assistants. McNamara paid a striking tribute to his wife whose personality, he said, "complemented" his own. She "was born wise . . . and was warm, open, gentle, extroverted, and beloved by all."[10]

Historians have argued that while McNamara consistently resorted to his proficiency in quantitative reasoning, he often rationalized decisions made more on grounds of sentiment or instinct. Although he claimed to want open discussion, he could not tolerate opposition and would humiliate dissenters, because he could not stand challenges to what he believed to be true. The secretary administered in a controlling manner, somewhere between the hierarchical and the authoritarian.[11] He dismissed those whom he thought were not verbally articulate or who could not match him in argument, but at times consciously used bad arguments to defend favored conclusions. He dominated decision making not by reason but by position and personality. Congressional opponents were often in awe of his command of information and ability to marshal material to support governmental policy. They were often also dismayed that he sometimes adjusted the truth to his own purposes in his appearance before legislators. He surely dissembled in the early 1960s when he regularly denied that there was friction between the civilians and the military in the Defense Department at a time when McNamara's assistants despised the military, and the soldiers hated the civilians. In a less duplicitous fashion McNamara would often avoid hard questions in public by transforming them into concerns that he was more comfortable in handling.[12] This is standard operating procedure for figures in American politics, and is only noteworthy because McNamara so vigorously claimed that he did not stoop to such conventional practices, when he certainly had done so. Then, in old age, he almost gleefully announced that not answering questions directly had been a long-standing strategy.[13]

IN RETROSPECT

McNamara wrote two books on the war, *In Retrospect* and *Argument Without End*. The earlier memoir, *In Retrospect*, concentrated on the deliberations of 1963–65, his realization that squeezing the north was not working, his disen-

---

[10] McNamara, *In Retrospect*, 6. Ward Just's appraisal, among others, can be found in "Roundtable Review," *Diplomatic History* 20 (1996), quote at p. 466.

[11] See Adam Yarmolinsky's Oral History (1980), p. 18, LBJ Library.

[12] An outstanding example appears in his 1964 testimony to the House Appropriations Committee reprinted in "The Joint Chiefs of Staff and the Defense Budget," in Tucker, *Modern Design*, p. 56.

[13] In Errol Morris's film *The Fog of War*.

chantment with the Johnson administration, and his anguish at leaving office. In retrospect, McNamara said almost thirty years later, American policymakers made faulty judgments and led the country astray, and for his part, the secretary intimated, he was sorry for his failed leadership.

Antiwar critics and hard-liners, on the one side, and establishment defenders, on the other, lined up on opposite sides in estimations of McNamara. A *New York Times* editorial took delighted opportunity to condemn him for waiting so long to make his doubts about the war public:

> His regret cannot be huge enough to balance the books for our dead soldiers. The ghosts of those unlived lives circle close around Mr. McNamara. Surely he must in every quiet and prosperous moment hear the ceaseless whispers of those poor boys in the infantry, dying in the tall grass, platoon by platoon, for no purpose. What he took from them cannot be repaid by prime-time apology and stale tears three decades late.[14]

Walt Rostow, still a defender of the war, argued that Vietnam was a good cause and that McNamara's apology represented moral confusion. At a notable presentation at Harvard, Graham Allison introduced McNamara, and Ernest May mildly criticized the book but recommended it as "excellent," "splendid," "forthright," "useful," and "wise."[15]

More worthy of note than the views of the secretary's friends and enemies was the mental outlook that the book displayed. It was hardly the work of a spiritual inquirer but rather an attempt at penance, overwhelmingly concerned with McNamara himself, and devoted to the correction of "errors." Two features of his writing stood out. First, he used the moral reasoning that emerged after the release of *The Pentagon Papers* to dilute responsibility for the war. Indeed, the authors of the report are repeatedly cited, construing McNamara's "radical" positions from 1965 to 1967 as challenges to the military (which they were). The secretary authorized the report in 1967; his associates carried out his wishes and laced *The Pentagon Papers* with references to McNamara's upright impulses; he quotes the studies thirty years later to show that he should be exonerated.

McNamara understood morality as a calculating utilitarianism in which the sorts of mistakes one might make in mathematics should not occur. The mistakes are intellectual in nature. When he said that the United States was "wrong, terribly wrong," in Vietnam, he meant that policymakers who had computed costs and benefits erred because some of their assumptions had been flawed. The defect was not "of values and intentions but of judgment and capabilities." McNamara got less than perfect information to measure means

---

[14] Cited from *In Retrospect*, p. 355.
[15] Cited from *In Retrospect*, pp. 422–23.

and thus was bound to make a bad evaluation.[16] To this by now long since conventional defense that the war managers and their defenders had constructed, McNamara added that he and his peers were too busy "to think straight" or "to take an orderly, rational approach." They faced too many urgent problems.[17]

The second feature of the writing is that McNamara imposed his own present ideas on the past in a way that evidence would not bear. This defect in his thinking was widely noted among his policymaker friends,[18] and in a way this characteristic embodied the same flaw that had angered critics thirty years before. For them the secretary just forced the world to meet his requirements of what it was appropriate to believe at the moment.[19]

Two examples—Cuba and nuclear weapons—stand out (both in *In Retrospect* and in other writings). McNamara recalled that except during the Bay of Pigs and the missile crisis the Kennedy administration did not contemplate the overthrow of the Castro regime. This position fit his view in the 1990s that such contemplation would have been a bad thing, but the evidence suggested otherwise in the early 1960s. For example, in early 1963, in what McGeorge Bundy described as "mood music," Kennedy took charge of a high-level meeting and expounded his views of international politics for forty minutes in a performance that all thought memorable. This was after the vague public American promise, brought on by the missile crisis, not to invade Cuba. As at least three accounts stressed, JFK spoke about the future "probability" of "hit[ting]" Cuba.[20]

Similarly, McNamara reiterated that JFK and those around him were opposed to the first use of nuclear weapons, the idea that had come of age in the 1980s. Yet in the early 1960s much of the evidence we have about McNamara's ideas tells us otherwise. In 1964 his assistant Adam Yarmolinsky said that McNamara "always recognized" the possibility of first use. There was no thought of a "no first use" position.[21] It was not just that McNamara misremembered, but that he put forward and defended his misconceptions.

McNamara desired to see his behavior in the past conform to what he thought best in the present. He could not grasp that his past self might not be

[16] *In Retrospect*, pp. xvi, 237–38.

[17] *In Retrospect*, pp. xvii, 277.

[18] See, for example, Bundy to Herring, September 9, 1998, Book Comments, Box 1; Bundy to Neustadt, October 23, 1990, File 1990 Chron, Box 2, Additional William Bundy Papers, Mudd Library Princeton University.

[19] Jones, *Death of a Generation*, pp. 365–68, discusses this aspect of McNamara's personality.

[20] Compare: Blight and Welch, *On the Brink*, pp. 244, 247, 257; and Blight, Welch, and Allyn, *Cuba on the Brink*, pp. 289–90, 376–77. To: Microfiche Supplements, FRUS, vols. 7, 8, 9, *Arms Control, National Security Policy, Foreign Economic Policy*, Documents no. 284, 285, 286, January 22, 1963.

[21] Yarmolinsky Oral History (December 1964), p. 50, JFK Library.

like the one he valued at the present. He had to make the past conform to his own contemporary standards of what was rational and good. He also had to see in the past a rationality and logic that accounting or economics might have. Yet while force of personality had allowed him to dominate politics for much of the 1960s, historical evidence proved more resistant to McNamara: it would not be budged. Nonetheless, the version of the past that the secretary put forward was based not on a lie but on a reluctance to admit that his present conception of what was appropriate belief and behavior had not governed everything in his life. In *Argument Without End* these two aspects of his thought bear analysis.

ARGUMENT WITHOUT END?

This book contains McNamara's musings about the war, his attempts to come to terms with it, and his desire to find closure to his leadership in that era. The effort built on a series of conferences that McNamara participated in from 1987 through 1992 on the missile crisis. These meetings involved Russian, Cuban, and American officials who were involved in the crisis, as well as a number of academics. Although McNamara still thought of the missile crisis as a great triumph, the conferences reminded him of various blunders that took place, and underscored how close an issue the Soviet-American contest was. He emerged from the symposia believing that he could apply the same strategy to learning more about the diplomacy of Vietnam, a failure instead of a triumph. *Argument Without End* printed the results of a number of colloquia that McNamara organized between a group of Americans and some Vietnamese officials and scholars. He arranged these meetings with difficulty. Many foundations refused to be engaged, and at a crucial point the Council on Foreign Relations withdrew its sponsorship. McNamara was not an inconsiderable figure in American public life, and these refusals testified to the suspicion in which influential people of varied ideologies held the former secretary. McNamara also had other trouble with people. By the midnineties many of the leading officials of the Vietnam period were dead. In the United States some who were still alive, such as Rostow, refused to participate. General William C. Westmoreland, who commanded American troops from 1965 through 1968, also declined to chew over what had gone wrong. In the end McNamara settled for some midlevel American civilian officials and was lucky to procure a few soldiers. On the North Vietnamese side McNamara did get, for more or less cameo appearances, General Nguyen Giap, who was Hanoi's chief military strategist, and Nguyen Thach, a retired foreign minister, who died in the middle of the proceedings. The rest of the "North Vietnamese Team," like the American one, consisted at best of second-level officialdom.

McNamara assembled his own "team" at the Watson Institute for International Studies at Brown University, which stayed with the project despite the defection of foundation money. In addition to former officials McNamara added, through Brown, a number of academics—mainly political scientists—to his group and listed them as subsidiary authors to this volume, although the book was McNamara's. Even a chapter entitled "U.S. Military Victory in Vietnam," written by Herbert Schandler, a former officer who had published on the war, did not depart from the secretary's views. McNamara requested that Schandler contribute an essay answering the question whether the United States could have won the war militarily at acceptable cost. In fifty-odd pages, Schandler dutifully said we could not—"definitively," as McNamara wrote twice. The chapter was thus not McNamara's in only a nominal sense, for this was just the answer that the secretary first gave vaguely himself in 1965 and had been elaborating on in public since 1995. It also reflected a contradiction at the core of McNamara's ruminations. When he wanted, he was able to speak "definitively" about Vietnam. When he worried about how his views might be taken, "argument without end" could occur.

The book contained partial transcripts of the conferences, commentary on them, a history of American and North Vietnamese policies in the 1960s, a catalogue of what McNamara called "missed opportunities," various explorations of how more astute diplomacy on each side could have abbreviated the conflict, and (related to the theme of missed opportunities) McNamara's view of the nature of history and the lessons that he drew for American foreign policy from this bit of history.

The Watson Institute had inherited the project from the Kennedy School, and taking a page from Neustadt, McNamara conceived of the meetings as a form of critical oral history, where civil interrogation on each side would reveal the truth. The secretary also made another Neustadt concept the keystone of his "method" for learning something positive from Vietnam. His accent was on matters that were fixable—miscommunications among top policymakers and between the United States and the North Vietnamese; the inadequacy of the enemies' attempts to understand each other's history; a lack of concern for how the opposing side felt about issues. These principles of bureaucratic politics were at stake when McNamara talked about "missed opportunities."

Finally, in terms of method, we must understand McNamara's master concept. One of many Americans who discovered "tragedy" in the late 1960s, McNamara used the term and its cognates at least fifty times. For the ancient Greeks, who gave us this term, tragedy was inevitable not because of circumstance but because of the character of the protagonist. McNamara reversed this meaning and ignored character for situation. For him a tragedy was something that the protagonists could have prevented if only they altered relatively trivial circumstances. For the Greeks Vietnam would have been a tragedy if it were destined to happen given the defects of the secretary and his associates. McNa-

mara followed many policymakers of the era who gave a new meaning to
"tragedy" after Vietnam. The war was a tragedy because greater social knowledge could have prevented it, and no one was to blame.

The secretary joined his sunny sense of the tragic to his version of bureaucratic politics. Opportunities were available in Vietnam that would have allowed each side to achieve its goals without the horrors of the period. But
mutual misperception, misunderstanding, and misjudgment caused diplomats
to miss the opportunities. The secretary later added inadvertence to this catalogue of foibles that could lead to disaster.[22] The "central failure" was one
of empathy because each side misread what McNamara regularly called the
"mindset" of the other. He saw most of these troubles as correctable failures
of knowledge.[23]

McNamara limited his interest to his personal responsibility in Vietnam.
The Vietnamese had to remind him that America had to worry about more
than the 1961–68 period. They thought that their involvement with the United
States began in 1945, and in response to their wishes the book detailed the
"missed opportunities" of the 1954 Geneva Conference, but McNamara
forced the spotlight on the period from 1964 through 1967. He was also unconcerned with what happened after he left office. His anguish about the
military strategy and, in particular, about the bombing of North Vietnam did
not extend to the Nixon period. McNamara lamented over and over that so
few contacts at high levels took place during his time in office. The necessity
of face-to-face meetings was one of the principles that he now advocated as
always beneficial to diplomacy. Yet no one analyzed what helpful or detrimental consequences followed from the extended talks between Henry Kissinger and the northern diplomat, Le Duc Tho, which occurred under Nixon.
Desperate to learn where he had gone wrong, McNamara was so alert to the
problems of his own watch that he ignored the pertinent experience of the
two chief Republican policymakers.

His treatment of the Vietnamese reinforced the personal focus. McNamara
traveled to the conferences convinced that both sides were to blame for the
missed opportunities that could have shortened the war and altered the 1960s.
In misreading its opponent, each side made matters more knotted than they
might otherwise have been. In a favorite example, McNamara believed the
Vietnamese misconstrued American intentions. He said that the Vietnamese
"projected onto the United States a kind of colonial mode of operation not
significantly different from that of French." On the contrary, related McNamara, Americans were "ambivalent about their global role." The Vietnamese

---

[22] Inadvertence appears in McNamara and James G. Blight, *Wilson's Ghost: Reducing the Risk
of Conflict, Killing, and Catastrophe in the 21st Century* (New York: Public Affairs, 2001), pp.
73–75.

[23] *Argument without End*, pp. 6, 376, 392.

wrongly thought that the Kennedy and Johnson administrations wanted "to destroy the Hanoi government." Time after time, McNamara told his old opponents they were "completely wrong" to believe that the United States was a neoimperialist or neocolonialist power, bent on exploitation in Vietnam. They must, he said, grasp the "psychological reality" of American policymakers in the 1960s. They felt on the defensive all over the world, and saw the North Vietnamese as the spear-point of advancing Communism.[24]

In looking to a group's "psychological reality" or "mindset" the secretary brought into play some popular concepts of post-1960s social science and got matters half right. Understanding a historical figure's worldview is an essential part of the historian's task, but only a part. Another part of the job explores what that reality meant to others at the time and what it means in light of our best contemporary knowledge. It is no great insight that people don't see themselves as others see them; that they usually think more highly of themselves than others do, and that they are often confused about their motives. No man, as we say, should be a judge in his own case. McNamara forgot these truisms. Grasping the "American mind-set" (or the Vietnamese mindset) no more explained Vietnam than grasping the Confederate mind-set would explain the Civil War.

McNamara asserted that in the 1960s the United States wanted to protect South Vietnamese interests and to give non-Communist impulses a fighting chance in a unified Vietnam. But, overall, he suggested that the United States would have accepted the neutralization of Vietnam and would have allowed the northerners to triumph over the long haul. The North Vietnamese, McNamara claimed, were wrong not to take hold of this aspect of American policy. They should have facilitated such a solution and permitted the United States to exit Vietnam gracefully. Instead they clung to their view of America as a neocolonial power. McNamara's argument hung on the possibility that the combatants could have steered clear of the worst disasters through a series of decisions that would have stepped down the war.

This view is peculiar, as is so much of McNamara's conception of Vietnam. Only a tiny minority of the men close to power had a relaxed vision of Communism in Asia in the 1960s. Commentators usually characterized the neutralization of South Vietnam (rightly) as "surrender on the installment plan" or "putting the fox in the chicken house." The Johnson administration rather wanted to transform the south into a bastion of American values. As LBJ put it to Ambassador Henry Cabot Lodge in March 1964, "Your mission is precisely for the purpose of knocking down the idea of neutralization wherever it rears its ugly head . . . nothing is more important than to stop neutralist talk."[25]

[24] *Argument without End*, pp. 22, 26, 38, 379.

[25] Quoted in George McT. Kahin, "*The Pentagon Papers*: A Critical Evaluation," *American Political Science Review* 69 (1975): 683n.

More important, *In Retrospect* had proposed over and over that neutralization had no sponsorship. McNamara reported that at the end of 1963 he, Rusk, and Bundy recommended that Johnson shun neutralization, which would only be a façade, and that the recommendation hardened a preexisting attitude of the president's.[26] In early 1964 the leadership again rejected the neutralist idea, and in early 1965, when the United States was deciding to escalate, officials identified neutralization with slow retreat and dismissed it on those grounds.[27] At the end of 1965, when McNamara first proposed a "compromise solution (entailing less than our objective of an independent non-Communist South Vietnam)," he said it received "no serious attention."[28] Later, in 1966, he and his assistant John McNaughton went further and "consider[ed]" that the United States might disengage and look the other way while South Vietnam slid under northern control, but McNamara said that "most of my colleagues view[ed] the situation quite differently." "Little support existed among the president's senior advisors" for the disengagement he had conceived.[29] Why, in further retrospect, did the secretary believe that such negotiations offered a plausible way out?

The Vietnamese were Communists and examined social relations and politics with Marxist preconceptions. Nonetheless, their perception of the United States in the 1960s was not as much off the mark as McNamara's. As he put it correctly at one point, leaders in Washington "had no interest in directly colonizing Vietnam,"[30] but they did want an American-oriented polity and would not have settled for disguised defeat.

The Americans wanted to prevent the south of Vietnam from being communized. The northerners were determined to unite their country. So fearful was the United States that it used extraordinary military means to achieve its goals. Vietnamese in both the north and south fiercely resisted. McNamara could not look squarely at this opposition. As a consumer of the bureaucratic politics model, he could not admit that basic policy disagreements were at the heart of the conflict.

Even using the language of bureaucratic politics, McNamara had trouble sustaining his view that, with more knowledge, positive alternatives had been available. He wrote of "ubiquitous missed opportunities," the "utter inability" of each side to understand the other, and the fundamental misreading of each side by the other. American ignorance of Vietnam was "immense," "astounding," "profound." Both sides sent "mutually incomprehensible sig-

---

[26] *In Retrospect*, pp. 106–7.
[27] *In Retrospect*, pp. 184, 187.
[28] *In Retrospect*, pp. 222–23.
[29] *In Retrospect*, pp. 260–63.
[30] *Argument without End*, p. 383.

nals." The incomprehension "seems to have been total and absolutely consistent."[31]

Yet McNamara's Vietnamese interlocutors did not believe that both sides shared the blame and that mutual understanding would have altered the outcome. Again and again they resisted the U.S. position that they misconstrued American intentions. Respectfully and politely the northerners dismissed McNamara.

> *Nguyen Thach*: I would say, with all due respect to Mr. McNamara, that the U.S. mindset, as he says was incorrect, but that the Vietnamese mindset— our assessment of the U.S.—was essentially correct. Essentially correct. That is all.
>
> *Luu Van Loi*: I am afraid I fail to see how, or in what way, we were wrong in our assessment of the U. S. That is my answer. Does this answer satisfy you?
>
> *Luu Doan Huynh*: Really, I think it was mostly your fault. You did not perceive things objectively. It was your mindset. . . . [F]or the failure . . . the primary reason is because of you gentlemen.
>
> *General Giap*: I don't believe we misunderstood you....Excuse me, but we correctly understood you.... you are wrong to call the war a "tragedy"— to say that it came from missed opportunities. Maybe it was a tragedy for you, because yours was a war of aggression, in the neocolonialist "style," or fashion, of the day for the Americans.[32]

In one dramatic moment that McNamara had the graciousness to print, he asked the Vietnamese why the devastating losses the Americans inflicted on them had not influenced them to negotiate. McNamara wrote that the Vietnamese misunderstood his question. He wanted to know why the Vietnamese did not respond to various U.S. peace probes. The Vietnamese, according to him, thought he was saying they were insensitive to the pain of their people. The interested reader should examine with care this whole section of the book, and we must always face the problem of translation. But it is clear to me that McNamara asked them why they were so callous as not to capitulate to the graduated escalation, designed to display to the Vietnamese how costly resistance to the Americans was, and how the cost to them would go up indefinitely. Why did they not adhere to the theories McNamara had learned in October 1962? Although the northerners did not say so directly, it is also clear to me that they felt McNamara was still insensitive to what he was doing, to his leadership of the bombing.

McNamara asks how they could ignore the suffering caused by the bombs. The Vietnamese believe he was responsible for the air war. Here is part of Tran

---

[31] *Argument without End*, pp. 376–77, 381.

[32] *Argument without End*, quotes, in order: pp. 47, 85, 139, 23–24.

Quang Co's answer, which McNamara said was delivered at "a fever pitch of emotion" and followed by a long silence:

> I must say that this question of Mr. McNamara's has allowed us to better understand the issue. . . . We understand better now that the U.S. understands very little about Vietnam. Even now in this conference—the U.S. understands very little about Vietnam. . . . If he thinks that the North Vietnamese leadership was not concerned about the suffering of the Vietnamese people, . . . then he has a huge misconception of Vietnam. That would be [speaks in English] "wrong terribly wrong" [the phrase from *In Retrospect* that had become well known in Vietnam].[33]

McNamara would not take a Vietnamese *no* for an answer. He said that, over the course of the meetings, the other side accepted that had diplomats on both sides not missed opportunities and displayed better judgment, they might have averted tragedy. It is difficult to know what to do with his declarations, for the Vietnamese are quoted, as above, in ways at odds with McNamara's line. To counter this impression from the transcripts, McNamara made much of minor concessions. Nguyen Thach, early on in the first conference, said, "So, you think it takes two to tango, eh? Maybe. We will talk more about this."[34] In general, in the texts presented, the Vietnamese yielded minimally about mistakes, although they were happy to talk and agreed that discussions were useful, even now. But McNamara did not get the admission of serious missed opportunities and of joint responsibility that he wanted.

The colloquy and the book were consistent with much of what we know about McNamara. Through aggressive energy and what has occasionally been described as intellectual harassment—though in the book it is just willfulness—he often bent discussions to corroborate his view. As McNamara said, when he first went to Hanoi, the big question for him was whether the Vietnamese "really want to play this game by our rules," that is, by admitting their mistakes and cogitating on the limitations of mind-sets.[35] The meetings between the two sides often displayed the American attempt to have the Vietnamese share U.S. perceptions, and often showed the Vietnamese objecting. McNamara did his best to force his ideas on his old opponents. They were modestly forthcoming, and perhaps his relentless character even swayed them a bit. He also extracted from the record everything that served his purpose. But the conference did not result in the adoption of his outlook by the Vietnamese, and one would have to be strange to think that they would.

At the start of the book, McNamara said that his primary concern was not the past. Rather, how could we use the experience to avoid disasters in the future? The last twenty-five-page chapter was called "Learning from Tragedy:

[33] *Argument without End*, esp. pp. 220–21, 253–56, quote at p. 255.
[34] *Argument without End*, p. 56.
[35] *Argument without End*, p. 22.

Lessons of Vietnam for the Twenty-First Century." The "payoff," "the ultimate justification" for historical research, was the search for durable lessons. McNamara did not think subtly in the human sciences, and he evinced his technocratic background when he wrote that we could raise the "probabilities" of preventing future conflict.[36] Like Neustadt and May he offered recommendations to nurture diplomacy.

Some of McNamara's proposals were clichés, though no less true and significant for that: recognize that some problems have no solution, and particularly not a military solution; organize and apply military power with care and thoroughness. Some rules of thumb might or might not be applicable in given situations: work with your allies, practice in foreign policy the democratic principles that Americans preach. Mainly, however, McNamara's lessons were relevant to conditions that knowledge can remedy: communicate with adversaries at a high level, understand the way their minds work, learn about their culture, and put a lot of effort into making thoughtful policies. McNamara did not see opposition of purpose. Such opposition would more or less vanish if we had adequate knowledge.

Even dealing with the Communist world, McNamara had no sense of a real enemy.[37] But he also had a personal motive for his position. Conflicts of purpose are subject to moral evaluations. Yet in his public reflections on Vietnam in the 1990s, an ethical appraisal of conduct was just what he wanted to skirt. When he said he was "wrong, terribly wrong," he believed that he had misapplied a geometric proof, not that he had acted in a morally reprehensible way. The Vietnamese told him this, though he would not listen. His definition of tragedy was not just new; it warded off the inspection of character. For the Greeks disaster could not be derailed because of the values of the protagonist, or his faults.

Argument Without End further worked out McNamara's guilt about Vietnam. He sorely desired to distribute blame and win absolution by using the "tragedy" to do good in the future. After spending his life showing that he could make policy decisions objectively, he titled this book *Argument Without End*, to suggest that on one historical issue where most people agreed that the blame was in large part his, we could argue forever on the distribution of the blame. Suddenly the great exponent of positivist rationality advocated historical relativism, and who was to say he was wrong?

McNamara was a figure like Albert Speer or Richard Nixon. Speer's *Inside the Third Reich* of 1970 made something of the same impact on views about World War II, as did *In Retrospect* about Vietnam. Nixon won a grudging respect after Watergate because he would never give up making his case. Again

---

[36] *Argument without End*, pp. 6, 374.

[37] An idea more prevalent in Europe; see John P. McCormick, *Carl Schmitt's Critique of Liberalism: Against Politics as Technology* (New York: Cambridge University Press, 1997).

and again he commanded attention with his version of events. McNamara was the same. He would not let American opinion alone.

WILLIAM BUNDY

McGeorge Bundy's brother, William, was also a high official in the executive branch of the Kennedy-Johnson administration, almost exclusively concerned with Vietnam, although at one level down from his brother, McNamara, and Walt Rostow. William was self-effacing but never masked ambition. After his government service ended with the defeat of Lyndon Johnson, Bundy edited the magazine *Foreign Affairs*. He at once began a book on American policy in Vietnam from 1961 to 1965. This effort remained in manuscript form, as did other historical writing, but later, in the 1990s, Bundy did complete *A Tangled Web*, a noted volume about the policies of the Nixon administration from 1969 to 1975.[38]

As one would expect of a policymaker turned historian, these works did not escape the framework of Cold War verities as they were promulgated in the United States from the end of World War II onwards. According to Bundy, American diplomacy was designed not just to construct a world in which the United States could flourish but more positively to protect the planet from the Soviet Union and the ideological evil of Communist totalitarianism. Unstable and vulnerable through the 1950s and early 1960s, Southeast Asia was one part of the globe that the revolutionary impulses of Communism threatened, and American intervention was an appropriate response. But in Vietnam in the 1960s "muddling through" was operative. Overworked men, Bundy thought, were able to conjure up few alternatives to the policies they followed, or to think of the wider implications of their efforts, although Bundy did not much criticize the United States. The worst thing he could say about the overthrow and murder of Diem (and his brother-in-law) in 1963, for example, was that their deaths "must be set against the virtual certainty that they themselves would have gone on to cause the deaths of many." The same could be said of JFK's assassination shortly afterwards. In the early 1970s Bundy found that benign motives and gradualism combined with the fear of Chinese expansionism had gotten the United States mired in what seemed to Bundy to be a never-ending and doubtful conflict.[39]

---

[38] The Vietnam manuscript, almost eleven hundred typescript pages, was written between 1969 and 1972, but is incomplete, just stopping in 1965. Bundy wrote in 1986 that it was not his last word (Bundy to Johnson, July 3, 1986, Bundy Papers, LBJ Library). *A Tangled Web: The Making of Foreign Policy in the Nixon Presidency* was published in New York by Hill and Wang in 1998.

[39] Bundy Mss: On murder: 104; on muddling through, 14–14; on gradualism, 454, 51, 9–29–30, 15A-3, 16–20.

Over twenty-five years later, with Nixon's help, Bundy put his own service in greater perspective and was firmer in his evaluations. *A Tangled Web* embodied a vision of foreign affairs in the whole postwar period and the way in which Democratic and Republican policies fit together. *A Tangled Web* argued that South Vietnam had achieved "enormous gains in confidence and stability" because of the "firm stand" the United States took in escalating the war in 1964–65. These gains, Bundy conceded, cost too much, and American policy-makers erred seriously. But, he suggested, after fighting the good fight and assisting a weak ally, the national security managers of the 1960s planned "a measured American policy of withdrawal from South Vietnam" before Nixon took office. Had the United States carried out this policy, South Vietnam and neighboring nations would have had "a substantial chance to cope with threats to [their] security," but the Democrat administration was ousted, and Nixon and Kissinger took its place.

Bundy gave Nixon—and Kissinger, for Bundy a player of almost equal weight with the president—some credit for the direction of foreign affairs. But overall, Bundy found inattention to detail and a concern for short-term political benefits. The inability of Nixon, in his second term, to concentrate on international politics because of the Watergate scandal also marred the record. Even more important for the "failure" of Nixon on his watch was his habitual deceit and lack of humanity, "morally repugnant" character defects that Bundy reminded us Kissinger shared.

Nixon too was interested in the "managed withdrawal" first promoted by Johnson but botched this effort, and made matters worse than they would have been otherwise. The negative results in extricating the United States from Vietnam were more "out of proportion" to the positive results than the disproportion in earlier periods. Bundy additionally found that the "sinister" theme in Southeast Asia was not the commitment in Vietnam, but the agony of Cambodia, for which Nixon and Kissinger alone were responsible.

Finally, although Bundy admitted to no knowledge of domestic politics, he dismissed the argument that the domestic unrest Nixon inherited in 1969 contributed to the "lack of scruple" culminating in Watergate. According to this argument (made prominently by Kissinger), Democrats, such as Daniel Ellsberg, had devised American policy in Vietnam in the early sixties. They then turned emotionally against it, and after Nixon's election undermined his strategy of disengagement. Their criticism and actions—for example, the leak of *The Pentagon Papers*—made it more difficult for Nixon to carry out whatever policies he intended, and surely contributed to Nixon's well-known distaste for "liberals" and his own aggrieved sense of the world. For Kissinger and for other commentators sympathetic to Nixon the destructive impact of the war on the civilities of American politics was a necessary context for understanding the abuses of power of the Nixon presidency. Nixon in part adopted questionable methods to combat a frenzy of antigovernmental activity that

Democrats spawned but that reached its height only when the Republicans took office.

Bundy would have none of this and indeed embraced an earlier view of his brother's about "the gravity of [Kissinger's] distortions."[40] Instead, William Bundy said that the central Watergate misdeeds simply aimed at Nixon's victory in the election of 1972 and at the augmentation of his personal power. Nixon would have done what he did regardless of Vietnam. Bundy stated that Nixon's past just caught up with him in 1974. The president was destined to fall in the classic Greek sense because of his overweening pride. Bundy too could use tragedy for his own purposes.

So here is the history of the United States during the Vietnam era à la Bundy. American diplomats, like him, resolved to prevent Southeast Asia from falling to Communism. In general, this policy, effective from the 1950s to the 1970s, was flawed. But men such as Bundy made courageous decisions, which looked better after the Nixon administration had been on the job than they looked to Bundy when he left the State Department in 1969. Had the slow winding down of the war and negotiations that Johnson (and Bundy) contemplated at the end of his elected term occurred, South Vietnam would have had a good chance of survival. But the electorate denied Democrats like Bundy the chance to carry out this policy. The duplicitous Nixon and his henchman Kissinger took over in 1969, and Indochina paid the price when the Communists triumphed in a much more destructive fashion than they otherwise would have. At home, the protests that antedated the accession to power of the GOP and, from all accounts, contributed to its victory had little influence on Nixon's malign purposes in winning his second term and subverting the Constitution.

---

[40] Bundy, "Reconsiderations: Vietnam, Watergate, and Presidential Powers," *Foreign Affairs* 58 (1979): 397.

IN THE THIRTY YEARS after World War II a variety of men committed to the application of ideas to conflict were prominent in American policymaking circles. Although some form of social-science understanding was critical to many of them, a countertradition hostile to the dominant assumptions was also in evidence. Whatever the intellectual stance, the university proved to be a major locale for the entrée of such thinkers into government. In Washington, however, a certain Darwinism was at work: only selected ideas became creditable, and experts on war might prune their theories to satisfy the demands of statesmen.

The call of reformers for the use of savants in politics produced minimal results. We did not have the sort of knowledge necessary to lift decision making out of the space of the contestable and into the space of the right, or even the nationally successful if Vietnam is kept in mind. Much of what strategists "knew" was wrongheaded or muddled, if not mistaken. Indeed, it is unclear that more knowledge, what policy scientists ordinarily assume they obtain by education and research, would assist decision makers, although we cannot conclude that we don't need more knowledge.

Decision making is based on what I have called agent knowledge, which differs from historical understanding. The knowledge that defense intellectuals and statesmen brought to contemporary issues was no greater than the knowledge that decision makers in earlier times had, not much more than that acquired by the astute reader of the press of record and leading journals of opinion, and certainly not more arcane. The statesperson had to be intelligent enough to keep before the mind the many elements of a situation that a decision would affect and other elements that themselves were influencing the decision. In addition to this intellective component, the decision makers needed the moral courage or political will to override opposition when they thought it unacceptably stood in the way of the preferred decision; and the judgment to sense what was unacceptable and what was not. Experts or advisors might provide detailed information. Or they might depict the competing interests at work and how they might react to a move, but a decision maker did not need an assistant who had the sort of esoteric knowledge generated in a doctoral program. Writers like Kennan in "The Sources of Soviet Conduct" might brilliantly codify the structure of the culture's foreign policy belief, but they were creatures of this culture and its beliefs and never offered advice that transcended the culture. None of the critical aspects of decision making had much to do with the prevalent model of American social science—"whispering in the ear of princes"—the middle-range generalizations supposedly necessary to benign policy and learned in a Ph.D. course.

We want a certain process of decision making. Certain primitive evaluative terms, which cannot be explicated, imbue the definition of this process as I have given it in the preceding paragraph. They are specific to American culture and to the nation-state system in which American diplomats function. Within the parameters established by international political life, we can say that good advice is that which plays its role in the process that I have described above, and that the decision making that evolves in such a process is responsible. We have intelligent people who try to assess all the factors involved, who consult widely and get honest advice. The individuals are of reasonable judgment and have the best information available.

Will such a process result in decisions that are better than others? Who can say? The alternatives that such a process will leave open will not be such as to enable us to distinguish a decision with a good outcome from other sorts of decisions. A decision is just what decision makers have to make when they do not know what will happen after they act. Decisions are acts of the creative imagination, made in tumult and semiblindness, when the available powers of action cannot at all be described as means to any end.[1] This brutal truth is key, for many theorists assumed that applying their models could result in decisions that were specifically and objectively superior to other decisions.[2] There was no way to reach this goal, for policymakers had no way to ascertain how or why the actual alternatives proposed in crises would make one decision more desirable than another. A "decision," as the Latin etymology of the word suggests, merely cuts the knot.

THE ROLE OF IDEAS

One standard argument about the foreign-policy history of this period is that intellectuals made an impact on policy (and in the 1960s led the United States astray in Vietnam). The correctness of the commitment in Vietnam aside, there is much to be said for the position that the *university-learned ideas* of the men of strategic studies had a minor causal role in the quarter-century after World War II, although those men among them in positions of power contributed with varying degrees of influence to the implementation of policy. The RAND social scientists most straightforwardly offered advice to politicians based on a clear model of what advisors ought to do and how they ought to do it. But both in the air force and the Department of Defense their formulations were

---

[1] Adapted from G. L. S. Shackle, *Uncertainty in Economics and Other Reflections* (Cambridge: Cambridge University Press, 1955), p. 9.

[2] David M. Barrett, *Uncertain Warriors: Lyndon Johnson and His Vietnam Advisors* (Lawrence: University Press of Kansas, 1993), usefully distinguishes between the rational and the wise, pp. 190–94.

subservient to politics. McNamara adopted the cost-benefit analyses of RAND but regularly used its lines of reasoning to defend or attack policies that policymakers wanted for reasons other than RAND's imprimatur. In this respect the secretary of defense operated much like the air force generals whom RAND had forsaken for McNamara: the brass had subordinated knowledge to service requirements. Overall, when it pleased policymakers with their own agendas to advance RAND recommendations, the policymakers did so. When the advice was at odds with what they wanted to do, the advice was ignored. RAND analyses became useful arguments for those on one side or another of a policy divide, but the reasoning ordinarily did not have an independent role and was a dependent variable.

The prestige structure of the academy and the ease with which many policyminded intellectuals could publish and disseminate their thoughts made them believe they were giants whose ideas could decisively influence the world. They were wrong. Rather, expertise often became a pawn in the power struggles that it was supposed to circumvent.

Vietnam was here a test case. Politicians used ideas of various sorts to legitimate activity engaged in on other grounds. These grounds were political, whereas the legitimating ideas were justificatory—at a level above the partisan clash. After the war, intellectuals continued to find new ways of understanding Vietnam that, if they did not lead people from the truth, at least obscured the involvement of the authors. Although other examples abound—the explanations of bureaucratic politics in addition to the RAND thinking for the air force—Vietnam is so compelling that it almost persuades one of Benjamin Franklin's lament that man is so conveniently a reasonable creature "since it enables one to find or make a Reason for every thing one has a mind to do."[3]

That is, it is tempting to conclude from the example of Vietnam alone that ideas only provide a framework for action, and do not cause any particular actions. Human beings inevitably talk about their decisions and elaborate a narrative in which their choices cohere. Like other people, diplomats needed some moral and political discourse to validate their efforts, to have policies make sense to themselves and others. Policymakers did what they wanted, though they had to come up with reasons for what they did. Defense intellectuals provided that talk. They fabricated the acceptable speech, the vocabulary and grammar, in which the participants formulated decisions and explained them to one another and to their various publics. The dialogue was necessary for decisions, but had one set of reasons not been available, leaders would have found another to realize the same decisions. If they wanted to make other decisions, they would have found other reasons. Some critics have claimed that this is the function of ideology. Rostow's modernization, for example, did not tell us about the world but provided a rationale for something done for

---

[3] Franklin, *The Autobiography and Other Writings* (New York: Penguin, 1986), p. 39.

more controversial reasons—the advancement of capitalist national interest and the subjugation of third-world countries. Modernization theory was a form of false consciousness.[4]

Such an analysis, however, would be mistaken. In its modern form as the examination of ideology the analysis assumes in any event that some ideas have a real causative power (the genuine reasons) while others (the ideology) function differently. Only some ideas are rationalizations. More important, the analysis fails when formulated as an empirical generalization. Ideas match up with the world in ways that the analysis rules out.

One extraordinary example stands out here—the diplomacy of Henry Kissinger. Over a twenty-year span in the academy, Kissinger developed a sense of how the real world might absorb ideas about foreign policy, and when he went to Washington, he put his "theory" into practice, most effectively from 1969 to 1972. I have called this development one in which a strategic concept emerges. Had Kissinger's ideas not been applied to American-Soviet relations in the early 1970s, the outcomes would have been different than they were. Certainly all his critics urged that his decision making was distinctive and consequential. He made ideas count in foreign policy, although this is not to say that the outcome was desirable.

There are other examples of such counting. The most important, however, has a different resonance—the strategic concept of Dwight Eisenhower from 1953 to 1957 (after which he seemed to tire and to become bewildered). The president combined a vision of the importance and fragility of the American economy, of the intentions of the enemy, of the superiority of the United States in respect to nuclear weapons, and of what he wanted to achieve for the country. This vision gave the United States a foreign policy it otherwise would not have had. Again, Ike's critics certainly made this claim.

The juxtaposition of Kissinger and Eisenhower suggests an important point about the period from 1945 to 1975. In some cases ideas were causally relevant, but policymakers' ignorance of something taught in a doctoral program did not hinder them from making decisions based on a strategic concept. Having learned something that was taught in graduate school did not make them better able to avail themselves of a strategic concept. It is difficult to see that ideas from the university, from centers of strategic thought, or from social science were distinctive in any way. Using them, moreover, did not mean that policy was better.

The sorts of ideas promulgated by Eisenhower and Kissinger were peculiar. When he was confident, Eisenhower disdained men of knowledge in the public arena. In the later 1950s when he was forced to listen to them, his own strategic concept fell apart. The added value of knowledge of foreign affairs that was

---

[4] There is an excellent and pertinent discussion of these issues in Latham, *Modernization as Ideology*, esp. pp. 1–29.

learned in a university setting was unclear. Kissinger's ideas were not arcane or complex. They depended neither on RAND quantification nor scholarship on bureaucracy. They did depend on an unappetizing but often accurate construal of the way statesmen and their states behaved. Critical for Eisenhower and Kissinger was their own reconstruction of the ideas absorbed from the general foreign policy culture, and the political will to act on these ideas. For Eisenhower events of the late 1950s compromised this will. In Kissinger's case Richard Nixon provided the will.

What are we to make of other periods in the era from World War II to Vietnam? Truman's decision making after Roosevelt's death in 1945 was makeshift—a number of changing hands, without much experience, took up and dropped the reins of diplomacy, even in their own eyes unsuccessfully implementing policy. From 1947 through 1949 experience and a more settled sense of what was necessary, a version of Kennan's containment, guided policy under Truman, although it was undone from 1950 through 1953. A settled sense, if not a strategic concept, is what one sees under Kennedy from 1961 through 1963. Kennedy's policies of 1963 represent (by my subjective standards) the high point of American statesmanship in the period under study, even though they produced the space in which Vietnam was to take place. The lack of a fully conscious strategic concept in this period of achievement intimates that success may not hinge on the imposition of articulated ideas on the world.

In one period, 1964–68, I am convinced that ideas played a legitimating role only and that nonideational variables explain policy—for example, Lyndon Johnson's feelings of insecurity and the desire for power his advisors displayed. The lack of a strategic concept is also suggested by the argument of most critics that although Johnson is responsible, any American president would have taken the United States into Vietnam. Americans were bound to get into a scuffle in Asia—and thus ideas were nugatory.

If there was a functioning concept at work during the period, it was "the domino theory," a simple comparison that Eisenhower had first suggested between the fact that a row of dominoes would all fall over if the first fell and the way in which losing one country to Communism would make it inevitable that others would follow. As commentators have pointed out, Eisenhower had expressed a central notion of the Munich analogy that was already part of the common belief system. Standing up to international aggression would stop it in its tracks. The irony of Vietnam is that the intellectual contribution may have been the regurgitation of an idea popularized by Ike and an item of popular currency—in movies and comic strips, for example.[5]

[5] For some citations see "Domino Theory" in *Encyclopedia of the Vietnam War*, ed. Spencer C. Tucker (New York: Oxford University Press, 1998), pp. 104–5; and Jardini, "Out of the Blue Yonder," pp. 281–82, 419–20.

The lesson is that the determinants of policy shift and alter from time to time, and that ideas in guise of strategic concepts will have a varying importance. But in the era I have studied we have not gone through a period in which graduate school teaching was substantively significant. The causal role of the ideas of intellectuals was modest at best. Nor can we even say that when strategic concepts were important, policy was better.

Questions of Method

Within the community of scholars who study international relations the connection of strategic theory to what it is supposed to be about—the political world—has embarrassingly eroded. An outstanding example here is the comparative estimate of Henry Kissinger and Thomas Schelling. The "sheer brilliance of . . . Schelling's insights," his "immense" contribution, "breathtaking in its brilliance" lamentably "obscured fundamental political realities." On the other hand, Kissinger was "not primarily a strategist," "never a full-blooded nuclear strategist. His strength was more in great-power diplomacy." "It is doubtful if Kissinger had a significant influence on the making of strategic policy."[6] The historian must wonder about the point of the exercise of strategic studies.

Indeed, as practical reasoners, sometimes *neither* social scientist intellectuals *nor* their opponents had much of a kinesthetic sense of international life. Kennan, at one extreme, and the RAND theorists like Wohstetter, at the other, were equally babes in the woods. Dean Acheson said that Kennan had a "mystical attitude" toward the realities of power, "which he did not understand."[7] Carl Kaysen remarked that one "did not have to be very subtle" to see that Robert McNamara, who brought similarly minded RAND strategists into the government in the early 1960s, had "a tin ear for politics," a view that Richard Neustadt echoed.[8] This tone-deafness may have contributed to the felt need to simplify for the public, and to the dread of the public that went hand in hand with the need.

It may be that different varieties of political ideas or theory should generate different prescriptions for action, but this book does not bear out that conclusion. There are representatives of antipositivism among the intellectuals we have studied—Paul Nitze and Henry Kissinger in addition to Kennan. But it cannot be shown that, because of their antipositivism, the policies they advocated were better than those of the formal scientists, nor even that the antiposi-

---

[6] From *Makers of Nuclear Strategy*, ed. John Baylis and John Garrett (New York: St. Martin's, 1991): their introduction, p. 9; Lawrence Freedman, "Henry Kissinger," p. 98; Phil Williams, "Thomas Schelling," pp. 120, 133; and Ken Booth, "Bernard Brodie," p. 55.

[7] See Miscamble, *Kennan*, pp. 175, 341–42; Mayers, *Kennan*, pp. 233–35, 307–9; and McLellan, *Dean Acheson*, pp. 157–59, 415–16.

[8] Kaysen, interview, March 27, 2004; Neustadt, interview, October 9, 2001.

tivists had different policies from others. Kennan galvanized everyone in1947 and 1948, but thereafter Kennan and Nitze were opposed. Kissinger and RAND shared many of the same thoughts on nuclear policy in the 1950s. Neustadt and Kissinger disliked bureaucracies in the 1960s. In the early 1970s, from afar, Kennan savaged Kissinger's policies

Hans Morgenthau argued at length that what he called the "liberal," "technocratic," or "engineering" style of political science and policymaking was distinctive of the United States and its stupid foreign policies.[9] But it would be difficult to make a case that the conduct of American foreign policy was worse in the postwar period than that of the Europeans, who in general had rejected positivistic social science, or the Russians, who adhered to a Marxist social science. And it would be difficult to argue that principles of method are important, one way or another, in a comparison, say, of American foreign policy in the postwar era to that of France in the early nineteenth century, or to Britain and Germany in the 1870–1914 period. The peculiar formulations of experts in the West over the past two centuries are not essential for understanding international politics.

It *is* worth noting the role of hubris among the intellectuals. The social expense of expertise was great. The men of knowledge did well by their society, yet their actual knowledge was minimal while their sense of self-regard and scholarly hand-waving was maximal. They did their best work in constructing ways of thinking that absolved leadership of liability, deserved or not. Undoubtedly there was a symbiosis between the defense specialists and the nonintellectual elite that wanted their services in places of power, but the culture paid a pretty penny for the expertise, especially when so many of intellectuals disdained a democratic public.

The civilian strategists were often the high priests of the national security state. From the 1950s to the 1970s their theories could not be falsified. By the late 1960s most establishment figures believed that Vietnam was a disaster, and it is hard to imagine why—on grounds of competence—they would reward the RAND strategists that Albert Wohlstetter had sent to the Department of Defense with further high positions in government; with powerful administrative positions outside of government; with profitable advisory roles; with new consultancies and lucrative research professorships; or with novel problems of organization. Yet these men barely missed a step after the war, and followers of Wohlstetter continued to hold forth on defense policy. Why was RAND not discredited when the organization and its supporters came to believe that its strategists were responsible for matters having gone awry? The sluggish mediocrity of bureaucracy, which RAND despised, saved the careers of many men.

---

[9] While the countertradition is often overlooked, there is a large literature on the instrumentalist-positivist strain. A good survey of the Cold War period is David Engerman, "Rethinking Cold War Universities: Some Recent Histories," *Journal of Cold War Studies* 5 (2003): 80–95. For the

In 1967, supposing that Robert McNamara was suicidal because of his anguish over (what he thought was) a disastrous war, Lyndon Johnson gave the secretary the World Bank to manage. Can anyone think that the president made this assignment on grounds of fitness? Did Johnson try to sabotage the bank? Were the slow-witted policies of the Eisenhower period worse than those that RAND advocated?

Indeed, a more appropriate comparison than to the theologian would be to the primitive shaman, in power no matter what the connection between his formulations and what the culture experienced. Yet in a society such as ours we do not want decisions based on the tools of the shaman—on the examination of entrails, on oracles, or on the dice—even though we do not know that acting on such procedures would be worse.

This is distasteful medicine. The defense intellectuals did not know very much. They frequently delivered obtuse judgments when required to be matter-of-fact, or merely offered up self-justifying talk for politicians. Yet there is little alternative to urging that scholars should do it better and with less pride and dogmatism. One could argue that, under these circumstances, a cultural lesson to be learned is that the best traits to be inculcated into specialists are humility and prudence, just the traits that vanish with their education and growth in expertise.

This counsel of modesty is especially relevant because of a final generalization about the period under study. While it would be mistaken to argue that ideas are not relevant to policymakers, the evidence repeatedly corroborates the observation that politics trumps knowledge. The strategists believed that their know-how could turn the state system in a better direction, and their learning leverage interests into the empire of justice. But politics was always the more powerful partner, and dragged the erudite into the dominion of partisanship, maneuver, and advantage. Politicians outranked academics; politics seduced scholarship.

---

earlier period the standard work is Dorothy Ross, *The Origins of American Social Science* (New York: Cambridge University Press, 1991). And also Bernstein, *A Perilous Progress.*

Acknowledgments and Methodological Note

THIS BOOK has used archival resources to chart developments in the history of academic institutions. I consider this technique essential, and would first like to thank the many archivists who cheerfully assisted me in examining the collections cited in the notes.

The book has also drawn selectively on literature in diplomatic history, intellectual history, political science and ancillary disciplines, and the philosophy of history. It is consequently subject to criticism from expertise in any of these areas of inquiry, but I have been saved from many errors by an assortment of readers: several anonymous critics; Elizabeth Block, Richard Freeland, Frank Gavin, Carl Kaysen, Walter McDougall, Jonathan Steinberg, Jeremi Suri, Marc Trachtenberg; and especially Sarah Igo, Leo Ribuffo, and Susan Schulten. A number of people allowed me to talk to them formally about the issues the book raises: Morton Halperin, Carl Kaysen, Richard Neustadt, Walt Rostow, Marc Trachtenberg.

I have taken up at some length controverted issues in the philosophy of history in my manuscript "Historical Knowledge."

As a history of the policy sciences, this book has its own position. While I have a sense of the limits of policy study, I do not share the criticisms of a certain genre of "left" scholarship about higher education in the Cold War. I would distinguish my approach from that of Nils Gilman, *Mandarins of the Future: Modernization Theory in Cold War America* (Baltimore: Johns Hopkins University Press, 2004); and authors like those in Michael Bernstein and Allen Hunter, eds., "The Cold War and Expert Knowledge: New Essays on the History of the National Security State," a special issue of *Radical History Review* 63 (1995); and in Christopher Simpson, ed., *Universities and Empire: Money and Politics in the Social Sciences During the Cold War* (New York: New Press, 1998).

On the other side, I believe my history is more interpretative, and interpretative in a different way, than the writings of such historians as Lawrence Freedman in "Vietnam and the Disillusioned Strategist," *International Affairs* 72 (1996): 133–51 (and many other able writings); David Halberstam, *The Best and the Brightest* (New York: Random House, 1972); and Jim Mann, *Rise of the Vulcans: The History of Bush's War Cabinet* (New York: Viking, 2004).

I would also set apart my line of scholarship from what, roughly, I would call practitioners' history—embodied for example in studies like that of David Baldwin, "Security Studies and the End of the Cold War," *World Politics* 48 (1996): 117–41; Campbell Craig, *Glimmer of a New Leviathan: Total War in the Realism of Niebuhr, Morgenthau, and Waltz* (New York: Columbia University Press, 2003); Colin Elman and Miriam Fendius Elman, eds., *Bridges and Boundaries: Historians, Political Scientists, and the Study of International Relations* (Cambridge: MIT Press, 2001); K. J. Holsti, "Scholarship in an Era of Anxiety," *Review of International Studies* 24 (1998): 17–46; Robert Jervis, "Security Studies: Ideas, Policies, and Politics," in Edward Mansfield and Richard Sisson, eds., *The Evolution of Political Knowledge*, vol. 1, *Theory and Inquiry in American Politics* (Columbus: Ohio State University Press, 2004), 100–120 (and many other writings); and Stephen Miller, "*International Security* at Twenty-Five," *International Security* 26 (2001–2): 5–39.

I am additionally not engaged in the attempt to bring together insights from political science and history in the way of Richard E. Neustadt and Ernest R. May, *Thinking in Time: The Use of History for Decision Makers* (New York: Free Press, 1986) or Marc Trachtenberg, *Historical Method in the Study of International Politics* (Princeton: Princeton University Press, 2006).

I have a great respect for James Scott's *Seeing Like a State: How Certain Schemes to Improve the Human Condition Have Failed* (New Haven: Yale University Press, 1998), but as a historian I have a far smaller interest in validating a thesis about policy ideas, or in engaging in social commentary. I have examined one small patch of ground involving the connection of knowledge to social life. In some ways the effort is akin to Steve Smith, "The United States and the Discipline of International Relations: 'Hegemonic Country, Hegemonic Discipline,'" *International Studies Perspectives* 4 (2002): 67–85.

I do not know if the trials of yesterday are those of the present in foreign policy, or what the contemporary role of intellectuals is. I do not know if academics had greater success in guiding domestic policy in the 1930s, the 1950s and 1960s, or the 1980s. I do not know about the relation of other social science specialties to public policy, yesterday or today.

More important for me is the basic presumption of the book that one can measure the legitimacy and influence of some past social analyses by holding them up against the historical truth of what was occurring. That is, our knowledge of the historical past is the criterion for judging the accuracy of the beliefs of my intellectuals from the 1940s, 1950s, and 1960s, and their causal impact. At the same time, even a basic acquaintance with history should tell readers that historical interpretations are disputed and contested, not exactly a reservoir from which to dispense an impartially objective source with which to judge belief.

One minor aspect of this issue is the way that I have often characterized the assumptions of one brand of midcentury political science. Sometimes I have used the ideas of a few prominent practitioners to illuminate the views of the field. At other times I have drawn from a wide array of different sources to indicate a common premise. In all these cases, I am confident that my attempt to articulate standard views is accurate, and the confidence is based on a wide reading of sources, not all of which appear in the notes.

I have used several strategies in the book to meet the more critical problem of how (my) history can stand as a norm to adjudicate belief. In some cases I have used self-critique to make the case. The new edition of Graham Allison's *Essence of Decision* is easily the best refutation of the adequacy of the first edition. In other cases—notably the founding of the Kennedy School of Government—my knowledge of the available primary sources and the small scale of the issues make me confident that my interpretation is justified. But such an argument won't do, for example, in grasping the history of American foreign policy in the period from World War II to Vietnam. Here the sources are so plentiful, the secondary literature so enormous, and historical disagreements so varied that it would be foolish to presume that I have written a narrative that will be acceptable to everyone. In this case, and others like it, I have made my judgments as catholic as possible, in the belief that they will still fortify the conclusions to which I have come. So, for example, I have been leery in characterizing policies as desirable or undesirable, avoiding many arguments about what was good or bad, in part because taking a position in such disputes has little relevance to the points I want to make.

But irenic judgments get the historian only so far. The question is whether my interpretation of the past is serviceable in acting as a standard to judge the competence of the postwar understanding of policy. The interpretation is subject to tests to which any historical elucidation is subject. The manner in which historians evaluate their analyses is complex and involves a dialectic of claims and counterclaims, the weighing of evidence, and an appraisal of the plausibility of alternative accounts. My history can serve as a norm only if, over time, it survives such evaluations, displays an ability to persuade other students of the past, and offers explanations that ward off criticism and that future research corroborates and enriches.

Index